WHAT UNIVERSITIES CAN BE

WHAT UNIVERSITIES CAN BE

*A New Model for Preparing Students
for Active Concerned Citizenship and
Ethical Leadership*

ROBERT J. STERNBERG

CORNELL UNIVERSITY PRESS
ITHACA AND LONDON

First published 2016 by Cornell University Press
Printed in the United States of America

Library of Congress Cataloging-in-Publication Data

Names: Sternberg, Robert J., author.
Title: What universities can be : a new model for preparing
    students for active concerned citizenship and ethical
    leadership / Robert J. Sternberg.
Description: Ithaca : Cornell University Press, 2016. | Includes
    bibliographical references and index.
Identifiers: LCCN 2016003659 | ISBN 9780801453786 (cloth : alk. paper)
Subjects: LCSH: Education, Higher—Aims and objectives—United
    States. | Education, Higher—Social aspects—United States. |
    Education, Higher—Moral and ethical aspects—United States. |
    Universities and colleges—United States.
Classification: LCC LB2322.2 .S74 2016 | DDC 378/.01—dc23
LC record available at http://lccn.loc.gov/2016003659

Cornell University Press strives to use environmentally responsible
suppliers and materials to the fullest extent possible in the publishing of
its books. Such materials include vegetable-based, low-VOC inks and
acid-free papers that are recycled, totally chlorine-free, or partly composed
of nonwood fibers. For further information, visit our website at
www.cornellpress.cornell.edu.

Cloth printing   10   9   8   7   6   5   4   3   2   1

This book is dedicated to my wife, Karin Sternberg, and my children, Seth Sternberg, Sara Sternberg Greene, Samuel Sternberg, Brittany Sternberg, and Melody Sternberg, who have put up with me while I learned what I could about how universities work.

Contents

PREFACE

I started thinking about the content of this book a few years ago—forty-seven to be exact, but who's counting? I was a freshman at Yale. I had a great experience, especially in a special program called "Directed Studies" that provided intensive education in how to think about the problems of the world. I wondered whether I could "bottle" some of the ideas in that program. Of course, over all those years, my thinking has expanded beyond that particular program. But it really was the way that program was taught—to encourage critical but also creative and wise thinking—that started my consideration of many of the issues I deal with here.

Over the course of forty-seven years in higher education, I have been a student at two universities—Yale and Stanford—and a university assistant professor, associate professor, full professor, endowed professor, dean, provost, and president. I have served at five institutions: Yale (thirty years), Tufts (five years), Oklahoma State (three years), University of Wyoming (less than one year), and now Cornell University (two years and counting and, I hope, until I eventually retire!). I also have been treasurer of the

Association of American Colleges and Universities. So I have seen universities from a number of different points of view, and my diverse experiences are reflected in this book.

The story of this book can in many respects be captured by a poem by Stephen Crane:

A Man Saw a Ball of Gold in the Sky
A man saw a ball of gold in the sky;
He climbed for it,
And eventually he achieved it—
It was clay.

Now this is the strange part:
When the man went to the earth
And looked again,
Lo, there was the ball of gold.
Now this is the strange part:
It was a ball of gold.
Aye, by the heavens, it was a ball of gold.
                    Stephen Crane

My ball of gold, in Stephen Crane's terms, has been to change the way teaching and assessment are done in this country to develop and assess a much broader array of skills than that measured by conventional standardized tests, such as the SAT, ACT, or Collegiate Learning Assessment (CLA). In particular, universities need to teach and assess progress in ways that take into account students' patterns of creative, analytical, practical, and wisdom-based/ethical skills. But our country has not moved forward in its teaching and assessment practices. In many ways, under No Child Left Behind and other well-intentioned but not-quite-thought-through pieces of legislation, the country has gone backward. The instructional and assessment programs sold to us by the educational establishment often seem like balls of gold, but only if seen from a distance. Up close, they often appear to be balls of clay, much as earlier programs were in the previous century.

When I attended elementary school in the 1950s, my school administered IQ tests every couple of years. At first I performed poorly on these tests, a little worse each time. But in fourth grade, I was fortunate to have a teacher who thought there was more to a student than his or her IQ, and I became an excellent student. In sixth grade, I was sent back to a fifth-grade classroom to take the IQ test with the younger children because the school thought the sixth-grade test would be too hard for me. Whereas I was scared to compete with children my own age, I had no anxiety at all about competing with what I perceived to be the "babies," who were a full year younger than I was. From that time onward, I never experienced test anxiety again.

As a result of this early experience, I became interested in intelligence and other intellectual abilities and have devoted my scholarly life to studying these abilities. I acquired at least some degree of renown for my "theory of successful intelligence" (e.g., Sternberg 1988, 1997a, 2003b). I became a professor of psychology at Yale and for thirty years did research on intelligence and these other related constructs. I became president of the largest association of psychologists in the world, the American Psychological Association (APA), and then of an organization larger than the APA, the Federation of Associations of Behavioral and Brain Sciences (FABBS).

Toward the end of my years as a professor at Yale, I was funded by the College Board to create a test for college admissions that would supplement the SAT. The project was marvelously successful. Our tests, measuring creative and practical as well as analytical skills (also measured by the SAT), doubled prediction of freshman-year GPA at the same time that they substantially reduced ethnic group differences. The work was published as the lead article by the premier journal in my field (Sternberg and the Rainbow Project Collaborators 2006) and was also carried by the media (e.g., McLoughlin 2005). Our reward was that the College Board, instead of giving us more funding, cut off our funding altogether. It claimed that the work could not be upscaled.

I had discovered that my ball of gold was a ball of clay: as a professor, I was unable to change the way that either instruction or assessment was done. I was at a dead end. So I switched into administration.

In my five years as dean of arts and sciences at Tufts and three years as provost and senior vice president at Oklahoma State University, I was able to effect major changes in those universities, establishing new teaching centers to help professors better teach to the way students learn, and also changing admissions processes so that they took into account creative, practical, and wisdom-based/ethical skills as well as analytical ones. But

I realized that the changes were in two universities and were not extending a whole lot further. I then went to the University of Wyoming as president and found myself unable to effect the kind of meaningful change I hoped for, so I resigned.

I am now back as a professor at Cornell. I have no illusions that up there in the sky must be a ball of gold. But I am hoping that this book will at the very least be a ball of silver—that it will encourage university professors and administrators to effect meaningful changes that will improve the lives of students and increase their readiness for the workforce. And I believe the ideas presented here at least suggest ways in which we might truly reach the ball of gold.

I believe this book is especially timely. University administrators are faced with unprecedented challenges. Students and sometimes faculty members are demanding changes that are new for the universities, for example, in how students are treated by their environments. Administrators need to listen and be properly responsive but also need to demonstrate principles of ethical leadership and out-and-out moral courage that perhaps once were not the indispensable features of leadership they have become today.

What Universities Can Be builds on articles I have published over the years in a variety of outlets. But it is the first time I have integrated all my work and further developed it, so that my ideas are unified, expanded beyond what previously has been published in the articles, and presented together in one place. For me, therefore, this work is the culmination of all I have done in forty years working in universities.

This book is addressed to several key audiences. First, it should be helpful for educational administrators who are looking for ways to enhance how they lead and manage their institutions. Second, the book is addressed to faculty members who better wish to understand the complexities of higher education today and who want to know how they can improve their performance within the context of these complexities. Third, the book should be useful for scholars in the field of higher education who wish to learn about the concept of higher education I propose, namely, what I call the ACCEL university. And finally, the book is addressed to general readers who wish to understand higher education today. It can be read by any educated adult, without a background in the field of higher education.

I have learned from many people over the course of my career, but my greatest inspiration was certainly Kingman Brewster, president of Yale University during the time I was an undergraduate there. His course, "The Idea of the University," taught with Professor Ronald Jager, first piqued my interest in the nature of universities and what we all could do to make them better. I remember President Brewster most fondly as the role model to whom we all, in universities, can aspire.

I am grateful to all the people who made this book possible. My mentors in my career as a professor—Endel Tulving, Gordon Bower, and Wendell Garner—helped me in countless ways. As an administrator, I learned a great deal, particularly from serving under V. Burns Hargis, president of Oklahoma State University. I also learned more than I ever could have hoped about liberal education from Carol Schneider, past-president of the Association of American Colleges and Universities. Those to whom I am especially grateful are from my early days as a student at Yale: Sam Chauncey, who was director of University Admissions and Financial Aid Policy and hired me for my first job, as special assistant to the dean of Undergraduate Admissions at Yale; and Kingman Brewster, for me, one of the greatest university presidents the world has seen.

WHAT UNIVERSITIES CAN BE

INTRODUCTION

When I was dean of arts and sciences at Tufts University, I found myself caught in the middle of an argument between what appeared to be two opposing factions of faculty members. One faction believed that the purpose of university education is to promote active citizenship and leadership. They were especially proud of Tufts' reputation for producing outstanding leaders. They rejoiced in the Jonathan M. Tisch College of Citizenship and Public Service, which provided opportunities for students to develop citizenship and leadership skills. The other faction believed the purpose of university education is to teach students how to think and learn throughout their lives. Some of them viewed the activities of Tisch College as something of a distraction and as less rigorous than the ideal for an intellectual center. Some of these faculty members felt that Tisch College might actually be corrupting the development of complex, higher-order thinking skills. Both groups of faculty meant the best for the students, but they viewed themselves as having very different conceptions of what "best" meant.

The main thesis of this book is that you can have it both ways—and that to have a proper university education, you must. The purpose of higher education is to develop active concerned citizenship, ethical leadership, and democratic participation through the nurturance of high-level creative, critical, practical, and wisdom-based and ethical skills. In other words, deep, reflective, critical thinking and active citizenship and leadership are complementary, not mutually exclusive. Promoting leadership skills in the absence of critical thinking produces graduates who are self-serving, if often charismatic, charlatans posing as servant leaders. Promoting higher-order thinking skills in the absence of leadership and active citizenship produces high-IQ, abstract analytical thinkers who are paralyzed in the face of practical, real-world problems and often respond in ways that show little knowledge of, and engagement with, the real world. Simply having a program that emphasizes leadership in the absence of higher order thinking skills does not produce excellent leaders, but neither does having liberal-arts courses if those courses fail to connect with the active-citizenship leadership challenges of everyday life. The bottom line is that we do not want to produce students who score high on tests but who are content to live in a dictatorship, nor do we want to produce students who value democratic ideals but lack the critical-thinking skills to say why.

This is a challenge: there are countries around the world inhabited by very "smart" people, going to academically competitive universities in those countries, who nevertheless live in thinly disguised dictatorships with the pretense of voting but with censure or imprisonment, even torture and death, for those who challenge the government. The only allowable form of active citizenship and leadership in those countries is that which supports the supposedly "democratic" governments. The last thing universities in these countries want is thinking that is deep, reflective, or critical. Rather, they encourage thinking that reaches its conclusion first and then finds evidence to support the preordained, government-approved conclusion. One might say, "It couldn't happen here." Undoubtedly people in those countries said that too—before it did happen. University education needs to make sure it truly can't happen here.

The goal of this book is to describe what universities can be. Universities in the United States have evolved in ways that originally represented adaptations to the peculiar needs of the country. For example, general education once focused on the roots and development of Western civilization when it was thought that this was some of the most important learning a student could have. But today, in many universities, the intent is broader. Courses in ethnic or LGBT studies that once would have been viewed with astonishment are now parts of general curricula. Athletics was once limited to a few intermural sports and now has expanded outwardly in many directions, both intramural and intermural. Many of the changes that have occurred over time have been adaptive, in the sense that they met the needs of the time.

We need to rethink what we mean by a great university: I suggest that we view as a model what I call the **ACCEL** institution—an institution that places its emphasis squarely in the education of students (and faculty) for **A**ctive **C**oncerned **C**itizenship and **E**thical **L**eadership. In this country, many people view the institutions highest rated by magazines or websites as their aspirational universities. These universities, however, may or may not represent what necessarily should be aspirational for many if not most universities, namely, an emphasis on developing ACCEL.

Our universities, for the most part, are centered on selecting students for academic knowledge and skills and then further developing these students' academic knowledge and skills, and they generally do a good to excellent job of it. The best students who go to the best colleges and universities are, for the most part, those with superior academic knowledge and skills, plus students who get in for other reasons (legacies, athletes, development cases whose parents are viewed as potential large contributors, and so on).

At some level, this mentality of admitting and developing students works. There have been two major studies of academically gifted (high-IQ) children—the Terman study (Terman and Oden 1959) in California and a study by Subotnik, Karp, and Morgan (1989) in New York. They both found the same thing: people with high IQs go to good schools, including colleges and universities; they get good jobs; they make good money; and not one person in either of these two large studies had any revolutionary, society-changing ideas. If we want to develop students who are going to change the world, we won't do it by selecting students merely on the basis of standardized tests or by teaching them in ways that develop only their academic knowledge and skills.

The ACCEL institution recognizes that the greatest problem we have in our society is not a lack of leaders with high IQs or sterling academic credentials, but rather a lack of transformational leaders who behave in ethical ways to achieve, over the long as well as the short term, a common good for all. Existing standardized tests are not going to identify these concerned active citizens and ethical leaders. They are not even going to identify deep, reflective, critical thinkers. Standardized tests, as they exist today, cannot measure deep thinking because they squeeze in large numbers of test items in short periods of time, often through a multiple-choice format. Indeed, there are many dictators with what appear to be very high IQs. They have to be pretty bright just to stay in power. Colleges and universities talk about developing leaders. What they lack is a viable proven model for doing so. ACCEL provides such a model, as described throughout this book.

Our system of evaluating universities and the people in it is warped. We use admissions procedures that do not measure and often do not even concern themselves with ACCEL, instead focusing largely on standardized test scores and high school grades. When we select faculty, we largely ignore ACCEL characteristics. And then we evaluate students and faculty alike in terms that are largely irrelevant to ACCEL. Indeed, faculty members in elite institutions who spend too much of their time serving a public good are at risk for not being tenured, and students who spend their time in a similar manner risk having little to show, except perhaps negatively, in their GPAs. They do often get a benefit—a better job—but should there really be a trade-off between what gets one a better job and what leads one to be more highly ranked in the university?

The world is full of high-IQ citizens and leaders who are failing to behave in ways that will help achieve a common good for all. How many contemporary major leaders in any domain serve as role models for the younger generation of today? Try naming them. Are you done yet?

Many universities claim to focus on leadership development in their educational program. The problem is that their claim is typically based on little or no real conception of what leadership is and no operationalization of a plan to develop leadership. Simply participating in athletics or student government or fraternities/sororities does not produce great leaders. Without either a conceptual or operational basis for a leadership-development claim, the claim is essentially so much hot air—a marketing strategy and not much more. How many colleges claim to develop leaders? How many actually have any validated program for doing so?

My own views on ACCEL are shaped by a theory of leadership I have proposed called WICS (**wisdom-intelligence-creativity-synthesized**) (Sternberg 2003a, 2007). The basic idea underlying this model is that active and engaged citizenship, and especially ethical leadership, require deep reflective critical thinking. In particular, they require individuals to synthesize (a) the creative skills to produce a vision for how they intend to make the world a better place, not just for them but for their family, their friends, their colleagues, and others; (b) the analytical intellectual skills to be able to say whether their vision, and that of others, is a good vision; (c) the practical intellectual skills to be able to execute their vision and to persuade others of its value; and (d) the wisdom-based and ethical skills to ensure that their ideas represent a common good, not just their own interests or those of their friends and family.

Educating students for ethical leadership entails transmitting deep reflective critical thinking, in particular—creative, analytical, practical, and wisdom-based/ethical skills, as well as a passion for leadership. A university that truly develops ethical leaders needs to be able to show explicitly how its curriculum, formal and informal, develops all of these skills plus passion. Waving hands is not enough. This book covers explicit techniques for developing these attributes of good and successful leaders.

One might ask what the big deal is: Why is it hard to develop the next generation of leaders? Why do we need any special model to develop leaders? If universities say they are developing leaders, why should we even be skeptical? I argue in this book that developing leaders for the next generation actually is quite hard. Many universities do not directly address how they should develop the skills needed for good and successful leadership. And if they do, they fail to consider a key fact: there are many forces that act *against* the development of creative, practical, wisdom-based, and even analytical skills. Universities do not automatically develop them. A lot happens in a university to counteract, for example, the development of creative skills, which require people to think in ways that defy the crowd, or ethical skills, which often require people to act in ways that bring disfavor on them.

On this view, the question of whether a university should focus more on the liberal arts or on development of preprofessional skills is misstated. The answer must be to place a focus on both—to teach the liberal arts as well as preprofessional skills in ways that develop the skills underlying ethical leadership. A great liberal-arts education is a huge plus for any student (see Bok 2013; Delbanco 2013). But there is much to be said for a liberal-arts education that also prepares students for the professional challenges they will face on graduation. No parent wants a child to be graduated from college and face dismal job prospects. But no parent wants a student to be graduated who has not learned how to think and cope with the challenges of the world besides those of a particular job. Students need more than good grades to compete successfully in the world.

There was a time when it probably made good sense to focus more on high school grades and standardized test scores in admitting students. For example, elite schools used to accept students largely in terms of the socioeconomic status of their parents (Karabel 2006; Lemann 1999). Test scores and grades were intended to put a focus on meritocracy rather than lineage (Sternberg 2010a). Unknown at the time was the high correlation between test scores and grades, on the one hand, and lineage, on the other. It is the parents with means who can buy the schooling and out-of-school experiences that help their children to excel academically and in other ways. So the benefits of good socioeconomic lineage translate themselves, effectively, into higher grades and standardized test scores.

College learning was once achieved through a small range of teaching methods—classroom instruction, textbooks, and perhaps tutorials. Today there is a staggering variety of means to promote college learning. Online courses play an increasing role in college education. This role can be a positive one. Whereas originally online courses were intended to enhance the learning needs of students, in some colleges they are more and more being seen as a way of enhancing bottom-line revenue. They can be done more cheaply than classroom learning (Bowen 2013).

Moreover, college athletics has served and will continue to serve as a way for young people to develop leadership, physical skills, and teamwork skills. But it has grown into an enterprise that now serves to spin off revenue, mostly from past athletic endeavors to future athletic endeavors. The current manifestations of athletics, especially in some Division I schools, are not always serving colleges, universities, and society as well at this point as they once did in their original adaptive form. Today they have, for some universities, been thoroughly corrupted by money, making it hard for the universities that house them to claim to value ethical or character development.

This book makes recommendations as to how we can move in the direction of making our universities adaptive to our crucial needs in society rather than to needs that may not be primary, or may even be in conflict with, what universities ideally ought to be accomplishing. Universities especially need to pay attention to being adaptive because they are often nonprofits, and thus under different pressures than for-profit businesses.

For-profit businesses have to adapt or they go out of business quickly. Nonprofit universities have the great disadvantage that, although they need to adapt, their timeframe for adaptation can be slower to the point that once they realize they are in trouble, it may be too late to save their quality of education, reputation, or in some cases, existence. They are lulled into a false sense of security by different forces—the seeming inevitability of some level of state funding for public institutions, the seeming inevitability of tuition payments and alumni donations for private nonprofit institutions, and the seeming largesse of the government in supplying financial aid to students who then can go, in some cases, to for-profit institutions. But the old model is not working.

A university, for example, may continue to function because it receives tuition payments, endowment revenue, possibly state support, and other sources of revenue from grant overhead and private donations. But the university may long ago have become mediocre, in which case the faculty and administration may do all they can to protect that mediocrity, wishing for nothing less than to be threatened by an influx of talent that makes the current authority figures look bad. Only a very dynamic, forward-looking board of trustees working with a transformational president is likely to change the dynamic. But such universities are unlikely to want to keep forward-looking trustees or presidents, because they threaten the existing order. In such cases, the proponents of mediocrity are not viewed as the problem; rather, the advocates for positive change are.

Universities, especially those below the top tiers, are starting to shut down, and even many top-tier institutions, such as the University of California, the University of Illinois, the University of Wisconsin, and the University of Colorado, have found themselves, from time to time, strapped for cash. Moreover, surveys by the *Chronicle of Higher Education* and Association of American Colleges and Universities reveal that businesses are dissatisfied with the skills of the graduates of our universities. In contrast, university administrators are quite satisfied, suggesting a disconnection between two worlds. If universities were more adaptive, they could fare much better. This book discusses how they can increase their adaptive fit to contemporary society.

It is fashionable these days to deride the education provided by our colleges and universities (e.g., Arum and Roksa 2011, 2014). Richard Arum and Josipa Roksa have claimed that our colleges and universities are doing an inadequate job of educating our students. I agree that our institutions could do better, but I also believe that Arum and Roksa's (2011) analyses are seriously flawed statistically (Sternberg 2011c; see also Astin 2011, for a statistical critique of Arum and Roksa's [2011] claims). Yet if our colleges and universities are doing such a bad job, why is it that the US economy, although far from perfect, is performing quite a bit better today than most economies elsewhere? Why do so many innovations, technological and otherwise, that are used around the world come from the United States? Why, despite all the flaws of our governmental system, do we remain a model (albeit, a seriously flawed one) of democracy? There are certainly countries that do much better on standardized assessments, but some of the places that do best on the tests are either out-and-out dictatorships or essentially one-party states where, if you disagree with the government, you go to prison. Perhaps there is something the Program for International Student Assessment (PISA) and other standardized tests don't measure. That is a major claim of this book. We can do better, but not by focusing on the kinds of standardized tests that Arum and Roksa, among others, focus on. We need to emphasize broad skills of thought and action, something recognized a long time ago by one of the great founders of our country and of the University of Virginia, Thomas Jefferson. I turn to some of his ideas next, as well as to the ideas of some of his approximate contemporaries.

Part I

A New Future for Universities

1

Three Traditions of Higher Education in Relation to Democracy

The roots of the notion of the ACCEL university lie, to a large extent, in the thinking of Thomas Jefferson, as described later in the chapter. In the United States, there are three traditions of democracy and its relation to higher education. What type of university one values most will depend, in part, on the tradition to which one adheres. What is best, therefore, depends on what one seeks in the first place. That said, I argue that one tradition offers certain kinds of opportunities for us as a society that the others do not offer—that is, the tradition that gives rise to the ACCEL university.

This chapter draws and builds on Sternberg 2014d.

Three Traditions of American Democracy and Higher Education

The Jacksonian Tradition: Education—Who Cares?

The first tradition, which I call "Jacksonian," derives from Andrew Jackson's belief that almost anyone could do any job if he or she put in enough effort. In particular, on this view, the leaders of society need not have a lot of formal education in order to be successful (see, e.g., Brands 2006; Wikipedia 2015). Jackson's views were controversial even in his own time. On the one hand, there were relatively far more jobs in Jackson's time for uneducated individuals than there are today. On the other hand, the kind of critical thinking taught by education would have been as relevant in Jackson's time as it is today. Today, in any case, formal education is, for the most part, highly prized. Too many jobs require high levels of formal knowledge and skills for the unschooled to be confident of meeting their own goals, as well as society's, for success. In some areas, for example, there certainly are initial jobs for those without a college education; it's getting the second, third, and fourth jobs—and even retaining the first—that can prove challenging for those who do not seek at least some level of higher education, which may be in the form of a liberal-arts degree but may instead be in the form of technical training, or might be some combination of technical training and liberal arts.

Some people, notably Peter Thiel, think differently. He has proven willing to pay select students to drop out of college (Wieder 2011). But the trend of paying students not to attend, or to leave, college has not caught on broadly, except perhaps among professional athletic teams. And the students Thiel has been willing to pay are anything but a random sample of those who go to college. They are the cream of the crop. For the typical student, trusting in the Jacksonian model to propel one to success might be a serious mistake. Society, at least in the United States, has largely abandoned this model, at the same time that no virtually no one questions the value of the dedication and hard work that Jackson promoted.

Is higher education an investment that pays off? Financially, on average, the answer is certainly yes (see, e.g., Baum 2014). But it is, I believe, a mistake to dwell exclusively on economic indicators such as those provided by Sandy Baum (2014). Rather, higher education pays off in terms of developing knowledge, critical-thinking skills, a lifelong network of friends and potential business associates, and an enriching set of experiences that cannot be duplicated in any other life context.

This is not to say that the Jacksonian model will not come back at some future time—or that unusually talented students cannot succeed without college degrees. But if one were to place bets, the better bet might be to finish college or some other form of higher education and try one's luck after finishing rather than before.

Going to college is not at odds with a so-called blue-collar occupation. Institutions such as Oklahoma State University at Okmulgee offer a combination of technical training and liberal arts. Students' employment rate on graduation is close to 100 percent. The advantage of such programs is that the students are ready for work on graduation but also have the liberal-arts background that will enable them to prepare for the future workforce, in which the job they trained for may be modified or even eliminated. But such programs are not strictly speaking Jacksonian, because even though admissions may be relatively unselective, only the more motivated students complete the programs, and it is completion that matters most for future job prospects.

The Hamiltonian Model—Educating the Elite for Leadership

The Hamiltonian tradition is the one that has been adopted most in the United States. It is based on Alexander Hamilton's notion that a society should first identify who among it constitute its elite members and then put them into positions of leadership (see, e.g., Federici 2012). In Hamilton's day, the elite were typically from the upper social and economic classes, which usually but not always corresponded. This emphasis on social and economic class has been present for much of the history of the United States. Things started to change, at least on the surface, in the 1960s, when the demands for high grades and high scores in standardized testing came to outweigh socioeconomic consideration in the college admissions of the 1960s. Although an emphasis on grades and standardized test scores has replaced the emphasis on socioeconomic class, the replacement is in large part cosmetic. Grades and test scores are highly correlated with socioeconomic class. And for students from lower social and economic classes who excel in grades and test scores, a further barrier awaits their entrance into elite and some not-so-elite institutions, namely, the cost of going to college. Test scores and grades today are the main (although not the only) entrance credentials to Hamiltonian institutions—those often hovering near the top of media ratings—and they are actually the credentials most likely to lead youngsters today into the higher social and economic classes.

The Hamiltonian tradition makes sense to the extent that one believes that one's potential to become an active concerned citizen and ethical leader is largely a function of grades and test scores derived from the high school years. In practice, the implementation of this model is compromised by the inability of many students to afford an education at Hamiltonian institutions, even after one takes into account scholarship aid. A second compromising factor is legacy admissions (i.e., children whose parents are alumni of the school to which nonlegacy students are applying). A third compromising factor is development admissions (i.e., children whose parents are viewed as potential large donors to the university, but only if the children are accepted for admission).

Elite institutions in many cases try to compensate for their high cost of tuition by offering scholarship aid. Such aid is useful but not sufficient for many students to attend. What the college believes to be sufficient resources for attendance may not jibe with what the family believes are sufficient resources, after factoring in all their other expenses. Moreover, many students never even think to apply to elite colleges, not realizing that they would have a chance of covering costs if granted scholarship aid.

The greatest problem, from my experience, is that we provide the best opportunities to children of very wealthy and of relatively poor families. Students who come from solidly middle-class families are often those who have the greatest difficulty attending elite colleges, because they do not qualify for massive amounts of financial aid but also have insufficient family resources to cover their costs. Their option, then, is to take out loans, which many of them do. But they then have to bet that their future income will justify the loans, always a dicey proposition that probably reveals more about a student's risk-taking propensities than about his or her ability to succeed in college.

The Jeffersonian Tradition: Higher Education for the Masses

The Jeffersonian tradition is, in a sense, a compromise position between the other two traditions (see, e.g., Meacham 2013). Like the Jacksonian tradition, it holds that almost anyone can become, at some level, an ethical leader in society. But also, like the Hamiltonian tradition, it suggests that the individual first must be educated to prepare for such a role. Education, then, provides an important key to ethical leadership, but high school credentials such as grades and standardized test scores are unlikely to tell us who will become an ethical leader. Moreover, a lot will depend on the kind of education the student receives. Land-grant institutions perhaps come closest to trying to realize the Jeffersonian ideal (Sternberg 2014b).

On this view, successful leadership requires the knowledge and often somewhat shallow analytical skills measured by standardized tests; but it further requires, among other things, ethical behavior, a strong work ethic, creativity and a vision of the future, common sense, a sense of responsibility, a willingness to subordinate one's personal gain to the gain of the large community of which one is a member, skill in teamwork, resilience in the face of failure, social and emotional intelligence, and, as in the movie of the same name, "true grit." Standardized tests and even high school grades assess only a tiny sliver of the skills needed for successful leadership. Moreover, there is a risk that someone who is very successful on such tests may actually come to over-rely on his or her IQ at the expense of the other skills required for leadership, to the detriment of his or her overall leadership skills. Such over-reliance is, in part, a product of our society's great emphasis (and, I believe, over-emphasis) on the purported role of memory and analytical skills in career success.

As an example, I am an honorary professor at a university in Germany. Its psychology department, in which I teach, is one of the most selective in the country. To be admitted as an undergraduate, a student has to have essentially a perfect high school record (the equivalent of a 4.0 GPA). A distinguished professor there commented to me that the result of this admissions procedure is students who are extremely good at doing what they are told to do but who may or may not be creative. The high school reward system is such that the best students are often those who are good at following directions rather than creating the directions others will follow.

Examples of Hamiltonian and Jeffersonian Universities

What do Hamiltonian and Jeffersonian institutions look like in practice?

Institution H

Institution H is a fairly large prestigious private institution in the Northeast. It embodies the Hamiltonian ideal.

It is very selective in admissions, with most students scoring in the high 600s and low to mid-700s on the SATs. The overwhelming majority of students enter in the top 10 percent of their high school class, and many of those are in the top 5 percent. The admissions office takes into account many factors besides standardized test scores and grades—letters of recommendation from teachers and guidance counselors, records of extracurricular activities, and application essays. But these additional factors are largely supplementary. Except in unusual cases (such as athletes and legacy applicants, students with highly atypical backgrounds), students are those who excelled in the academic system of high school. Most students come from upper-middle-class and upper-class backgrounds, with a sprinkling of students from working-class backgrounds, most of whom receive large amounts of scholarship aid. The students who have the hardest time matriculating are middle-middle-class students, who typically qualify for aid but not necessarily enough for them to attend the university.

Instruction is geared toward academically high-performing students. There are virtually no true remedial courses. Professors are somewhat at a loss as to how to deal with students who are not academically adept. Although there is an academic-counseling center, it is equipped to handle only a small number of students, for the most part those with certified learning disabilities or attention disorders. Although there are many extracurricular activities offered at the university, the stress tends to be on academics.

Institution J

Institution J is a large public institution in the Midwest. It embodies the Jeffersonian idea, which has given rise to the concept proposed here of the ACCEL university.

Institution J accepts students largely on the basis of ACT scores and high school GPAs. However, the bar for admission by these standards is relatively low—an overwhelmingly large majority of students are accepted—and students who do not reach the bar can gain access through alternative routes, such as by taking supplementary courses in a community college or by showing personal qualities such as leadership that the admissions office believes indicate that the student could succeed academically as well as nonacademically in the university.

Instruction is geared toward typical college students, with extensive opportunities for remediation and extra help provided by a student-success center. The extra help is available to all students and is utilized by almost one-third of them at some point in their college career, mostly in the first year. Students at this institution often place a lot of emphasis on extracurricular activities such as athletics, Greek life, and various student organizations.

Comparison between Institutions H and J

It might sound like the main difference between Universities H and J is in their selectivity at the time of admission, and indeed that is a major difference. But I would argue that a larger difference is in institutional beliefs regarding modifiability and breadth of abilities. Institution H generally adopts a view of abilities as fixed and as well assessed by high school grades and high scores on standardized tests. Institution J, although using these criteria, tends more toward the view that education modifies abilities and that abilities are broad, extending far beyond test scores and grades. This institution emphasizes access in part because of a belief that when students are high school seniors, it is hard to predict who will succeed in life in the sense of making a positive, meaningful, and enduring difference to the world.

Simply by virtue of its high selectivity and the criteria for that selectivity, Institution H makes a statement to students, parents, and society as to what it stands for—namely, identifying at the high school level those whom it believes will be the future elite of society. Institution J does not place quite so explicit a bet, giving students whose academic records are weaker a chance to prove themselves.

An institution could be unselective but still not be a Jeffersonian institution. If its stakeholders believe that it is not simply a selective institution but rather one that accepts those who might wish for but cannot gain access to elite schools, it may not be Jeffersonian at all. Rather, it may view itself as a repository for weaker students with weaker prospects than those at more elite schools. In this case, it would be more, at best, of an aspiring Hamiltonian institution and, at worst, a Hamiltonian "also-ran."

The Hamiltonian tradition dominates conceptions of higher education in the United States of today. But ethical servant leadership is in no great supply in our society. As a result, there is almost certainly an important place for the Jeffersonian tradition as well—the historical and philosophical tradition underlying the ACCEL university. This latter tradition is not well appreciated or measured by ratings such as one finds in the media and even in scholarly publications. Perhaps that needs to change. And we need to remember that rankings for universities, like rankings for cars, depend not on what the media value but on what each of us values in educating our citizenry and our children. If we value giving every student a chance to succeed as an active concerned citizen and ethical leader, the Jeffersonian view is the one to adopt. What is the mission of the university in the Jeffersonian tradition—of the ACCEL university? We consider that in the next chapter.

2

THE MISSION OF THE ACCEL UNIVERSITY

Universities have many different missions. I suggest, though, that an important mission of the university is to teach students how to do deep, reflective, critical thinking and at the same time to educate the next generation of active concerned citizens and ethical leaders who will make a positive, meaningful, and enduring difference to the world. We educate these students by developing their knowledge base and their creative, analytical, practical, and wisdom-based and ethical skills. Again, I refer to universities that buy into this mission as ACCEL (**A**ctive **C**oncerned **C**itizenship and **E**thical **L**eadership) universities. In other words, successful ACCEL university graduates succeed when they make the world a better place in which to live.

When people think of *leadership,* they often think of someone bossing others around or at least showing people what they should do. The term "leadership" is used in this book in an entirely different way. *Leadership* as defined here refers to setting out on a path whereby one makes a positive, meaningful, and enduring difference to the world, at some level. That level may be the family, the community, the state, the nation, or many nations. Leaders, in this sense, are people who leave the world looking different and better than it did before they were in it. Thus, in preparing leaders, we are preparing people who make the world a different and better place, at some level.

One might ask, doesn't the world need followers too? In the end, aren't most college graduates followers rather than leaders? This question assumes that people are either leaders or followers. In fact, except in absolute dictatorships, all leaders are also followers. In a publicly traded company, and in many privately owned ones as well, even the CEO is responsible to a board of directors. And the board of directors is responsible to shareholders, as well as to consumers, government regulators, and, arguably, even a common good. So being a good and effective leader means being a good and effective follower as well. No one except an absolute dictator lacks responsibility to others beside himself or herself. That is, leadership and followership are not mutually exclusive categories—they are two sides of the same coin. So one could equally say that followers need to make a positive and meaningful difference to the world. And if a leader is behaving irresponsibly, it falls to followers to remedy the failure of leadership, usually peacefully, but not always (as in a revolution).

One might also question why college graduates should need to take on the great amount of responsibility that leaders often assume. But when I speak of leadership, I speak of it at multiple levels. For me personally, the most important leadership role I have ever taken on is in my family. Many, if not most of us, seek to make a positive, meaningful, and enduring difference to our family.

One also might wonder about the whole concept of "ethical leadership." Who is to define what is "ethical"? I discuss this question further in chapter 3, but for now, I would like to distinguish between "moral" and "ethical." I use the term "moral" to refer to issues of right and wrong. What we learn in religious-school classes is, for the most part, what is moral—do not kill, do not steal, and so forth. When I refer to "ethical leadership" here, I refer to a process of how problems are solved and decisions are made based on some kind of code of behavior—that decisions are made and problems solved not just on the basis of what will bring profit, or please shareholders, or even please consumers, but also on the basis of what will be the right thing to do. That is, the "ethical" part of leadership is in the process of thinking. It is asking what is the right thing to do and forming a careful chain of reasoning (described in chapter 3) as to how to reach the right course of action, or correct a wrong course of action. So my goal in this book is not to rehash Sunday School morals—I am not the right person to do that; there are others who would do it far better—but rather to discuss what steps a leader would have to go through in his or her problem solving and decision making to be considered an *ethical* leader.

People have always disagreed as to what is "ethical" and as to how ethical decisions can be made and ethical behavior enacted. What I would hope they would agree on is the importance of taking ethical considerations into account in leadership roles. It has become fairly clear, in today's world, that many leaders do not take such considerations into account, or that if they do, it is in a cavalier or even cynical way.

Great leaders differ in many ways. George Washington, Abraham Lincoln, Mahatma Gandhi, Winston Churchill, Franklin Roosevelt, Martin Luther King Jr., Mother Teresa, Aung San Suu Kyi, even young Malala Yousafzai, appear on the surface to share little in common. They have varied in age, race, sex, background, and even political and other beliefs. For the most part, they have led flawed lives, as have almost all of us. What they have in common is a strong ethical code and *moral courage*. In the end, the strong ethical code and moral courage to do the right thing are what matter more than anything else, especially in difficult times.

Washington took a leading role in the revolt against the British; Lincoln led the way in the fight against slavery and secession; Gandhi fought to lift the British yoke; Churchill led the British fight against the Nazis; Martin Luther King Jr. fought for civil rights. All of these leaders put not only their followers but also themselves at risk, realizing that in times of trouble, sometimes there is nothing left except the "good fight."

Today, as in much of the past, purchasing an insurance policy to keep one's job as a leader often means being a politician—it means knowing just how much to give, and possibly a bit more, to ensure that one retains one's position of leadership. This is true in politics—where it is becoming more and more difficult to find leaders who are anything more than self-serving and, increasingly, narcissistic—and it is becoming true in all domains of leadership, including universities. Increasingly, I believe, leaders are focusing on the concessions they believe they need to keep their jobs—and they may well be right—rather than on the stances they need to take to do the right thing. In one sense, who could blame them? How many leaders want to do the right thing and then be obliged to resign—or worse, be fired? But what the greatest leaders had in common is that they risked their jobs, and often their lives, to follow the morally courageous path. What college students are seeing today is a form of leadership—in their colleges, in our corporations, in the nation—that scarcely provides the kinds of role modeling they need to lead them to find the courage that moral leadership demands. Compromise is good, but only up to the point where it is morally defensible. Today lines of what is morally defensible seem to be in the process of being blurred in the name of political gamesmanship.

Compromise is especially difficult, even for the most moral leaders, because often what we think other people think is not what they think. For example, Michael Barnes and I conducted a study some years ago on the extent to which partners in intimate relationships understood what each other wanted. We computed the correlation between what one partner actually wanted and what the other thought he or she wanted. On a scale of 0 to 1, the correlation was a meager 0.3 (Sternberg and Barnes 1985). In other words, even people in intimate relationships don't know very well what the other wants.

The stakes for understanding our partners' wants in an intimate setting are pretty high. Equally high in value for academic marketplaces are the stakes for understanding what employers want in college graduates. Students pay many thousands of dollars for a college education in order to prepare themselves for the job market. If the college or university is providing the wrong stuff, that's a poor investment for the students.

Preparation for Jobs and Life

Reading the recent literature in the field of higher education, you might notice that what some educators think employers want involves several trends:

1. Employers want students to have college majors that provide them with readily transferable job knowledge and skills. The more professional the major is, the better it prepares students for later life.
2. They want students who have had access to top-quality means of knowledge transfer. In this view, perhaps MOOCs (massive open online courses)

are attractive to some because, in the ideal, the lectures would cost the students (and the colleges) next to nothing and would be taught by the most famous scholars in the world.

3. They want students who have demonstrated, through grades and standardized-test scores, that they are high achievers. In addition, employers want evidence of knowledge acquired in college.

The problem is that none of those three assertions holds up well, at least according to a recent survey of what employers really want, conducted by the Association of American Colleges and Universities (AAC&U, for which I was a member of the Board of Directors at the time; see Association of American Colleges and Universities 2013; see also Humphreys and Kelly 2014).

The AAC&U surveyed employers in the business and nonprofit sectors to find out what they most value in hiring college graduates. The survey was particularly concerned with the interface between the world of college and the world of work.

With regard to Trend No. 1, 93 percent of the employers surveyed said that they wanted a demonstrated capacity to think critically, to communicate clearly, and to solve complex problems. They viewed these skills as more important than a candidate's particular undergraduate major. They were not saying that a student's major does not matter, but that, overwhelmingly, the thinking, problem-solving, and communication skills a job candidate has acquired in college are more important than the specific field in which the applicant earned a degree. Looking at successful leaders in business and in the nonprofit sector, you find that they have majored in everything under the sun. Many ended up, by choice, pursuing careers in fields other than the one in which they majored.

On Trend No. 2, the association's survey found that more than nine in ten employers surveyed said it was important that job candidates show ethical judgment and integrity, intercultural skills, and the capacity for continued new learning. Furthermore, in excess of 75 percent of employers said they wanted to see more emphasis on five important skill areas, namely, critical thinking, complex problem solving, both written and oral communication, and application of knowledge to real-world settings.

Those are not skills optimally developed through passive learning in lecture settings, including MOOCs. Rather, they are skills developed through active learning in settings that encourage dialogue, give-and-take, real-world problem solving, and active mentorship. Put another way by the association, employers were especially interested in active learning, emphasizing practices such as collaborative problem solving, meaningful internships, senior projects, and engagement with the community.

As for Trend No. 3, educators seem to assume that employers want concrete evidence of achievement, in the form of grades, for example. But, the AAC&U survey found, employers consistently rank outcomes and practices that involve application of useful learned skills over merely the acquisition of discrete bodies of knowledge, whatever they may be. High grades on tests just don't cut it alone in terms of the broader knowledge and skills that employers value.

If we were to summarize the survey results, we might say that employers want the knowledge and skills that will be crucial not only to a student's first job but also to his or her second, third, and fourth jobs. They want a student who has learned how to learn and how to adapt flexibly to rapidly changing demands. ACCEL universities excel in developing these skills. Employers are not as concerned about specific majors or things like what gets academic credit and what does not.

The *Chronicle of Higher Education* also conducted a survey of employers, with similar results (see Supiano 2013; see also Fischer 2014). It found, for example, that employers tend to place more emphasis on practical work and internships than on academic work. The *Chronicle* survey also reported:

1. College graduates were most lacking in written and oral communication skills, in adaptability and their ability to manage multiple priorities, and in decision making and problem solving.
2. Only 19 percent of employers seek graduates from specific majors and are unwilling to consider candidates without those majors; the majority of employers—78 percent—will consider students from any major.
3. Employees in the executive ranks were those least interested in considering only candidates with specific majors (14 percent). Indeed, many of those executives themselves were liberal-arts majors.

Again, the survey did not say that major does not matter—simply that other qualifications matter more.

Why are many of educators' impressions about what employers want not entirely, or even barely, correct? At the very least, several current emphases in the higher-education literature do not seem to match well with the real demands of employers. Given that many students' main goal in going to college is to find a good job, why do we read so much about MOOCs, majors, and college-credit acquisition? Those issues may be important, but—according to the employer surveys—they are not central to generating the skills that best lead to employability.

Daniel Kahneman and Amos Tversky, two of the great cognitive psychologists of all time, proposed that many of our errors in thinking are a result of cognitive habits that work some of the time but not all of the time (see Kahneman 2013). Two such habits are representativeness and availability.

Representativeness is the degree to which something is similar in its essential characteristics to whatever population of things it is viewed as representing. The college major, for example, seems representative of what employers look for, because a major in a particular field seems to be what employers in that field want in a candidate. The student's major is viewed as representing the job. In some cases, it well may. But the association's survey makes clear that employers care more about ethics, critical thinking, creative thinking, and common sense. So in that case, representativeness leads us astray.

The cognitive habit of availability is thinking that what comes easily to mind must certainly be important. The more we hear about college majors, MOOCs, and college credit for knowledge acquired outside the campus, for example, the more we may think that those things are important and provide the answers to our problems, whatever the problems may be. So solutions to other problems somehow seem to become solutions to the problem of employability, even though they are not.

For those who really care about most students' primary concern, employability, it would behoove them to read the results of the AAC&U and *Chronicle* surveys carefully. They tell us what employers really want—not just what we imagine they want—and, more important, what students need to succeed in life. And they tell us that creative, critical, practical, and wisdom-based decision-making and problem-solving skills, along with a mindset of lifelong learning and a strong work ethic, are far more important than current fads in the literature. Employers want the qualities developed in ACCEL institutions, which often are not those emphasized by universities today.

Going Beyond Shallow Ratings

Many people, including university faculty, staff, and administrators, are uncomfortable with rankings of colleges and universities, such as those found in *U.S. News & World Report*. Perhaps they don't like the idea of measuring the quality of an institution of higher learning, or they don't like the way the measurements are done.

At some general level, colleges and universities near the top of the *U.S. News* ratings, such as Harvard and Yale, probably excel in some meaningful way over those institutions near the bottom of such rankings, just as people with higher composite ACTs have certain academic skills that are more developed than those in people with lower composite ACTs. But such global assessments miss the qualities that make institutional differences, like individual differences, interesting, and most of all, that distinguish ACCEL institutions from others. They can fool people into missing what is most important in distinguishing entities, whether individuals or institutions. For example, the University of California at Los Angeles and the University of Virginia, tied for the second rank among public universities in recent *U.S. News* ratings, would provide very different experiences to undergraduates (as anyone who has visited UCLA and the University of Virginia would likely notice). They differ in the roles of undergraduate versus graduate students, social traditions, and, of course, campus ambiance, among other things.

When students (or faculty or staff, for that matter) select an institution of higher learning, overall rankings may obscure the information that individuals most need to make an informed choice. Some of the best research institutions in the country show relatively little concern with teaching, and some of the best teaching institutions put only modest emphasis on research. Of course, there are institutions that care about both teaching and research and even those that care about neither (so long as they meet their projected bottom line). If one were to select an institution solely on overall quality, one would miss these important differences and many others, such as size, view of undergraduate versus graduate versus professional students, kind of campus life, role of religion on campus, salience of athletics on campus, availability of particular degree programs, pride in traditions, and so forth.

As with individual qualities of mind, one can and probably should become even more specific when evaluating institutions. With regard to research, one institution may excel in basic research, another in applied research. With regard to teaching, one institution might have fine teaching in large lectures but few small seminars because of a large ratio of students to teaching faculty; another institution might have excellent teaching, most of it through small seminars. Such differences are consequential for students because they provide different kinds of education. Overall ratings fail to take these differences into account (Sternberg 2011b). For example, college students may think that higher rankings mean a better education when in fact they may mean that professors are less available to college students, not more.

At some level, students applying to college and scholars looking for jobs know all this. But they, or their parents or other family members, may be willing to overlook the particular qualities that make institutions differentially great in favor of some overall prestige or reputational factor, possibly the result of evaluations by people who know little or even nothing about the schools they are evaluating. In the human-abilities field, one can see the same problem when some institutions become enamored of composite standardized test scores while largely ignoring the individual qualities that make a particular applicant unique. But if people—whether students or employees—are unhappy with their institutional choice, it will likely be not because of overall prestige but rather because of the mismatch of the institution to their personal preferences and goals (Sternberg 2004b).

A further obvious problem is that the presidents, provosts, and admissions deans making some of the ratings generally know very little about the large majority of the institutions they are evaluating, and are likely to fall into the trap of giving ratings on the basis of stereotypes. So, at least in "reputational ratings," one may learn more about prevailing stereotypes than about institutional qualities. It is perhaps embarrassing that people in top positions would rely on stereotypes—or that anyone would ask them to do these ratings—but we all are susceptible to falling into these traps in various aspects of our lives (Sternberg 2013e).

If evaluators of institutions truly wanted to perform a service for seekers of instruction and of jobs, they would rate the schools in terms of the dimensions that matter to potential applicants and pay little or no attention to overall ratings, which may mean relatively little. Indeed, providing such an overall rating may tempt people to simplify their evaluations in a way that ultimately hurts both the institution and themselves. Evaluators of institutions could learn from psychological research that often the most interesting information is not at the top level of a hierarchy but somewhere in the middle (Smith and Medin 1981). At this middle level is the information that will matter most in decision making about institutions of higher learning.

A first-class university does not have to be number one in national media ratings, which are based in large part on vague "reputational" elements that often are themselves based on the previous year's ratings. Other kinds of analytical ratings look at measures of faculty quality but fail to take into account the value added by the university education. Consider instead a different framework.

1. *Access versus exclusion.* Some elite universities take pride in rejecting as many applicants as possible. ACCEL universities, in contrast, emphasize access to qualified applicants. They want, at least in principle, to admit every student who is capable of doing the work and optimizing the university experience. Their mission is to reach out and support social and economic development by contributing to the creation of a highly educated workforce. Because the ultimate quality of a university resides so much in the value it adds to those who participate in it, there is much to be said on focusing on access for those who can profit from the university and profit it as well.

2. *Abilities as modifiable versus fixed.* College-admissions tests, such as the ACT and the SAT, are fundamentally based on a notion of abilities as fixed. Their publishers often take pride when studies find that interventions change scores minimally or not at all. Institutions that focus on students with scores only at the top of the distribution are buying into the notion that abilities are fixed. ACCEL institutions, in contrast, take pride in their view of abilities as modifiable. They are betting that some students with lower test scores and even grade-point averages, if they work hard, can become smarter through education. Indeed, the purpose of education, they believe, is to make students smarter. They thus look

carefully not only at grades and test scores but also at motivation and desire to give back to society.

3. *Abilities as broad versus narrow.* Standardized tests, as they now exist, measure primarily memory and analytical abilities. When admissions officers focus on test scores, they are implicitly buying into a notion of a person's potential as susceptible to being captured by a number. But positive and successful leaders show the creative skills to formulate a vision, the analytical skills to ascertain whether their vision is a good one, the practical skills to implement their vision and persuade others of its value, and the wisdom-based and ethical skills to ensure that their vision helps attain a common good. Great leaders further have a strong work ethic, a sense of responsibility, the skills needed to work smoothly on a team, the willingness to learn from their mistakes, humility, high motivation to achieve, integrity, and resilience in the face of failure. Standardized tests do not measure these essential leadership skills.

4. *Education for the world versus only for the "life of the mind."* In some institutions, professors harp on college as developing the "life of the mind." Nothing is wrong with this unless, from their point of view, the more removed an institution is from the complexities and harshness of the everyday world, the better. ACCEL institutions, in contrast, emphasize an education that prepares for and promotes interaction with the world—one that prepares students not only for their first job but also for their second, third, and fourth jobs. ACCEL universities want students to be job-ready on Day 1 as they enter the workforce. They do not believe in an education divorced from everyday reality. In ACCEL universities, both general education and specialized education teach students to think, to reflect, and to appreciate how others before them have approached and solved life's problems.

5. *Strong versus weak accountability.* Some institutions of higher learning have a weak accountability structure. For example, at some for-profits, it is not even clear from promotional materials who the faculty are or what they have accomplished. Even at many private institutions, accountability rarely goes much beyond a board of trustees, which may have been picked in part by the previous board. ACCEL institutions have a responsibility to their community, state, and nation and the world. They cannot afford to be anything less than fully and publicly transparent because they exist to serve. They cannot risk turning inward or battening down the hatches.

Seeing Things in a Different Way

No doubt there are other standards by which universities can be judged. But this rubric shows there is a viable alternative to "one-size-fits-all" published ratings—standards relevant specifically to the mission of the ACCEL university.

Our nation needs to broaden what "greatness" in a university means. At the very least, we need to expand our conception of greatness to a multidimensional notion, not just a notion of the unidimensional rankings that appear in certain magazines. ACCEL universities focus on changing the world in a positive, meaningful, and enduring way. They do not all choose to be elite like Ivy League schools, because Ivy League schools attain their elite status, in part, by being highly selective in admission of students and selection of faculty in ways that most institutions cannot equal. Ivy League institutions can be ACCEL institutions, but ACCEL institutions need not be Ivy League or anything close. ACCEL institutions perhaps best represent the very core of what greatness means in American society—namely, equal opportunity for all and, through it, the chance to make our society and the world a better place in which to live.

Thus, ACCEL institutions do not have to be perceived as being among the most "elite" universities of the nation, although some will be. Yet they accomplish some things that are truly extraordinary.

First, whereas many selective institutions in the country are highly focused on entry value—seeking students with the highest grades, test scores, and high school records of "extracurricular activities"—ACCEL institutions are particularly focused on "value added," that is, producing the future leaders who will make the world a better place. Typically, ACCEL institutions willingly and even gladly take students with a wider range of grades and test scores because their mission is to provide access, not to restrict entry. A necessary qualification, of course, is that the students admitted are able to do the work, either on admission or with remediation and enrichment, and that they are prepared to profit from and profit the university. ACCEL institutions generally have honors programs, but often the focus is not just on how academically smart you are but on how much of your smartness you can give back to the world. What is important in an ACCEL institution is developing future ethical leaders who will enrich their communities and their societies, in whatever way.

Some of the most selective institutions, of course, are also concerned about adding value. But their admissions numbers, with selectivity rates often in the single digits, may result in the message to many students that they may be good but not quite good enough. Ratings such as those of *U.S. News & World Report* reward institutions that reject lots of applicants. The game becomes somewhat perverse: get lots of applicants so you can reject them to prove how exclusive you are as an institution. In ACCEL institutions, providing access is especially important for students from low-opportunity households whose only chance to go to college may be at the ACCEL university. Often their education and socialization have provided them with only minimal scaffolding for a college education.

Second, graduation from an ACCEL institution may not always give students the same level of brand equity as they would obtain at the most elite institutions, although there are many employers who are impressed with the initiative and hard work that so many students from ACCEL institutions are prepared to offer. The ACCEL diploma should be a ticket to improve yourself sufficiently that so that later you will be in a position to prove your worth. It has proud brand equity. Usually, the student's initial job placement will be determined by accomplishments more than by the brand equity of his or her school. It will be up to the student, in the American tradition, to raise himself or herself by the bootstraps. At some future time, perhaps, members of our society will realize more and more the extraordinary value that may be hidden behind the ACCEL university diploma.

Third, in admissions, the most selective institutions tend to be organized around a relatively fixed notion of human abilities and skills. Requiring sky-high SATs and ACTs make sense as important (although not exclusive) bases of admission only if one believes that they measure relatively fixed traits that project the future potential of the applicant. If abilities are highly modifiable, in contrast, then such test scores assess potentials largely at certain intervals in time. In this case, one can look at the college or university as providing a "zone of potential development" to help students use the ability levels they are at as starting points, not just as ending points (Sternberg 1997a). From the point of view of the ACCEL mission, access provides a way for students to achieve the equal opportunity our society promises. Abilities are indeed modifiable, so the institution can help each student reach the outer level of those abilities—to translate abilities into competencies, and competencies into expertise.

Fourth, ACCEL institutions tend to have a broad sense of what abilities are. In our society, in part as a result of the No Child Left Behind Act, we place so much emphasis on narrow abilities and knowledge that often students who are the "best" academically have had little incentive to develop the emotional intelligence, practical intelligence, and wisdom-based skills that are needed to lead the institutions of society (Sternberg 2004a). Hence one can end up with leaders who were educated at elite institutions—who are very smart in an SAT sense—and then sometimes prove unable to connect with the rest of the population and who create financial and ethical messes because their analytical skills were never adequately complemented by the creative, practical, and wisdom-based skills they need to truly succeed as leaders.

Fifth, evaluation of scholarship and research takes on a particular cast in an ACCEL institution. All institutions are, or at least should be, pleased when a scholar publishes in the journals with the best reputations and citation rates. But in many institutions, it matters little or not at all whether the work has any implications for the betterment of the state and society, not only in the short run but even in the long run. Sometimes work that has implications for the betterment of society is actually viewed with suspicion. The result is a kind of curious disconnection between the university and the society. In an ACCEL institution, traditional scholarly quality still matters, but work that gives back to society receives special plaudits. It thus becomes easier for the people of a community or state to see why research is important to them, not merely to the advancement of individual researchers' scholarly careers.

Sixth, service and outreach have a particular meaning in an ACCEL institution. In many institutions, research, teaching, and service all count toward promotion and tenure, but often service is in last place in this triad. In an ACCEL institution, service is more integrated into the fabric of teaching and research.

Finally, in the ACCEL institution, the emphasis on give-back leads to the centrality of ethical leadership and wisdom as the core values of the learning experience. "Smartness" is valued, but as a means of giving back. Wisdom is the use of one's smartness and knowledge for a common good through the infusion of positive ethical values, and because the ACCEL institution must give back to the community, state, and country in order to fulfill its mission, its graduates cannot be viewed as truly successful unless they embody this ideal.

Whereas some of us may think of ACCEL institutions as needing to emulate the most elite institutions, perhaps these elite institutions, if they have not already done so, would benefit from adopting some of the ACCEL values. As our society becomes ever more socially and economically stratified and the middle class vanishes, and as correlations become even higher between educational opportunities and socioeconomic status, we have an obligation, as a society, to ask whether things are going where we want them to go. What kinds of leaders do we want to develop? Is it possible that the huge emphasis on memory and analytical skills reflected by tests such as the SAT and ACT, and embodied in college-admissions processes, are having effects opposite to what we as a society might hope for? Are we producing leaders who are analytically adept but who fail in a wise and emotionally connected way to engage deeply with the crises our society is currently facing? Do we want a society in which we care more about how narrowly smart people are than about how wise and ethical they are? ACCEL institutions in many ways reflect the ideals of the American dream. They have a unique role in helping to achieve that dream that is not being captured by magazine ratings based on narrow criteria. These ideals are not reflected by typical published ratings of universities.

What Should Be "Rated"?

If conventional ratings are not so useful, what are criteria that would be relevant in evaluating ACCEL institutions? How can one concretely assess how well an ACCEL institution is doing its job?

1. *Access.* What percentage of qualified students who apply are admitted? ACCEL institutions are supposed to provide access, and the more they do so, the better they are serving their function. Note that *U.S. News*, in contrast, rates institutions more highly that are extremely selective in their admissions. Access in an ACCEL institution means not only providing admission to a relatively broad range of potential students but also doing so in a way that is affordable and will not burden students with undue amounts of debt. To the extent institutions need to be selective, it

should be with regard to the full range of attributes that might predict active concerned citizens and ethical leaders.

2. *Admission policies.* To what extent do admissions reflect the ACCEL mission of access for those who will become active concerned citizens and ethical leaders? You really can't tell much when students are in high school about their future potential for citizenship and leadership. If the criteria are set too high (e.g., in terms of high school GPA or standardized test scores) or too narrowly (e.g., just grades and/or standardized test scores), the institutions probably are not doing their job. You want the bar set high enough to ensure that students have a chance to succeed academically, but that bar should be based on research regarding real student outcomes at the university and in later life, not on some arbitrary standard, such as top X percent of a high school graduating class. (Note that *U.S. News* rates institutions more highly solely as a function of their having higher admissions standards.) At some institutions, a holistic path to admission that looks at the whole person and not just at test scores and grades facilitates realization of the ACCEL mission. Holistic admissions procedures include essays and other activities that measure key ingredients of ethical leadership, namely, creative, analytical, common-sense, wisdom-based, and ethical reasoning skills.

3. *Scaffolding and support for student collegiate success.* Whereas in some institutions, all or almost all admitted students will have superb academic preparation for college, in an ACCEL university that is doing its job, many students will enter with academically challenged preparation. Retention and four-year (or five- or six-year) graduation is more of a challenge for many ACCEL institutions than it is for other types of institutions that do not seek to maximize access. Yet for an ACCEL university to prepare active concerned citizens and leaders, it must get them through to the degree. College administrators can talk all they want about how high schools could or should do a better job in preparing students, but once the students are admitted to institutions of higher learning, they are the institution's responsibility. This means that the institution needs a full-scale student-success center, providing support for students who (a) need to fill in deficiencies in academic preparation, (b) need to learn the ropes of what it means to be a successful college student, (c) have yet to come to believe that they can be academically successful, (d) have to learn better self-regulation skills, (e) require financial counseling, (f) need counseling regarding the

relation between their college career and their job aspirations, or (g) simply require close mentoring in choosing courses, a major, and a career.

4. *Meaningful job placement.* Because ACCEL institutions are intended to give a worldly education, job placement is key. The issue is not only the percentage of graduates who are employed within, say, six months of graduation, but also the percentage who are employed in jobs they consider meaningful and career-relevant. ACCEL institutions thus need to have educational services that promote employability—regardless of students' majors—and excellent job-placement services.

5. *Development of active concerned-citizenship and ethical-leadership skills.* Many if not most colleges and universities say they promote active-citizenship and ethical-leadership skills, but what concretely do they do to promote such skill development? One thing they could do is to institute an ethical-leadership track that would enable all students who so choose to take courses infusing ethical-leadership case studies into their course curricula. The program would be coordinated with student affairs, and participants would attend seminars and other discussion groups. The capstone requirement would be a paper or project that would show how students have applied what they learned in their courses to their leadership in extracurricular activities. ACCEL institutions must have concrete means of promoting ethical-leadership development, not just messaging proclaiming that they do it.

6. *Quality of instruction.* In order to serve their stakeholders, ACCEL institutions need to provide superb instruction. Instruction should be evaluated both by peers and by students. Moreover, it should be evaluated on multiple dimensions, such as with regard to quality of in-class instruction, usefulness of assignments, fairness of tests, and usefulness of grading in pointing out means for improvement. ACCEL instruction should also enable all students to capitalize on their strengths and to compensate for or correct their weaknesses. In other words, it should enable them to optimize their patterns of abilities.

7. *Availability of instruction.* Students should be able to take the courses for which they wish to enroll. They should not be turned away because course enrollments fill up. To the extent that students are turned away, the institution is failing to meet its obligation to its students.

8. *Value added by university experience.* ACCEL universities are more interested in value added by the instructional experience than they are in

entry-level credentials. They recognize that students' knowledge and skills are modifiable and hence subject to change through the university experience. Some universities use standardized tests to measure value added, but such tests tend to measure a narrow band of skills. Electronic portfolios (e-portfolios) tend to be broader and more comprehensive measures of students' achievements over the course of their college careers.

9. *Contribution of the university to the economy of the community, state, and nation.* ACCEL institutions should serve not only those who study or work in them but society at large as well. A major component of such service is their contribution to the economy in terms of job creation, outreach and extension and other services, patents for inventions, and so forth.

10. *Usefulness of research to academic discipline, state, and nation.* The same measurements that apply to the evaluation of research at any other university also apply to ACCEL universities: What is the quantity, quality, visibility, and impact of the research being done? In ACCEL institutions, however, utility not only to the academic discipline but also to the community, the state, and the world takes on special significance. Such utility is especially realized through outreach and extension efforts, which should be evaluated for effectiveness.

So now we have discussed the mission of the ACCEL university. The next question that arises is precisely what skills the ACCEL university develops in students which serve to fulfill the university's mission. This question is considered in the next chapter.

3

The Skills ACCEL Universities Should Develop

What skills should universities concentrate on developing?

Critical (Analytical) Thinking

When colleges and universities teach for critical thinking, too often it is in contexts that do not transfer to students' everyday lives (Sternberg 2007). For example, students could take a logic course and become masters of formal abstract syllogistic reasoning, but people do not go around in their lives solving Aristotelian syllogisms. Or students could learn critical thinking in literature or history or even physics, for that matter, and still make the same dumb decisions in their lives. Indeed, the fact that people can be smart on paper and stupid in their lives led to my editing of the book *Why Smart People Can Be So Stupid* (Sternberg 2002).

Although people reason all the time, not all inferences or conclusions are correct or justified by the data. Scholars have attempted to classify and study the various kinds of erroneous inferences (rickety reasoning) that people can make. In classifying types of inferences, they refer to everyday fallacies. It is in this realm of everyday thinking that colleges and universities most need to intervene but rarely do.

In contrast, the kinds of critical-thinking skills measured by the SAT and by IQ tests (of which the SAT essentially is one) are not all so relevant to everyday reasoning. The SAT and similar tests measure critical thinking in solving problems that are abstract, emotionally barren, and devoid of motivations for personal or institutional gain. When people reason in everyday situations, they deal with concrete, emotionally laden problems in which there are powerful motivations for gain, such as making money or acquiring friends, romantic partners, clients, or allies. Reasoning skills applied to idealized situations are modest predictors of the messy reasoning of everyday life (Stanovich 2010) and are largely different in kind from reasoning skills applied in everyday life (Nisbett 1993).

What I am proposing to emphasize in teaching for critical thinking is rather different from what is sometimes emphasized when students write papers or do projects and is very different from the skills that would be taught in an SAT preparation course. I would encourage universities to emphasize the critical fallacies people make in their everyday reasoning. Consider some examples.

Fallacies of Relevance

Fallacies of relevance are committed when the premises of an argument have no bearing on its conclusion. The conclusion is irrelevant to the line of reasoning that led up to it. Arguments of this type are referred to as non sequiturs (from the Latin *non sequitur*, meaning "it does not follow"). Concerned citizens, of the kind developed by ACCEL universities, need to be able to decide on what bases to support political candidates, for example. Political candidates, for the most part, encourage citizens to vote on the basis of reasons that are largely irrelevant to how they will perform in office: "You should vote for me because I have a beautiful family, I go to church every Sunday, and I'm handsome."

The statement sounds a bit absurd on its face, and yet many candidates gladly circulate posters and pictures of themselves with their families—with everyone looking lovely—and emphasize their strict religious principles. None of these things is terribly relevant to being elected, but the strategy often seems to work.

Sales pitches for products take a similar form. When I was young, my family was offered a *World Book Encyclopedia*. It was free—a good deal. We would not have to pay for the encyclopedia, only for some number of years of annual updates. Of course, the cost of the annual updates was really the cost of the encyclopedia, so it was irrelevant whether the money was for the annual updates or the encyclopedia. But that's how encyclopedias were sold in those days and it worked. And yes, we bought the encyclopedia—what a great deal!

The point is that political candidates and encyclopedia salesmen do not sell their wares just to people with low IQs or SAT scores or whatever. They sell to people, many of whom are quite intelligent. Indeed, stupid people might want nothing less than an encyclopedia. Why bother? Really, almost all marketers sell their wares on the basis of irrelevant stimuli— beautiful women for the purchase of perfumes, airplane pilots for watches being sold to people who will never fly a plane in their lives, happy carefree young people for tobacco products. Companies invest billions of dollars in ads that appeal to fallacious reasoning. The products sell, even to people with high SAT scores.

Straw-Man Arguments

Straw-man arguments attempt to refute a claim by replacing it with a less believable statement (the straw man) and then attacking the straw-man claim rather than dealing with the original claim. An interesting aspect of this argument is that it may contain good reasons against the straw-man claim, but these reasons will be irrelevant to the original claim.

Consider again the role that deep critical thinking needs to play in active concerned citizenship of the kind developed by ACCEL universities. As an example, a politician recommends targeted cutting of defense spending and is then called "weak on defense." Another politician supports a woman's right to choice on abortion and is said to support murder. Or a politician does not support a woman's right to choice on abortion and is said to be anti-woman. The point is that, in each case, a straw man is created that may, but probably does not, support the politician's true position, and then an opponent attacks the straw man rather than the original position.

Representativeness

The representativeness heuristic is used in making a judgment regarding the probability of an uncertain event according to (a) how obviously the event is similar to or representative of the population from which it is obtained and (b) the degree to which the event reflects the noticeable features of the process by which it is generated (such as randomness) (Kahneman and Tversky 1971). Consider some examples:

All the families having exactly six children in a particular city were surveyed. In seventy-two of the families, the exact order of births of boys (B) and girls (G) was G B G B B G. What is your estimate of the number of families surveyed in which the exact order of births was B G B B B B?

Most people judging the number of families with the B G B B B B birth pattern estimate the number to be less than seventy-two. Actually, the best estimate of the number of families with this birth order is seventy-two, the same as for the G B G B B G birth order. The expected number for the second pattern would be the same because the gender for each birth is independent (at least, theoretically) of the gender for every other birth, and for any one birth, the chances of a boy (or a girl) are one out of two. Thus, any particular pattern of births is equally likely, even B B B B B B or G G G G G G.

Why do people believe some birth orders to be more likely than others? They do so because they are using the representativeness heuristic. For example, people believe that the first birth order is more likely because, first, it is more representative of the number of females and males in the population and, second, it looks more random than does the second birth order. In fact, of course, either birth order is equally likely to occur by chance.

Similarly, if asked to judge the probability of flips of a coin yielding the sequence—H T H H T H—people will judge it as higher than they will if asked to judge the sequence—H H H H T H. Thus, if you expect a sequence to be random, you tend to view a sequence that "looks random" as more likely to occur. Indeed, people often comment that the ordering of numbers in a table of random numbers "doesn't look random," because people underestimate the number of runs of the same number that will appear wholly by chance. Another example is the lottery—if you are given the choice between picking the number sequence 12–43–7–22–35 and the number sequence 1–2–3–4–5, which set would you be more likely to pick?

Most people would pick the first set of numbers. Maybe you would, too, if you hadn't just read this section. But, of course, in a fair lottery, there is no cause-and-effect relationship between the particular numbers picked and the odds of winning.

Consider another example that is more relevant to active concerned citizenship: Penny has been trying to decide whom to vote for. She keeps hearing that Mr. Jones, who is running for the legislature, is an upstanding family man who puts his family first and takes care of his children. She decides to vote for him because she wants someone who has a sense of responsibility and who looks at his constituents as part of his greater family.

In this particular instance, Penny assumes that the politician's behavior toward his family is representative of his behavior outside it. But she has no logical basis for assuming that the politician's behavior toward his family will represent the politician's behavior outside the family situation. Indeed, many Nazi officers were "good family men." Moreover, in all likelihood, she knows nothing of the politician's behavior toward his family. Many of the politicians caught up in prostitution and other stings previously had conveyed an impression of being "good family men."

Creative Thinking

The worst way to assess creativity is through multiple-choice questions. Nevertheless, let's start with a multiple-choice question:

> Which airline will you not be flying anytime soon? (a) Northwest, (b) Texas Air, (c) Braniff, (d) Eastern, (e) all of the above.

The correct answer is (e) because all of the airlines mentioned have disappeared. Airlines are like every other business. If they do not innovate, they die. The list of failed businesses seems endless. Businesses fail when their owners lack the creativity to adapt flexibly to new circumstances and constraints in the environment.

Good and responsible employers do not want individuals who just blindly do what they are told. They want to work with individuals who can think outside the box and respond flexibly to novel tasks and situations.

It is not only businesses that need to be creative. So do the governmental leaders for whom we vote. As we listen to politicians campaign for the next election, many of the messages we hear are that we have to stop making the stupid mistakes of the past and move on toward a brighter future. The problem is that, at age sixty-five, I've been hearing that message my entire life. Politicians seem better at reframing the same message than they are at actually acting on the message. An ACCEL university should help students come to see the difference between empty promises and consequential actions.

Creativity is skill in coming up with ideas that are novel and useful in some way. Creative people constantly ask themselves whether what they were doing yesterday is what they should be doing today, tomorrow, or the next day. Active concerned citizens and ethical leaders need to be creative because what works or seems to work at one point in time in a family, or job, or society often does not work at another point in time. When we look back on past practices in our own society—absence of suffrage for women, slavery, internment of American citizens of Japanese descent during World War II, McCarthyism—we sometimes properly gasp in horror. It is only through creativity and realizing that any society, no matter how good, can be better that we can see through our own flaws and improve our society and its elements.

Some people believe that creativity is an ability with which people are born. But creativity is not genetically determined. Rather, creativity is a decision process. It's a decision not just to follow the crowd but rather to consider unconventional paths or methods that could lead to similar or better outcomes than those originally intended. And it's not just about esoteric decisions among scientists, writers, or artists. It's about everyday decisions of all kinds. Behind the decision to consider other paths or methods are several attitudes toward life:

- *Thinking outside the box.* Creative people change their patterns of thought. They do not keep doing things the same way just because things have always have been done that way.
- *Being willing to take sensible risks.* Creative people are willing to take risks and even to fail. They know they will make mistakes, but they are ready to learn from them.
- *Being resilient in the face of obstacles.* If one lives a creative life, the question is not whether one will encounter obstacles but rather what one will do in the

face of them. Creative people always get pushback, often from people who are threatened by change. And those who are threatened are often in powerful positions.

- *Realizing that creative ideas don't sell themselves, that people need to be persuaded of their value.* The hardest part of creativity often is not coming up with novel and useful ideas but rather persuading others to accept them.
- *Realizing that what works at one time or in one place often does not work at another time in a different place.* Many people have a creative idea at some time or another, and they can't let go of it. Long after the value of the idea has passed, they stick with it. Their early creativity thus degenerates into a lack of creativity later on.

A problem in our educational system is that schools do not always encourage creativity and sometimes inadvertently discourage it, both in instruction and in assessment. By the time students get to college, they often find it hard to rediscover their creativity. What's to be done?

- *Inform young people that creativity is a learned skill, not an inborn ability.* Many students are not creative because they think they can't be. If they tell themselves they are not creative, they won't be because they will never try.
- *Role-model creativity.* Students will model what they observe, not what they are told. If you want young people to think creatively, show them how to do it.
- *Provide opportunities for young people to think creatively.* You won't get creativity if you always tell youngsters what to do and how to do it. Nor will schools truly value creativity if they limit their assessments to short-answer and multiple-choice tests. Provide opportunities for young people to do independent projects, products, and portfolios that enable students to display their creative powers. Creativity is not just for art or writing class: it's a learnable skill for making all of the choices that we make in all of the things that we do.
- *Encourage creativity.* Don't just hope for students to show creativity. Tell them explicitly that you value their thinking outside the box.
- *Reward creativity.* When students show creativity, praise them and tell them you are proud that they are thinking for themselves, not just following what others tell them to think or do.

Employers want creative employees. Societies need active concerned citizens and ethical leaders who are creative. But how much do universities do to promote creativity? Often the universities say they want students to be creative but actually do little to encourage creativity.

If we admit students with a wide range of abilities, we need to teach them in ways that reflect how they learn. If we are looking for qualities like creativity—which we hear so much about today—but teach students primarily in a way that rewards how well they memorize, then we are setting them and ourselves up for failure. Most people can agree that creative ideas are valuable to individuals and to our society. But those ideas are often rejected because the creative innovator must stand up to vested interests and defy the crowd.

Educators, then, need to do a better job teaching students to mobilize their creativity successfully. Here are twelve ways to encourage creativity in the university classroom (Sternberg and Williams 2001).

1. *Redefine the problem.* Universities can promote creative performance by encouraging students to define and redefine their own problems, projects, presentations, and topics for papers, subject to approval; to choose their own ways of solving problems; and sometimes to choose again if they discover that their approach was a mistake.

Professors cannot always offer choices in the classroom, but having choices is the only way students learn how to choose. Giving them latitude helps them develop taste and good judgment, both of which are essential elements of creativity. In large lecture classes, where it sometimes is difficult or even impossible to give creative assignments, a professor can role-model the redefinition of problems by showing how phenomena in the field about which instruction is taking place can be perceived in a variety of different ways. For example, when I teach about intelligence, my disciplinary specialty, I point out how there are different metaphors that can be used to understand intelligence—for example, as a static IQ, as an information-processing program, as a social construction—and that the metaphor one accepts leads to very different research and conclusions.

2. *Question and analyze assumptions.* Everyone has assumptions, although they are not always widely shared. Questioning assumptions is part of the analytical thinking involved in creativity. Professors can help students develop this talent by making questioning a part of the daily exchange. It is more important for students to learn what questions to ask—and how to ask them—than to learn the answers. Faculty members need to avoid perpetuating the belief that their role is to teach students the facts, and instead help them understand that what matters is their ability to use facts.

3. *Teach students to sell their creative ideas.* Everyone would like to assume that his or her wonderful, creative ideas will sell themselves. But they do not. When I was a first-year assistant professor, the second colloquium I was invited to give was at a large testing organization. I was delighted that the company was apparently interested in adopting my ideas about intelligence, even though I was only twenty-five years old. My career seemed to be off to a spectacular start. I took the train to Princeton, New Jersey, and gave the talk. It was an abject failure. I went from fantasizing about a dazzling career to wondering whether I would have a career at all.

I would like to imagine that my ability to sell ideas has increased with age. But I'm not confident it has. I have been lobbying for changes in the way universities do admissions for years, and in all those years, little has changed.

Students need to learn how to persuade other people of the value of their ideas. Selling is part of the practical aspect of creative thinking.

4. *Encourage idea generation.* Creative people demonstrate a "legislative" style of thinking (Sternberg 1997b): they like to generate ideas. The environment for generating ideas can be constructively critical, but it must not be harshly or destructively so. When suggested ideas don't seem to have much merit, don't just criticize. Instead, suggest new approaches, preferably ones that incorporate at least some aspects of the ideas that seemed overall not to have much value.

5. *Recognize that knowledge is a double-edged sword.* Some years ago, I was visiting a famous psychologist who lived abroad. As part of the tour he had planned for me, we visited the local zoo. We went past the cages of the primates, who were, at the time, engaged in what euphemistically could be called strange and unnatural sexual behavior. I, of course, averted my eyes. My host, however, did not. He began, to my astonishment, analyzing the sexual behavior of the primates in terms of his theory of intelligence. I realized how knowledge and expertise can be a double-edged sword.

On the one hand, people cannot be creative without knowledge. Quite simply, they cannot go beyond the existing state of knowledge if they do not know what that state is. On the other hand, those who have an expert level of knowledge can experience tunnel vision, narrow thinking, and entrenchment. It happens to everyone.

Many students have ideas that are creative with respect to themselves but not to a field. I tell my own students that the teaching-learning process goes two ways. I have knowledge they do not have, but they have a flexibility I do not have—precisely because they do not know as much as I do. By learning from—as well as teaching—our students, professors can open channels for creativity.

6. *Challenge students to identify and surmount obstacles.* The question is not whether one will encounter obstacles. The question is whether the creative thinker has the fortitude to persevere. I have often wondered why so many people start off their careers doing creative work and then vanish from the radar screen. I think I know at least one reason: sooner or later, they decide that being creative is not worth the resistance.

Faculty members can prepare students for disappointment by describing obstacles that they, their friends, and well-known figures in society have faced while trying to be creative; otherwise, students may think that they are the only ones confronted by obstacles.

There comes a time, of course, when one has to know whether to fight or fold. During my brief tenure as president of a university in which I had not previously taught, I attempted to make a number of changes in the way the university operated. The university ranked at a less than stellar level in evaluations of the quality of universities, and I had some ideas about how it might achieve much higher-ranked status. I did not find, nor was I able to create, a receptive audience. I tried to overcome the obstacles; I just did not succeed in doing so. I resigned. Perhaps I should have fought even harder to overcome the obstacles, as I have with most obstacles throughout my life. At some point, one has to decide which battles one wishes to fight and, as well, which battles are worth fighting.

7. *Encourage sensible risk-taking.* When creative people defy the crowd, they take risks. But there are levels of sensibility. Creative people take sensible risks and produce ideas that others ultimately admire and respect as trend-setting.

To help students learn to take sensible risks, faculty members can encourage them to take some intellectual risks with courses, activities, and what they say to adults—to develop a sense of how to assess risks.

8. *Nurture a tolerance of ambiguity.* There are a lot of grays in creative work. Artists and writers working on new projects often report feeling scattered and unsure.

A creative idea tends to come in bits and pieces and develops over time. But the period when the idea is developing is often uncomfortable. When a student has almost the right topic, it's tempting to accept the near miss.

Instead, faculty should encourage students to accept and extend the period in which their ideas do not quite converge.

9. *Foster self-efficacy.* Many people reach a point where they feel as if no one believes in them. Because creative work often doesn't get a warm reception, it is extremely important that creative people believe in the value of what they are doing.

There is no way to know for sure that an idea is good. There are, however, some questions to ask:

> Is there any empirical evidence to support the idea?
> Does the idea follow from any broader theory whose elements may have support?
> Is there some way of testing the idea?
> Have similar ideas been supported?
> Will you pursue an unpopular idea?

Professors need to help students find what they love to do. This is different from what the professors love to do or the students' parents love to do.

10. *Teach students the importance of delaying gratification.* Part of being creative means being able to work on a project or task for a long time without immediate rewards. The fact of the matter is that, in the short term, people are often ignored or punished when they do creative work.

11. *Provide an environment that fosters creativity.* There are many ways to do that. The most powerful is to be a role model for creative thinking. Students develop creativity not when they are told to but when they are shown how.

12. *Teach students that creativity is an attitude toward life.* Creativity is not something you are born with. It is an attitude toward all aspects of your life—that you are willing to think in novel ways and have the courage to stand up for those ideas in the face of likely opposition.

In sum, active concerned citizens and ethical leaders need to be creative in order to avoid getting stuck in the traps or antiquated practices of the past. Creativity can be developed in elementary and secondary schools but also, and most importantly, in universities. If we merely teach students knowledge and how to think analytically about it, we may end up with citizens and leaders who know what was done in the past and what needs to be changed; we won't end up with citizens and leaders who know what to do about what needs to be changed.

Common Sense

Common sense, as it is sometimes said, is anything but common. Yet there are few things more important for an active concerned citizenry and for ethical leaders than to have basic common sense. But what, exactly, is common sense? Common sense is what one needs to know to succeed in life that typically is not explicitly taught and often is not even verbalized.

Standardized tests don't measure common sense. Really, grades don't measure common sense, and neither do any of the other conventional measures used in college admissions. Yet common sense is truly important in life in any society.

Over the years, my colleagues and I have done a number of research studies on common sense, which we studied under the rubric of practical intelligence (Sternberg et al. 2000). Our goal in this work has been to understand how common sense functions, how it can be assessed, and how much it contributes to success in life.

The way we have measured common sense is to present to people the kinds of problems such as they would encounter in their everyday lives. In our college admissions work, for example, we showed movies with various scenarios (Sternberg 2010a). In one scenario, roommates discuss how to divide payments among them, given that the sizes of the rooms in their flat are unequal. In another example, a student enters a party where he does not know anyone present. In yet another example, a student approaches a professor to ask for a letter of recommendation, only to discover that the professor does not know who he is. In one more example, a college student and his girlfriend are starting to make out on a couch when a friend knocks on the door and wants help with a problem. Finally, in another example, students are trying to maneuver a bed up a winding staircase that clearly will not accommodate it. In each case, the movie stopped in the middle of the scene and students were asked how they would handle the situation.

In work on managers, we presented managerial personnel with problems they might encounter in their management work, such as dealing with a difficult subordinate, dealing with a task that somehow never seemed to get done, or dealing with a boss who could never be satisfied (Sternberg et al. 2000). We had similar problems for military officers, salespeople, and individuals in other occupations.

The question, of course, was how well individuals taking the assessment could solve the problems. Their responses were scored in a variety of ways. In one method of scoring, responses of test-takers were compared with those of experts in their fields. In another method of scoring, responses were scored in terms of how practical they were with respect to time, place, and available material and human resources, as well as with respect to how persuasive they were.

Our findings were quite similar from one domain to the next and one subject population to the next. They suggested that IQ is a more limited construct than many people have realized.

First, common sense is correlated with IQ, but only minimally. Someone could be high in common sense but not in IQ, high in IQ but not in common sense, high in both, or low in both. Quite simply, IQ and common sense are not mutually good predictors of each other.

Second, scores on measures of common sense are correlated with each other across domains. In other words, if you are high in common sense, say, as a manager, you probably will have fairly good common sense as a salesperson. The correlations are by no means perfect, but common sense in one domain is a better predictor of common sense in another domain than is IQ.

Third, common sense predicts performance in jobs, at least for managers, at about the same level as IQ. Because it is only minimally correlated with IQ, both measures—common sense and IQ—can help to predict who will be a successful manager.

Fourth, common sense predicts success in college over and above the prediction obtained by scores from standardized tests. In our research, the increment has not been large, but it has been statistically significant.

Fifth, common sense is not the same as personality. One cannot get a good reading on a person's common sense by administering a personality test to the individual.

Sixth, common sense in a domain increases with experience. However, our research suggests that it is not experience per se that predicts gains in common sense but rather what one learns from the experience. From this point of view, simply asking a person how much job experience he or she has is not likely to tell you a whole lot about the person's common sense as relevant to that job. You need to figure out what the person has learned from the job.

Seventh, common sense does not always transfer well from one cultural or subcultural context to another, because what is considered common-sensical in one environment may be considered foolish in another. There is thus always risk in crossing cultures. Crossing cultures does not pertain only to going from one country to another. Businesses have different cultures and so do universities. So what is common sense in one university environment may be anything but in another. For example, at a Research I university, it is common sense that a professor had better publish in prestigious journals if he or she wants to achieve tenure. But at a community college, publishing in such journals may count little or even negatively because it could be seen as taking away time from teaching. One has to figure out the lay of the land before one draws conclusions.

I have referred to the problem of how to apply common sense in challenging environments as the problem of dealing with murky environments (Sternberg 2014c). Let me explain: I was attending an international convention in a foreign city reputed to be somewhat dangerous. I went to take a walk in a neighborhood near my hotel. When I returned to the hotel and mentioned to the concierge that I had walked in that area, he was flabbergasted. He told me I was lucky not to have been mugged or even killed. But the neighborhood had not looked dangerous to me. Some of my colleagues at the convention were not so lucky. No one got hurt in that neighborhood, to my knowledge, but at least two colleagues got mugged on escalators in shopping malls, where one mugger situated himself in front of the target and the other behind. Who's afraid of escalators? It could have happened to anyone and certainly to me.

Unbeknownst to all of us, we were negotiating what proved to be murky environments. And murky environments are everywhere to be found in academic settings, which are, in a sense, themselves "foreign cities reputed to be somewhat dangerous." Common sense is in large part our skill in negotiating murky environments.

A murky environment is one that is unclear, hazy, obscure, confused, or otherwise obfuscated. Murky environments are local. Each has to be understood in its own terms. They pose serious career challenges because we often feel like we should understand them or we think we do understand them but we don't.

If you think about it, almost any personal or business situation is murky to some extent. In this respect, it differs from a standardized test problem, which typically needs to be crystal clear. The problem is that skill in solving crystal-clear problems often does not transfer well to solving murky problems, because so much of solving murky problems is seeing through the haze.

During the course of a career, almost everyone enters multiple murky environments, ones where one thinks one should know the rules but then begins to question whether one knows anything at all about how the place works. The experience is somewhat analogous to what airplane pilots or underwater divers go through when they experience spatial disorientation. They lose their frame of reference and even find themselves uncertain as to what is up and what is down. They are more likely to experience spatial disorientation in murky environments, such as hazy skies in which a pilot can no longer make out the horizon or turbid water in which it is not clear where either the surface or the bottom of the body of water is. Airplane landings are especially risky in such environments, because local conditions are different at each airport.

Often one does not recognize the murkiness in a local environment until it is too late. A colleague of mine had worked hard toward tenure and was told just before tenure time that she had too many grants and publications, leading her fellow faculty members to question her commitment to teaching, which she now was told was the main function of the university. Yet in graduate school and up to that moment, she had always believed she would be rewarded for her research productivity. In contrast, another colleague was told that his teaching and research were excellent but that he made his colleagues uncomfortable and was not perceived as a good fit to his department. He had been unaware of this problem before and had no clue as to what its origins were, other than that he seemed to be outperforming those who were judging him.

Academics are typically judged on one or more of three usually explicit factors: research/scholarship, teaching, and service (to institution and profession). But academics are also typically judged on two criteria that are less likely to be made explicit: perceived fit to the institution and reputation.

All of these criteria can be sources of murkiness, even if they are presented as being crystal clear.

With regard to research, the supposedly clear mandate is that a professor should do good research, and enough of it. What is often less clear is how quality or quantity is to be measured. Some tenure committees make their own judgments by reading candidates' research, but more and more committees emphasize the levels of citations for the journals in which one publishes. Some committees are fine with purely online journals, whereas others are still skeptical of them. And what if the research is cited but by academics in fields other than the one in which the candidate is to be judged? Judgments of quantity are no easier, well, to quantify, in that it is challenging to decide how much a book is worth versus an article, or a longer book versus a shorter one, or a chapter in an edited book versus an article in a refereed journal.

It is no simpler with teaching. Student evaluations are often counted, but who really puts great stock in them, knowing that they are affected by less than relevant variables such as easiness of grading, level of entertainment the professor provides, ease of exams, and relatively lower levels of homework? Peer ratings are used by some institutions, but much can depend on who the peers are and which particular classes they happen to observe. Often the most important teaching is done outside formal teaching contexts, such as through one-on-one advising; but such advising may or may not be explicitly counted, and if it is, evaluating it can be difficult.

Service is equally murky. What counts as service? How does one compare departmental service, university service, and service to one's field? And what about the argument that service is what is most likely to kill the tenure chances of junior faculty?

Fit to the environment is about as murky as one can get—it often becomes a euphemism for whether colleagues like a candidate. It probably includes some assessment of match of the values of the candidate to the institution, but often those values are not clearly delineated, nor is it clear how they can be measured. One sometimes has the feeling that members of committees reach decisions in large part on the basis of perceived fit and then try to find a way to make the other, more tangible categories— research, teaching, service—appear to be responsible for the decision. The committee members may not even be aware of what they are doing: fit is often something one feels emotionally rather than reflects on rationally—and consciously.

With regard to research, teaching, service, and fit, there are two separable issues on which new faculty will wish to seek guidance—performing at one's best level and demonstrating that performance. As a dean and a provost, I saw many sad cases in which junior faculty members had paid attention to the former but not the latter. You need to know what counts for performance evaluation and also how you can demonstrate that performance. In one institution, giving a professional talk on one's research at a major convention may "count" for displaying research prowess; at another institution, one may need to have published the work in a top-of-the-line refereed journal for it to "count."

Reputation would seem to be some unknown combination of all of the above factors, but often it is not. Ask virtually any senior faculty member and she or he will tell you that there are people with reputations that simply don't make sense—professors with strong reputations despite weak academic records, and others with much weaker reputations than they deserve. There is a correlation between reputation and academic record, but the level of correlation is far from perfect. Perhaps charisma or other personality-based factors also enter into reputation, but they are certainly no easier to measure than anything else.

If one is in a murky environment in one's career, one needs to make an "instrument landing." The problem is that, unlike in a plane, one has to create one's own instruments and there often is little guidance as to precisely what these instruments need to tell you. So what does one do?

There are no electronic instruments that will guide a person through a murky environment where the murkiness is a result of human nature. One needs common sense, or practical intelligence of a kind that existing assessments just don't measure well. The only reliable guidance for human-induced murkiness is human guidance. But just as you cannot suddenly acquire electronic instruments when you are in an airplane (or a diver's suit) entering a period of disorientation in a spatial environment, you generally cannot suddenly acquire human instruments when you enter a period of disorientation in a human environment.

Basically, what aviation instrumentation does is to give a pilot a comprehensive set of readings regarding how and where the plane is situated. If things go awry, the instruments also visually instruct the pilot how to correct course. Some instruments, such as the attitude indicator or altimeter, may be more important than others, but the set of them may be necessary in cases of spatial disorientation (e.g., without the attitude indicator, the pilot will not be able to tell instantly whether he or she is right-side-up or upside-down).

If there were electronic instruments for each of the causes of murkiness, one would need an instrument for each. Unfortunately, it often is not even clear what the nature of the murkiness is or what causes it. Because one will need human guidance, which is fallible, one most likely will need more than one instrument for each potential source of murkiness, although the sources of guidance may be overlapping. One needs mentors and one needs them quickly—preferably before one ends up feeling disoriented. A major role of faculty members, in general, and of advisers, in particular, is to guide students through and teach them how to respond to murky environments.

What does one do when one realizes, whether gradually or suddenly, that one is in the midst of a murky environment? First of all, take it seriously. Pilots who experience spatial disorientation and are unable to recover are liable to go into what is called a graveyard spiral—they lose control of their aircraft and it spirals down to the ground. Deep-sea divers, too, may think they are heading toward the surface, only to find out too late they are heading toward the bottom. A graveyard spiral is what is generally considered to have killed John F. Kennedy Jr. and his wife when he was flying at night to Martha's Vineyard in hazy weather.

Pilots learn that they should never fly in murky weather if they are not instrument-rated. Kennedy apparently had limited experience with instruments, and in such cases, pilots are liable to make the mistake of trusting their senses instead of their instruments. The problem is that in spatial disorientation, one's senses typically give conflicting information, so their sensory input and one's cognitive processing of it are faulty.

In careers, as in flying, there are different kinds of murky environments. The most important task is to recognize the environment as murky before it is too late, to figure out if possible the source of the murkiness, and to have mentors ready to advise you on how to navigate ahead. Five frequently encountered types of murkiness are:

1. *Foggy.* The environment can be foggy, so that one simply cannot see what is the right thing to do. In foggy environments, there is usually either

deliberate or inadvertent obfuscation of the best course of action. Just as in driving, dangerous objects are often closer than they appear to be. For example, no one tells you what it means to "fit" because they want to have flexibility in deciding whether to keep you. So they fog things up because being clear about criteria would take away some of their flexibility.

2. *Stormy.* The environment can be stormy, so that what was right even a short time ago no longer is right. Such environments occur when there are new presidents, provosts, deans, chairs, or others who change the conventions under which faculty may have operated in the past. For example, teaching counted a lot for tenure until a new dean came in who decided that she wanted to accelerate the institution's research reputation, and quite suddenly, and with much turbulence and agitation, things changed.

3. *Windy.* In a windy environment, headwinds may seem to constantly thwart your attempts to progress in your career. Headwinds can be caused by colleagues who want to see you fail, spreading yourself so thin that you can't get anything done, or by a funding environment that makes it extremely difficult to get support for your empirical research. If you are lucky, you will experience tailwinds, in which others, granting agencies and colleagues alike, help you achieve goals that you probably would not have achieved on your own. Winds can be sudden and they are not necessarily preceded by warnings. Everyone who has experienced "clear air turbulence" in airplanes knows how suddenly it can come on and how disorienting it can be.

4. *Icy.* No matter where you try to move, you find yourself slipping (or losing altitude). You can't seem to get the footing you need to move forward in your career.

5. *Topographically challenging*. You find you simply don't understand the terrain you need to navigate and it is getting the better of you. You are expected to make too steep a climb or too many turns.

In dealing with murky environments, you face three big risk factors. The first is recognition. If you do not recognize murky environments, you may be in trouble. The environment may be murky without your sensing it. The second risk factor is an attempt to transfer a solution that worked in some previous environment to the present one. Murky environments are local. Pilots know, for example, that each airport presents a different challenge. Similarly, dealing with murky environments requires knowledge relevant to each environment. Your knowledge about how you dealt with a different murky environment may help you in a new murky environment—or it may impede you. Finally, murky environments do not respond well to generalized solutions. You need local informants, not merely distant sources of advice or general articles that deal well with generic situations but not your special one.

The bottom line is that the murky environments in which we live do not respond well to the crisp kind of analytical thinking that is measured by standardized tests and is often taught in university classrooms. Murky environments are negotiated through the informal knowledge of common sense. Because almost all the problems faced by active concerned citizens and ethical leaders are murky in some degree, unless we are teaching common-sense thinking skills for real-world environments, we are not preparing university students for the challenges they will face in the world outside the classroom.

Wisdom and Ethics

When I tell colleagues and friends that the chief goal of a university ought to be to educate its students for active concerned citizenship and ethical leadership, I sometimes get objections, such as that (a) universities should not be in the business of teaching ethics; instead, that is the job of parents and churches; (b) on the contrary, the purpose of the university should be to instill the knowledge that students will need for success in their careers and their lives; (c) if teachers emphasize to students that they should just do the right thing, that should not take more than about five minutes; or (d) you can't really teach ethics, can you? Here is what I answer back (see also Sternberg 2010b).

First, few leaders in any field—business, education, law, medicine, politics, even clergy—fail because they lack points on standardized tests. More likely, they fail because they lack ethics. Almost every day, newspapers and other media cover some kind of serious ethical scandal on the part of our leaders. Look at today's newspaper—whatever day you read this book. Chances are, there will be a report of an ethics scandal. Even worse, sometimes citizens learn of these scandals and just shrug their shoulders— for example, reelecting politicians who have demonstrated serious ethical breaches in the performance of their duties. (One such politician was elected to Congress in my own state of New York, despite a conviction on major tax evasion. He later resigned his seat—under pressure from party leaders, not, apparently, from his constituents. More recently, the leaders of both houses of the legislature in New York State were convicted—a sad commentary on the state but also on how we are preparing and then choosing our leaders.) Our society will fail our next generation if we cannot educate our youth to do better than what they often see in the world around them. Sure, knowledge is important, but knowledge without ethics is empty.

Second, almost any educator will tell you that ethical lapses—plagiarism, cheating on tests, outright lying, and the like—are on the increase. In my own field of psychology, ethical lapses are harming the field's reputation, both internally and externally (Sternberg and Fiske 2015). Maybe it's the Internet—it's easier than ever before to lift text from an online document and paste it into one's own document without making proper attribution. Maybe it's cell phones, which can be used in various illegitimate ways to communicate exam answers. Or maybe it's just a loosening of societal standards, whereby students hardly even see as cheating what students in the past would have viewed as gross violations of integrity. Whatever the reasons for the increasing ethical lapses, they are not going to fix themselves. College is one of our last chances to work with students to teach them that ethical lapses are not okay—that society expects better from them.

The importance of ethical leadership is shown in the university setting by athletic programs such as those at Penn State and, more recently, Oklahoma State (my own former university, for which I have very high regard), which have had serious ethical violations. These instances show that programs can spend tens and even hundreds of millions of dollars on athletics, and then essentially throw it all away—plus potentially much more in court cases and even loss of reputation—through lack of ethical leadership. Without ethics in leadership, one has nothing.

Third, contrary to some popular views, it often is not easy to do the "right thing." Nor is it even obvious to everyone in many cases what the right thing is, as successive debates over military interventions in faraway countries have shown. Ethical debates are often complex, and what colleges can do best is to teach students how to reason ethically and thereby draw conclusions that they can support and defend. In my own research on ethics, I have argued that ethical behavior is sometimes challenging because there is not just one step in ethical thought and action but rather eight. Examples of such steps are deciding (a) whether an ethical lapse is even taking place; (b) whether a lapse is serious enough to justify anyone's intervention; (c) whether the lapse, if it exists, justifies one's own personal intervention or is none of one's business; (d) how to cope with the consequences if one's ethical action backfires and one loses friends or even one's job; and (e) how to translate one's ethical thinking into ethical action.

Consider the position of a member of senior management in a large corporation. In every decision she makes, she has ethical responsibilities to at least four different groups of constituents: to herself and her family, to her company's shareholders, to her company's employees, and to all of the company's numerous stakeholders (e.g., customers, suppliers, competitors) who will be affected in any way by the decisions that she and her company make. In any single decision situation, these four responsibilities can and often do conflict with each other. Such conflicts are ethical conflicts, can be very complex, and for their solution require ethical reasoning far more advanced than the training traditionally provided in the home or in Sunday school. Institutions of higher learning have an obligation to prepare their students for such complex decision situations, not only for their own sake but also for the benefit of the society that they serve.

Fourth, students best learn about ethical leadership not only through studying abstract principles of the kinds that tend to be taught in ethics courses or even at home and in church, but also through concrete case studies in their fields of endeavor whose applications to their own lives and work the students can immediately see. For example, as a youngster, I learned about ethics at home and in Sunday school, but I did not learn how to apply these principles in my own field of psychology, such as in issues of informed consent, statistical testing of hypotheses, client relations, and the like. I hope to see an ethical-leadership track instituted in universities and opened to all students; such a program would provide specially designated courses that infuse principles of ethical leadership into disciplinary instruction. That is, students would encounter ethical challenges in their own field of endeavor, be asked to apply what they learn to their extracurricular activities, and be required to do a capstone project applying what they learned in their courses to their own ethical leadership. In such a track, teachers don't "teach ethics" per se but rather create opportunities for students to learn for themselves, through guided instruction, how to think and act ethically in their life and their work.

One can scarcely open the newspaper without finding examples of smart, well-educated people who have behaved in ethically challenged ways: for example, Bernard Madoff and the numerous investment advisers who have come to be called mini-Madoffs because their Ponzi schemes were similar to Madoff's. President Obama called the bonuses awarded to some of the same Wall Street executives who helped to create the current economic mess "shameful" (Stolberg and Labaton 2009). Even some of the president's own proposed political appointees had to withdraw for ethically questionable behavior. And then, of course, there are people like Rod Blagojevich, the former governor of Illinois, and Kwame Kilpatrick, Detroit's former mayor, who seem to have had few ethical standards at all.

What is frightening about ethical lapses is not that they happen to the ethically outrageous but that they can sneak up on just about all of us. An informal classroom "experiment" I performed recently illustrates that slippery slope.

In a course I have taught called "The Nature of Leadership," I have told students from the first session that I would be presenting them with situations, sometimes hypothetical, that would challenge them to think in ways they may not have thought before. I also told them that often it would not be clear which situations were hypothetical and which were real. I believe that dealing with such situations is necessary for the development of ethical leadership. Sometimes the results of my challenges to the class surprised me.

"I am very proud of myself," I told the seventeen undergraduates in my seminar. I had just returned from a trip, I told them, and felt that the honorarium I was paid for my consulting on ethical leadership was less than I deserved. I felt badly that I had decided to accept an engagement for so little compensation. I then told the class that I had been about to fill out the reimbursement forms when I discovered that I could actually get reimbursed twice. The first reimbursement would come from the organization that had invited me, which required me merely to fill out a form listing my expenses. The second reimbursement would come from my university, which required me to submit the receipts from the trip. I explained to the class that by getting reimbursed twice, I could justify to myself the amount of work I had put into the engagement. (Full disclosure: I did not really seek double reimbursement.)

I waited for the firestorm. Would the class—which had already studied leadership for several months—rise up in a mass protest against what I proposed to do? Or would only a few brave souls raise their hands and roundly criticize me for what was patently unethical behavior? I waited, and waited, and waited. Nothing happened. I then decided to move on to the main topic of the day, which, I recall, was . . . ethical leadership. The whole time I was speaking about that main topic, I expected some of the students to raise their hands and demand to return to the issue of my double reimbursement. It didn't happen.

Finally, I stopped talking and flat-out asked the class whether anyone thought anything was wrong with my desire for double reimbursement. If so, I asked them, why had no one challenged me? I figured that all of them would be embarrassed for not having challenged me. Indeed, many of them were. Others thought I must have been kidding. Still others thought that, since I was the professor and a dean to boot, I must have had a good reason for doing whatever I wanted to do. What I did not expect, though, was that some of the students would commend me for my clever idea and argue that, if I could get away with it, I was entitled to receive the money—more power to me!

That experience reminded me how hard it is to translate theories of ethics, and even case studies, into practice. The students had read about ethics in leadership, heard about ethics in leadership from a variety of real-world leaders, discussed ethics in leadership, and then apparently totally failed to recognize or at least speak out against unethical behavior when it stared them in the face. Moreover, these were students who by conventional definitions would be classified as gifted. Why is it so hard to translate theory into practice, even after one has studied ethical leadership for several months?

John Darley and Bibb Latané (1970) opened up a new field of research on bystander intervention. They showed that, contrary to expectations, bystanders intervene when someone is in trouble only in very limited circumstances. For example, if they think that someone else might intervene, bystanders tend to stay out of the situation. Darley and Latané even showed that divinity students who were about to lecture on the parable of the Good Samaritan were no more likely than other bystanders to help a person in distress.

Model of Ethical Reasoning and Action

Drawing in part on Darley and Latané's model of bystander intervention, I have constructed a model of ethical behavior that applies to a variety of ethical problems (see Sternberg 2015a). The model's basic premise is that ethical behavior is far harder to display than one would expect simply on the basis of what we learn from parents, school, and religious training. To intervene, to do good, individuals must go through a series of steps, and unless all of the steps are completed, people are not likely to behave ethically, regardless of the ethics training or moral education they have received and the level of other types of relevant skills they might possess, such as critical or creative thinking.

Consider these eight steps of behaving ethically and how my students responded, or didn't respond, to the ethical challenge I presented:

1. *Recognize that there is an event to react to.* The students were sitting in a class on leadership, expecting to be educated about leadership by an expert on leadership. In this case, I did not present the problem as one to which I expected them to react. I was simply telling them about something I was planning to do. They had no a priori reason to expect that something an authority figure did, or was thinking of doing, would require any particular reaction, except perhaps taking notes. So for some students, the whole narrative may have been a non-event.

That is a problem that extends beyond this mere college-classroom situation. When people hear their political, educational, or especially religious leaders talk, they may not believe there is any reason to question what they hear. After all, they are listening to authority figures. In this way, cynical and corrupt leaders can lead their followers to accept and even commit unethical acts such as suicide bombings and murder of those with divergent beliefs.

2. *Define the event as having an ethical dimension.* Not all students in the class defined the problem as an ethical one. It became clear in our discussion that some students saw the problem as utilitarian: I had worked hard, had been underpaid, and was trying to figure out a way to attain adequate

compensation for my hard work. In that definition of the problem, I had come up with a clever way to make the compensation better fit the work I had done.

Thus cynical leaders may flaunt their unethical behavior simply by defining it in other, plausible-sounding ways. For example, when Robert Mugabe and his henchmen seized the land of white farmers in Zimbabwe, the seizure was presented as a way of compensating alleged war heroes for their accomplishments. What could be unethical about compensating war heroes?

3. *Decide that the ethical dimension is significant.* In the case of my plan to seek double reimbursement, some of the students may have felt it was sketchy or dubious but not sufficiently so to make an issue of it. Perhaps they themselves had "double-dipped." Or perhaps they had sometimes taken what was not theirs—say, something small like a newspaper or even money they found on the ground—and saw what I was doing as no more serious than what they had done. So people may recognize an ethical dimension but not see it as sufficiently significant to create a fuss.

Politicians seem to specialize in trying to downplay the ethical dimension of their behavior. The shenanigans and subsequent lies of Bill Clinton regarding his behavior with Monica Lewinsky are an example. Eliot Spitzer, former governor of New York, misbehaved for years until his misdeeds were exposed.

4. *Take responsibility for generating an ethical solution to the problem.* My students may have felt that they were, after all, merely students. Is it their responsibility, or even their right, to tell a professor of a course on leadership how to act, especially if the professor is a dean? Perhaps from their point of view, it was my responsibility to determine the ethical dimensions, if any, of the situation.

Similarly, people may allow leaders to commit wretched acts because they figure it is the leaders' responsibility to determine the ethical dimensions of their actions. Or people may assume that the leaders, especially if they are religious leaders, are in the best position to determine what is ethical. If a religious leader encourages someone to become a suicide bomber, for example, that person might conclude that being a bomber must be ethical; why else would a religious leader suggest it?

5. *Figure out what abstract ethical rule(s) might apply to the problem.* Perhaps some of the students recognized the problem I created for them as

an ethical one. But if they had never had to figure out reimbursements, it might not have been obvious to them what rule, or rules, apply. Or even if they had dealt with reimbursements, might there be some circumstances in which it is ethical to be reimbursed twice? Maybe the university supplements outside reimbursements, as they sometimes do with fellowships. Or maybe the university does not care who else pays, as long as they get original receipts. Or maybe I had misspoken; maybe what I meant to say was that I would get some expenses paid by the university and others by the sponsoring organization. Especially in unfamiliar situations, it may not be clear what constitutes ethical behavior.

6. *Decide how abstract ethical rules actually apply to the problem, in order to suggest a concrete solution.* Perhaps the students did know of relevant ethical rules but did not see how to apply them. Suppose they thought of the rule that one should expect from others only what one deserves. Well, what did I deserve? Maybe they saw me as deserving more than I did simply because I said I did. Or suppose they reflected on the maxim that one should not expect something for nothing. Well, I did something—I was only trying to get something back that adequately reflected my work. In the end, the students may have had trouble translating abstract principles into concrete behavior.

When US forces kill suspected terrorists in other countries, some residents of the United States may be happy that the evildoers got what they deserved. But what if foreign forces entered the United States and started killing people whom a foreign government suspected of being terrorists? Does the ethical principle of "do unto others as you would have them do unto you" mean, concretely, that if we do not want foreign forces in our country, we should not have our own forces elsewhere? Or does it mean that if we in the United States have forces elsewhere, those forces should not kill anyone, regardless of who that person is killing and what terrorist acts he or she may be planning? In many instances, understanding exactly how to apply an ethical principle forces us to grapple with deeply held values.

7. *Formulate an ethical solution, at the same time possibly preparing to counteract contextual forces that might lead you to act unethically.* Suppose you sit in a classroom and hear your teacher brag about what you consider to be unethical behavior. You look around: no one else is saying anything. As far as you can tell, no one else is even fazed. Perhaps what you

think is the right course of action isn't. Maybe you're the one who's out of line, and speaking up will only embarrass you in front of your peers.

In Darley and Latané's work, the more bystanders there were, the less likely it was for one to intervene. The investigators saw that people tend to think that if something is really wrong, someone else witnessing the event will take responsibility. You are actually better off having a breakdown on a lonely country road than on a busy highway because a driver passing by on the country road may feel that he or she is your only hope.

Sometimes the problem is not that other people seem oblivious to the ethical implications of a situation, but that they actively encourage you to behave in ways you define as unethical. In the Rwandan genocides, Hutus were encouraged to hate and kill Tutsis, even if they were family members. Those who were not willing to participate in the massacres risked becoming victims themselves. In Hitler's Germany, those who tried to save Jews from concentration camps risked being sent to the camps themselves, or having family members sent. Obviously an individual has to decide what he or she is willing to risk for the sake of doing what he or she believes is right.

8. *Act.* In the end, you could be a wonderful ethical thinker, figure out all you need to do, be prepared to do the right thing, and then do nothing. One has to make the leap from thought to action. For example, most people know they should have only safe sex, but not all of them do, even if they know they have an illness that they could spread through sexual contact. In Rwanda and more recently in Syria, there were countless discussions about what needed to be done to behave ethically. In the end, the most difficult thing was not getting people to talk about action but getting them to engage in it.

We would like to think that peer pressure to behave ethically leads people to resist internal temptations to misbehave. But often exactly the opposite is the case. In the Enron scandal, when Sherron Watkins blew the whistle on unethical behavior, she was punished and made to feel like an outcast. In general, whistle-blowers are treated poorly, despite the protections they are supposed to receive.

I have argued that ethical behavior typically requires eight steps, and that if you miss any one of them, you are not likely to behave fully ethically. College can produce students who are smart and knowledgeable but ethically challenged. When students are alerted to the steps in ethical behavior and the potential difficulty of going through them all, they may come to understand why it is so easy to slip into unethical behavior and thus they may be more likely to think and behave ethically. Given the problems we face in today's world, that seems like an urgent priority. Consider the child-abuse scandal at Penn State.

Here is the lesson people want to learn from the Penn State scandal: there are some smarmy folks out there who, through a combination of mindless groupthink and fear of antagonizing important people, will do unimaginable things, like not reporting child abusers to the police; perhaps there are other "Penn States" out there or possibly there are even people at our own institution who are hiding seriously dirty linen about which we know nothing. The one thing we know for sure is that we never would act the way those people did.

That's the wrong lesson. Here's why.

In the 1960s, Stanley Milgram did a series of studies while a faculty member at Yale University (see Milgram 2009). Although the initial studies are old, they have been replicated many times since, across time and place. Milgram would have two study participants enter a room. One would be assigned, seemingly at random, to the role of learner and the other to the role of teacher. Unbeknownst to the teacher, who was a naive subject, the role assignments were rigged and the learner was a confederate of the experimenter's.

The teacher and learner were informed that they would participate in an experiment on the effects of punishment on learning. On successive trials, the teacher would read to the learner a list of words to be learned and the learner, in a separate room, would repeat back the words he remembered. When the learner made a mistake, the teacher would use an apparatus that would deliver an electric shock to the learner.

The apparatus was designed so that each successive shock would be heavier than the last one. Shocks on the device were arranged in increments of 10 volts, ranging from just 10 volts up to 450 volts. The switches at the high end, near 450 volts, had labels such as "slight shock," "moderate shock," "extreme shock," "danger: severe shock," and at the top of the scale, "XXX." The teacher was given a sample 45-volt shock to show him that the apparatus really did deliver shocks and that they were painful.

Once the experiment started, the learner began to make mistakes. So the teacher shocked him. (In the initial experiments, participants were male, but later experiments involved female participants as well.) After a while, the teacher heard the learner groan, later scream, still later complain about his heart, yet later demand that the experiment stop, and finally fall silent. It might seem that the teacher would stop delivering shocks once the learner started to protest, but the experimenter would reply, when the teacher indicated he wanted to stop the experiment, with responses ranging in a graded sequence: "Continue please." "Go on." "The experiment requires that you continue." "It is absolutely essential that you continue." "You have no choice."

As you may know, the experiment was not really on the effects of punishment on learning but rather on obedience. Psychiatrists who were asked to estimate what percentage of subjects would administer the maximum level of shock estimated that it would be less than 1 percent. In fact, it was roughly two-thirds.

When I have taught introductory psychology, I have asked my 150 or so students how many of them would have gone to the end, and typically, only one or two jokers say they would have. The rest of the students strenuously deny they would have administered the maximum shock. Yet roughly two-thirds of them would have gone to the end of the shocks, even though they cannot imagine they would have. They do not yet realize the harm of which they are capable. We all are susceptible to believing that only other people act in ways that are heartless, cruel, or indifferent and then possibly rationalizing them as humane.

Fortunately for the learner in the Milgram experiments, the shock machine was a phony and, as mentioned earlier, the learner was a confederate and a trained actor. The experiments as originally conducted would never pass muster with today's ethical requirements because subjects could not be adequately debriefed. No matter what the debriefing said, roughly two-thirds of the subjects in a typical running of the study left the experiment knowing that they might have killed the subject had the shocks been real.

The usual interpretation of the Milgram experiment has been that people are remarkably obedient and that it is because of this typically unrealized potential for obedience that horrors like the Nazi or Rwandan genocide or the brutal reprisals in Syria could take place. Stephen D. Reicher of the University of St. Andrews and his colleagues (2012) have suggested that agents of tyranny identify actively with their leaders. Moreover, they are motivated to display "creative" followership in working toward goals that they believe their leaders set. In other words, people don't just passively obey; they behave proactively to curry favor with their admired leaders or role models. Sound familiar?

In a related demonstration, Philip Zimbardo, formerly a professor of psychology at Stanford, randomly assigned college students to one of two groups: prison guard or prisoner (see Zimbardo 2008). He placed them in the basement of the Stanford Psychology Department and then observed how they acted. To his dismay and the dismay of anyone who has since learned of the study, many guards rather quickly started acting like sadistic prison guards and many prisoners started acting in ways betraying learned helplessness—they were essentially browbeaten into submission.

In yet another study, John Darley and C. Daniel Batson (1973) found that even most divinity students on their way to give a lecture on the Good Samaritan failed to help a person in obvious distress if their other priorities, such as arriving on time for the lecture, were more important to them at the moment. The study showed that intense ethical training provides relatively little protection against bad behavior in an ethically challenging situation. Since that study was published, revelations of horrendous abuse of children at the hands of clergy, while other clergy in the know stood idly by, have reinforced this lesson in painful detail. Really, no training offers ironclad protection.

Ethical Drift

If there is one thing that social psychologists have learned over the past decades, it is the enormous but often hidden power of situational pressures. The lesson of the Penn State tragedy is not that there are heartless bureaucrats out there who are willing to sacrifice the well-being of children for the sake of the reputation of the university and its athletic teams. Almost certainly there are. However, the real lesson of the Penn State tragedy is that, given certain situational constraints, virtually all of us could behave the way those administrators allegedly did. These circumstances include severe pressures to conform accompanied by fear of punishment for noncompliance, desire to please or curry favor with one or more persons in a position of power, rationalization of one's actions, and what I have called "ethical drift"—one's declining ethical standards in the face of group norms to the point that one is not even aware that one's standards are dropping (Sternberg 2012a).

To be clear: the power of situational variables in no way excuses bad behavior. Rather, such variables should help us understand, in part, why such behavior occurs in certain situations, why we are all potentially susceptible to it, and most importantly, what we can do about it.

As I was writing about ethical drift, fourteen officials of FIFA, the world soccer organization, were indicted. If ever an organization has experienced ethical drift, it has been FIFA under the leadership of its then president. Worse, two days after the indictments, the president was reelected as though the indictments had never happened. In what other enterprise could one's top staff fall and one go on to get reelected to a top position? At roughly the same time, the former Speaker of the House of Representatives in the United States was indicted for financial misdealings and lying to the FBI, allegedly because of hush payoffs to a victim of his sexual abuse many years ago. Can we teach students about ACCEL in universities if we accept such behavior in our societies? We need to care about ethical drift not only in the classroom but also in the lives we supposedly role-model for today's younger generation.

How do you avoid falling into the trap of ethical drift? How do you teach university students to learn to avoid this trap? First, you need to realize that almost anyone, including yourself, is capable of behaving abysmally under certain circumstances. Second, you need rather regularly to ask yourself whether situational pressures are leading you to behave in ways that once would have seemed totally inappropriate and wrong to you. Third, you need to ask yourself whether you are rationalizing behavior that once would have seemed unacceptable to you. And fourth, you need to be willing to take a stand and do the right thing, realizing that although there may be serious short-term costs to acting ethically, you are willing to accept those costs so you can live with yourself and others over the long term.

One last thing: you may still be thinking that although other people may fall prey to ethical drift—or even a sudden drop off the ethical cliff— you would never succumb to situational pressure to conform. For example, you may feel positive that you would not have gone to the top of the shock apparatus or have let a child abuser continue to abuse children, regardless of the situational pressures placed on you. You may be right, but research has not found any personality characteristics that reliably predict who will succumb to such extreme pressures and who won't.

Put another way, we all have to be in the situation to know what we would do, so you may wish to reserve judgment for now. When, sooner or later, you are in an ethically challenging situation, as the Penn State administrators were, you will have an opportunity to learn something about yourself. If you resist succumbing to the temptation just to go along, then you will be able to feel pride in yourself, as would we all. As for me, I find what happened at Penn State absolutely abhorrent and cannot believe that I would have acted in the way some administrators appear to have, but I know I cannot be absolutely sure of what I would do unless I found myself actually in such a situation under comparable pressures.

When crowds of fans shouted, "We are Penn State!" they did not realize just how right they were. Potentially, at least, we all are Penn State, in both its best aspects and its worst.

Moral Disengagement

No matter how much students are taught to behave ethically, there will be instances in which they transgress. We all are susceptible to what Albert Bandura (2016) calls *moral disengagement*. Put another way, people who generally view themselves as moral and upstanding act in reprehensible ways because they disengage themselves from their immoral actions. According to Bandura, they blame and devaluate their victims, obscure responsibility for their acts, minimize the harmful effects of their acts, and generally rationalize reprehensible behavior to view it as neutral or even positive.

Unfortunately, universities are far from blameless when it comes to moral disengagement. Penn State, of course, provided one example. But moral disengagement by no means applies only to athletics. Students and faculty who engage in bullying behavior often justify what they are doing as being in the service of some noble cause. In the next chapter, I discuss how students and faculty members alike have acted extremely aggressively toward each other in the name of being protected from aggression. Moral disengagement often results when one is prepared to fault others without looking first in the mirror.

Passion

If there is one consistent finding in the literature on creativity, it is that people do their most creative work in fields about which they are passionate (Kaufman and Sternberg 2010). In the absence of passion, it is simply hard to marshal one's resources to do creative work.

The practical implication of this finding is that parents and professors alike, if they want the young people for whom they are responsible to succeed, need to emphasize the importance of finding one's passion. In the ideal case, the child's passion fits his or her parents' desires. More often, the young person's passion is a mismatch for the parents' ambition. As a professor, I cannot even count the number of unhappy undergraduates I have met who felt stifled by their parents' ambitions for them. On the one hand, they wanted to please their parents. On the other hand, they wanted to find themselves. And parents range from being mildly disappointed when their children find their own dreams to threatening to withhold funds if the children do not comply with the parents' wishes. In one case, a student told me that his parents offered to pay for college as long as he studied engineering. Although the pressure is not usually quite so blatant, it is often intense.

There is a lot of pressure in society today to major in a field that will make one a lot of money. The irony is that if one looks at successful people, defined only in terms of income, large numbers of them majored in the liberal arts (Association of American Colleges and Universities 2013). Science and engineering majors tend to start out with higher salaries, but in the long run, liberal-arts majors do at least as well economically. Perhaps this is because the skills they learn in the liberal arts translate well into success in higher-level positions but not necessarily in lower-level positions, where one is often paid to do what one is told rather than to think one's own thoughts.

I have tried to practice what I preach in this domain. Both of my adult children ended up majoring in political science. I had no idea what they would do with this major, but political science was what interested in them and so I encouraged them to pursue their passions. It worked out just fine: Seth is a successful entrepreneur, and Sara is a law professor. I now have three young triplets and plan to give them the same advice I gave my older children: to succeed in life, follow your passion. The worldly perquisites will follow—or they won't. But at least one will lead a satisfying life.

When I went to college, more than half my graduating class matriculated in law school. It was the thing to do at the time, just as financial services is today. As I attended reunions over the years, I was impressed by the fact that those who had gone to law school because they truly were interested in law tended to be happy with their professional lives, on the whole, whereas those who had gone to law school because they thought it was "the thing to do" ended up rather unhappy, feeling trapped because family and other responsibilities made it difficult for them to switch to a career that truly interested them.

My best friend from college went to law school and became a lawyer. He never seemed very excited about the work. After he retired—early—he found a way to pursue his passion for history and became the president of a history museum. He now seems, at least to me, happier than he ever was as a lawyer. This is not to say that one cannot find happiness as a lawyer; rather, it is to say that happiness is best to be found when one pursues one's passion, whatever it happens to be. I argue in the next chapter that one fares best, at least in terms of the values of ACCEL, when one pursues happiness in an environment that encourages and actively promotes diversity.

4

Diversity

To be excellent, a university must be diverse. And to develop the skills that lead to active concerned citizenship and ethical leadership, a university must be diverse. You cannot be an active concerned citizen if your only concerns are for people you view as like yourself; you cannot be a true leader if you can only lead people like yourself. Most colleges and universities seek diversity in their student bodies and their faculty as well as staff. This is often one of two major goals for these institutions, the other of which is academic excellence. But whereas the importance of academic excellence to a college or university may be self-explanatory to the general public, it is not always obvious why colleges believe diversity to be important. Is concern for diversity merely a form of political correctness, or is there really some educational benefit to a diverse student body and faculty?

Why Diversity Is Important

There are several reasons why diversity is truly important in institutions of higher education and especially in ACCEL institutions. Consider each in turn.

Learning

First, students learn more from others if the others are different from themselves in significant ways. Imagine, in some strange world, that everyone in a university was a clone of everyone else. Students would learn almost nothing from each other, because they would all be identical. Diversity promotes learning by exposing students to different ways of seeing the world, different points of view, and different assumptions about how the world works. Much of learning is outside the classroom—it is in the informal curriculum of the university. One's learning from friends is as important as one's learning from books and lectures. And diverse friends expose one to different experiences. When I was a freshman, I had friends from Illinois, Louisiana, Maine, Pennsylvania, Texas, Georgia, New York, Alberta (Canada), and other locales. I learned from them in a way that would not have been possible if all had been from my home state of New Jersey.

I have been a faculty member in institutions that cover the gamut in diversity, from very diverse to very uniform. My observations convince me that being a student in a relatively homogeneous environment reduces the quality of the learning. In a nondiverse environment—one in which all students are from a particular geographic area, or of a particular ethnic group, or of a particular socioeconomic level, for example—students see lots of other students (and, often, professors and staff) who think more or less the way they do. The lesson they learn is not "Oh, I'm in a homogeneous environment and I'm not learning to think about problems in diverse ways." Rather, the lesson they learn is that people whom they view as diverse, whether or not they are, tend to think the same way and believe the same things. The students may even come to believe that there is something odd or even wrong with people who do not see things the way they do. The problem is that they do not realize how much diversity in viewpoints there is, or even that such diversity is healthy.

Promoting Interaction

Second, diversity helps promote understanding that can be lacking when different groups fail, or even refuse, to interact. In 1968, the Flemish- and French-speaking factions of the University of Leuven decided that they could not get along, and they split, leaving two universities, Leuven (Flemish-speaking) and Louvain (French-speaking). The repercussions of this and other, similar splits can be seen in contemporary Belgium, which has not had a functioning government since April 22, 2010. The country has been on the verge of splitting apart because people of different linguistic and cultural groups have failed to work together successfully. The split has negatively affected the economy and, obviously, the morale of people in the country. South Africa, for many years, had "black" universities and "white" universities, and never the twain did meet; the consequences were extremely negative for education and for the country as a whole. Bringing diverse people together creates bridges across cultural, linguistic, racial, and other divides.

In some respects, the division in Belgium represents a better case because at least the Flemish and Wallonian groups know and understand the differences that exist between them. It is harder to deal with situations in which people are uncomfortable with or even hostile toward each other without quite acknowledging it or understanding why. One sees this clearly in racism. The worst racism is often that which is under the surface—in which people openly act as if they have no prejudices or biases but underneath seethe with hostility and resentment.

Attracting Excellent Students, Faculty, and Staff

Third, diversity helps attract the best students, faculty, and staff. Suppose everyone at a particular university is a member of Group X, whatever group that may be. It is safe to say that no matter what the group, many of the people who could contribute most to the university will be members of other groups. But members of other groups will likely be reluctant to go to a university where they will find no one like themselves at all. The result is that the university will scare away many of the most able potential constituents.

Of course, there will be some members of groups who are in minorities who go to institutions that are relatively homogeneous, sometimes lured by financial aid. The challenge in such situations is for them to be fully integrated into the university community, as opposed to forming their own social and other groups that fail to interact with the groups of people in the mainstream in that institution. I remember during my own undergraduate days an institution that was fully integrated on the surface but in which students of different socially defined racial groups often clustered together tightly within their own group and only very loosely and occasionally outside it.

In one university with which I am familiar, when I suggested to people at the highest level of governance that it might make sense to have a vice president for diversity, some of them stared at me with disbelief. They just could not understand why one would want to spend money on such a thing. This particular university, unfortunately, was notably unconcerned about diversity and did not even recognize it as an issue.

Those who view appeals for diversity as thinly disguised appeals to political correctness (PC) can, under some circumstances, have a point. Many of us have seen situations in which the powers that be seem more concerned about their diversity statistics (we need some of these, some of those, and some of still others) than about the importance of diversity for quality education. Moreover, an oft-heard complaint is that people of a certain kind are admitted under a lower standard in order to ensure that there are "enough" of them.

Messaging

When I grew up in the 1950s, diversity was not particularly prized. Opportunities for women were severely restricted. African Americans were overtly discriminated against, in the North as well as the South. Jews were looked at askance—a local country club where I grew up did not admit them. Gays were, for the most part, in the closet, and with good reason given the way they were treated. Immigrants were expected to assimilate fully and, to the extent possible, put any customs from their countries of origin behind them. One could argue about what things are like today, but certainly, with respect to diversity, they are better than they were then. Yet I doubt that anyone with her or his eyes open would claim that problems of diversity have been fully solved. As I write, a major immigration debate is occurring in the United States, with many prominent politicians now, as then, taking a loud and principled stand to restrict it as much as possible. (What else is new?)

If a university wants to take a position in favor of opportunity for all, then it needs to actively promote diversity. Diversity brings together people with different backgrounds, different ideas, different ways of seeing things. It thus promotes intellectual excellence and broad-mindedness. If universities do not publicly take a stand in favor of these goals, what institutions will?

Actually, universities have not always taken such a position. Even into the middle of the twentieth century, universities quietly discriminated against a variety of groups—women, Jews, Catholics, African Americans, and others. But such discrimination is at odds with the intellectual goals of the university and so puts the university at odds with itself.

There are universities today that continue to discriminate, some covertly but others openly. For example, some religious institutions admit or hire only individuals with approved points of view. That is their prerogative. But under such policies, they will never be ACCEL universities, because they cut off the very diversity that is needed to reach the top rungs of excellence.

How Multicultural Backgrounds Develop Different Knowledge and Skills

Campus diversity is sometimes mistakenly taken to be about the number of faculty or students who look like this or that. That is not the issue. Rather, the issue is different kinds of enculturation, socialization, and world views. World views may differ between people in North America and Africa, but they may also vary within continents, such as, say, between Appalachia and the Hamptons in New York.

The standards problem is a tricky one because when diversity is sought, some groups may have lower means on certain indices, such as standardized test scores or GPAs. In this regard, it is useful to understand just how great cultural differences can be. I cite some of my own research in order to illustrate this point.

A Study in Rural Kenya

Consider a young person in a small Kenyan village. I first learned something of these children in a discussion with a parasitologist, then at Oxford University. The parasitologist, Catherine Nokes, mentioned that young people in rural villages in Kenya would know the names of eighty, ninety, or even one hundred natural herbal medicines that could be used to combat parasitic illnesses. Such knowledge is extremely relevant for adaptation by these children because parasitic illnesses are endemic in the regions in which they live and interfere greatly with their ability to function, to the point that they may have to stay home from school or work because they are too ill to be effective.

If knowledge of natural herbal medicines was just a proxy for general intelligence (*g*) or academic knowledge, then a teacher might predict the young people's knowledge from conventional tests, standardized or otherwise. But suppose that such knowledge was not predictable from conventional tests. Then knowing something of children's ability to learn, as evidenced by their knowledge of natural herbal medicines, might be useful information for a teacher to have in assessing which children could be more successful in learning tasks than perhaps they appeared to be on the basis of their schoolwork. Oddly, it might even be relevant to admissions officers in universities because it would show how well young people adapted to their own environments, not the environments that are relevant to people living in circumstances very unlike their own.

The young people's prospects in some of these Kenyan villages are rather limited. Schooling beyond the early years is largely considered a waste of time because there is little need for academic skills. But there is a need for a knowledge of natural herbal medicines that can be used to treat the various parasitic illnesses prevalent in the region, such as malaria, schistosomiasis, hookworm, whipworm, and the like. Consider one of a number of problems we posed to such young people (Sternberg et al. 2001):

A small child in your family has homa. She has a sore throat, headache, and fever. She has been sick for 3 days. Which of the following five Yadh nyaluo (Luo herbal medicines) can treat homa?

1. Chamama. Take the leaf and fito (sniff medicine up the nose to sneeze out illness).*
2. Kaladali. Take the leaves, drink, and fito.*

3. Obuo. Take the leaves and fito.*
4. Ogaka. Take the roots, pound, and drink.
5. Ahundo. Take the leaves and fito.

There are multiple correct answers, which are asterisked here. Once again, no one would expect a typical US college professor or student to be able to answer such questions at better than a chance level. Why should they? The knowledge probably has no real adaptive value for them (unless they are studying cultural psychology or anthropology). But for young people growing up in an environment where the major threat to adaptive success is parasitic illness, such knowledge is extremely important. And imagine what such young people might have to teach students for whom parasitic illnesses and the threats they pose are as far from their experience as is life on Mars (were there to be any)!

Some of us may tend to assume that the knowledge and skills we often value—such as those measured by standardized tests—are important anywhere. On this view, if a group of students score more poorly on standardized tests, they simply are intellectually inferior. Perhaps they are not. Perhaps they have knowledge and skills that are important elsewhere that would be hidden if one were to rely exclusively on conventional standardized tests. Teachers and admissions officers alike would do well to know of the practical knowledge and adaptive competencies that students from diverse environments have acquired, because such knowledge and skills may tell us more about their learning abilities than do scores on conventional tests.

We also tested the rural Kenyan children for their vocabulary levels in Dholuo, their home language, and in English. Such measures assess socalled crystallized intelligence. We also used geometric matrix problems to measure their so-called fluid intelligence, or ability to think in novel and flexible ways. Our expectation, based on work we had done on what we have called "practical intelligence," was that the knowledge of the natural herbal medicines would show at most a weak positive correlation with scores on the standardized ability tests.

To our surprise, there were significant correlations, but they were negative. This left us, at first, puzzled, and might leave other psychologists puzzled as well because tests of fluid and crystallized abilities typically show a positive manifold, that is, a pattern of positive correlations throughout that yields a general factor, signifying what is known as general intelligence (*g*), when the tests are factor-analyzed. But we came to see a logic to the negative pattern of correlations. What the correlations showed is the extent to which patterns of relationships among assessments may be influenced by characteristics internal not only to individuals but also to the environmental contexts in which they live. Young people who were learning the knowledge that was most relevant for adaptation in their environments were not the best at learning school knowledge, and those who were most adept at picking up school knowledge were not learning what was most adaptive in their home environments.

The question, of course, is whether one should admit into universities those who are not as finely tuned academically but have shown a great mastery of practical knowledge. Are these individuals any less likely to become active concerned citizens and ethical leaders? The answer depends on what one is trying to maximize. If one's goal is to admit that student group whose academic achievement will be maximized, by all means one should go with the standardized tests. But if one's goal is to admit students who will be adaptive to, and even shape, whatever world they live in (and many students from abroad go back home after college), one might choose to go with the students who are higher in practical knowledge. At the very least, a case could be made either way. If we want to admit students who will impact the world as active concerned citizens and ethical leaders in ways that go beyond high academic performance, we need to think outside the box of standardized test scores.

One might be inclined to think that the phenomenon we observed in Kenya is limited to cultures remote from ours, but that is not the case. In our culture as well, gaining more education can lead to reduced societally valued outcomes, such as money. For example, students with a two-year MBA will generally earn substantially more money than students with a PhD earned over four, five, six, or more years. In Silicon Valley, the entrepreneurs who run start-up companies are often individuals who have nothing more than a bachelor's degree, if that; they hire PhDs to work for them, at salaries considerably lower than their own. The grade level at which additional formal schooling leads to certain reduced societally valued outcomes is different, but the principle is the same: at some point, additional schooling and acquisition of associated academic knowledge and skills may lead to a reduction rather than an increase in certain societally valued outcomes. This is even more the case in most other countries of the world, where college and university professors are paid far less than they are in the United States. German universities, for example, generally pay less than American universities, and the national pay scale for professors there was recently reduced.

A Study among the Alaskan Yup'ik

One might think that the phenomena we observed in Kenya would be found only in developing countries. Such is not the case. In my colleagues' and my work with Native American Alaskan Yup'ik youth, for example, we discovered Native American young people who were able to navigate on a dog sled from one distant village to another across what to us (and probably you) would have seemed to be a perceptually uniform field of vision (Grigorenko et al. 2004). If you or we or the young people's non–Native American teachers attempted to go from one village to another on such a dog sled, all of us would probably get lost in the wilderness and die. Signals for navigation are there; we just would not see them. Similarly, the Puluwat people of Micronesia can navigate across long distances in the sea under circumstances in which meaningful signals also would elude us.

The importance of context is shown by the kinds of practical knowledge that children develop in order to adapt to their environments. Consider two examples.

Imagine living in a hunting-gathering society. Many Yup'ik Eskimos in Alaska live in such a society, where hunting and gathering are joined by fishing as means of putting food on the table. The knowledge and skills you need to survive in such an environmental context are rather different from those of, say, an individual who has spent his life as a professor. The professor (or college student, for that matter) might do well on an SAT question or on a question about what or how to order in a restaurant. He or she might not fare as well on a question we developed for assessing Yup'ik young people:

When Eddie runs to collect the ptarmigan that he's just shot, he notices that its front pouch (balloon) is full of ptarmigan food. This is a sign that:

- there's a storm on the way.*
- winter is almost over.

- it's hard to find food this season.
- it hasn't snowed in a long time. (Grigorenko et al. 2004)

The correct answer is asterisked. Of course, there is no reason why the typical college student or professor would need to know the answer to the question about the ptarmigan. But similarly, it is unclear that the Alaskan Yup'ik student would need to do well on the SAT or restaurant question if he or she plans to live in a coastal Yup'ik village. The knowledge that is useful depends on the context. One could argue, of course, that it is not the mission of universities to educate those young people, but do we really want higher education to be only for those students who come from, or plan to live, in more urban settings?

We found that urban students (from Dillingham, a city in Alaska that, although small by the standards of most states, would count as fairly large in Alaska) outperformed rural students on conventional tests of fluid and crystallized abilities, but that the Yup'ik Eskimo young people outperformed the urban children on tests of knowledge of adaptive competencies relevant to the Yup'ik environment. Moreover, tests of practical knowledge predicted hunting skills whereas conventional standardized tests did not.

When we in the United States create tests of intelligence, which is what college-admissions tests are, we inadvertently rely on culturally bound implicit theories, or folk conceptions, of what intelligence is. We may think we know what intelligence is—for example, general ability or fluid/crystallized abilities—but we nevertheless rely on implicit theories that are not widely shared across cultures around the world. In particular, in the university world, we may be tempted to equate being smart with having high scores on standardized tests. And if our goal is to admit the brightest students, we may default to high standardized test scores. That's a shame, because we may admit students who are culturally attuned to mainstream US culture, but we are not necessarily admitting the students with the greatest potential for active concerned citizenry and ethical leadership.

Folk Conceptions of What It Means to Be Smart

To understand what people around the world mean by "smart," we need to study folk conceptions, or implicit theories of intelligence across cultures, not just in our own culture. Implicit theories do not tell us what intelligence is, to the extent that the question is even answerable; rather, they inform us about folk conceptions of what people believe intelligence is. Folk theories drive many psychological phenomena, including even what we know and remember about ourselves.

One might ask why implicit theories are important. After all, why should we care what laypeople think intelligence is? Shouldn't we be more concerned about the opinions of experts? The main reason folk theories matter so much is that 99+ percent of the judgments that are made about people's intelligence are based on people's implicit theories, not on IQ tests or SATs or ACTs or related tests. These judgments are made on dates, in job interviews, after listening to someone talk at a party, during a business negotiation, or when we read an article about someone in the newspaper. Implicit theories, not explicit theories of experts, are what makes the "world go 'round."

My colleagues and I have studied implicit theories across cultures and have found that, indeed, our implicit theories are not all that widely shared. In a set of studies we did in the United States (Sternberg et al. 1981), we found that people's implicit theories were well characterized by three factors: practical problem solving, verbal ability, and social competence. Note that only one of these factors—verbal ability—is seriously measured by conventional tests of intelligence.

In a study Shih Ying-Yang and I did in Taiwan, four factors emerged from people's implicit theories of intelligence: traditional cognitive abilities, but also interpersonal competence (understanding others), intrapersonal competence (understanding oneself), knowing when to show you are smart, and knowing when not to show you are smart (i.e., have a "poker face") (Yang and Sternberg 1997). Again, only one of these factors is measured by conventional tests of intelligence, namely, traditional cognitive abilities.

In studies in a very different part of the world—rural Kenya—we found that cultural conceptions of the nature of intelligence were quite different from those in either Taiwan or the United States. Four qualities seemed to underlie people's implicit theories of intelligence: *rieko* (knowledge, abilities, skills), *luoro* (respect), *paro* (initiative), and *winjo* (comprehension of the complexities of a social problem-solving situation (Grigorenko et al. 2001).

One view of all this would be that these implicit theories cannot all be right. According to this view, the results show the futility of relying on implicit theories, since they vary so widely. But an alternative view is that the results show precisely the opposite—namely, the need to take implicit theories seriously. If implicit theories differ so widely, it is clear how attributes that are valued highly in one culture might not be so highly valued, or might even be devalued, in another culture. Note also that unless one does implicit-theory studies in a variety of cultures, one is likely to make the mistake of thinking that the implicit theories of one's own culture typify other cultures as well. But even the small sampling of cultures described here reveals large differences in implicit theories across cultures. Standardized tests scores, in sum, reflect a relatively narrow implicit theory of what intelligence is. We will not admit truly diverse classes to the extent we rely on standardized tests to tell us who will be the students with the most potential to add value to, and receive value from, our universities.

How Implicit Theories Affect Teacher Behavior

I claimed above that implicit theories affect people's behavior. An important example is that of teachers. Teachers, like everyone else, have implicit theories of intelligence. They use these implicit theories to evaluate their students. If the students look smart according to the teachers' implicit theories, the teachers are likely to treat the children differently from, and perhaps better than, the students who do not look so smart.

In one set of studies Lynn Okagaki and I conducted in San Jose, California, we looked at how the match between teachers' and parents' implicit theories of intelligence would affect the teachers' views of young people from different ethnic groups (Okagaki and Sternberg 1993). We queried parents of Anglo American, Latino American, and Asian American young people regarding their implicit theories of intelligence. We also queried the children's teachers. We found that parents of Anglo American and Asian American young people emphasized cognitive skills more than social skills in their conceptions of intelligence, whereas Latino American parents placed more emphasis on social skills. The young people's teachers, however, like the Anglo American and Asian American parents, emphasized cognitive skills. Perhaps partially as a result, the teachers viewed the

Anglo American and Asian American students as generally more academically able. But which skills will be more important in life after college—or even, arguably, life in college—cognitive or social skills? Who will make the successful businesspeople, social workers, salespeople, or whatever? Do we really want to limit our conceptions of who the most able students are to those who do the best on standardized tests?

If one reflects on these various studies of diverse children from diverse backgrounds, one must question whether standardized tests are telling us all, or even most, of what we would want to know about the students whom we consider for admission to our universities. Students may have tremendous potential in terms of the ways in which they were enculturated and socialized, but because these ways do not correspond to the rather narrow skills measured on standardized tests, the students may come out of the experience looking far less able than they really are. We overemphasize tests and then wonder why it is so hard to achieve a diverse student body. In effect, the tests knock out the diversity we prize.

Objections to the Seeking of Diversity

I value diversity in the student body. Perhaps you do too. But not everyone does. I would like to review the three main concerns I have heard from individuals who do not particularly value it, at least as it pertains to university admissions and hiring.

The Political-Correctness Objection

One objection is that the seeking of diversity is nothing more than political correctness run amok. I hope I have dealt with this issue in the discussion above. The seeking of diversity can become a form of political correctness when it is done for the sake of appeasement of certain groups or without due regard to the quality of the applicants being selected for positions as students, staff, or faculty members. But if one considers the advantages of diversity discussed above, as well as the range of skills that diverse people can bring to the table, one at least needs to reconsider what one means by "quality." Diversity may or may not be politically correct: it is important in a university setting, nevertheless.

The "It's Not Important" Objection

An ACCEL university takes the position that diversity is necessary for quality. If everyone thinks and sees problems the same way you do, then you are not likely to learn much from them and, on the contrary, you are likely to come to the false conclusion that anyone in his or her right mind will think the same way you do.

In one of my administrative positions, I had a discussion with a member of the university board of trustees. He (and some of his colleagues) did not particularly value diversity, and when, as mentioned above, I mentioned the idea of creating a position of vice president for diversity, some of the people looked at me as if I were from another planet. An issue for people who grow up in nondiverse settings is that they may come to believe that others should think as they do, and if others don't, then they should just be in another place where people think the way they do. In other words, people who are not exposed to diversity may not think it has value and instead may judge others not by the quality of their ideas but rather by the extent to which the others' ideas correspond quite precisely to their own.

A state politician in one of the states in which I worked commented on the importance of a particular industry to the state, and suggested that people who see things another way just find another state in which to live. I expected widespread condemnation of the politician. Instead, within the state, there was widespread praise. With that attitude, it is challenging to see why people from diverse backgrounds would want to live in the state or study in a public university within the state. Homogeneity breeds more of the same and the view that one's own culture and mores are superior to those of others.

The "It's Unfair" Objection

The toughest objection, I believe, is the feeling that when one admits or hires an individual in order to increase diversity, there is someone else who may be more qualified who is not getting that slot. And that objection may have some justification to it in some instances. I personally do not believe in hiring a less qualified person simply to increase diversity. As an administrator, I always argued for admitting and hiring the most qualified individuals. But too often, as I noted above, our notions about what constitutes a "qualified" person are excessively narrow. Although we think our view of qualifications is that we seek the best person for a particular slot, often we end up seeking the person who is most like us. As I discuss later in the book, we tend to be attracted to people who are like us. In effect, we confound similarity with quality.

In a study I did with some colleagues years ago, we asked people to rate their own intelligence. The mean rating, on a 9-point scale, where 5 was average, was between 7 and 8. So people very much think they are above average, even though, by definition, half of people need to be below average (assuming a so-called normal, or bell-shaped, distribution). Most people, thinking they are above average, want to associate with others like themselves. They figure that they've reached the heights, and hence others who reach the heights presumably are much like them. Unfortunately, they are wrong. But if they are used to nondiverse environments, they may never have been exposed to the diversity of people who would show them the folly of their own narrowness.

When Diversity Turns on Itself

I am writing this book at a time (late 2015) when, in some institutions, diversity has turned on itself. By this, I mean that some members of campus communities—students, faculty, and staff alike—have decided that they do not want to tolerate or even hear diverse points of view or ways of approaching the world. In some universities, they have decided—in the name of protection of diversity—that those who disagree with their views on matters cannot be tolerated. Some of these students want "protection" or "safety" against points of view they find offensive.

Regrettably, in an era in which campus leadership often is more oriented toward job preservation than toward doing the right thing, some administrators have capitulated to demands that individuals with points of view different from those of a vocal group on campus not be allowed on their campuses. Some of those on campuses with different points of view already on campus have been shouted down and sometimes targeted by obscenities and worse. Oddly, diversity is being stifled—in the name of diversity.

The benefit of diversity is to open up a university to varying lifestyles, points of view, and ways of looking at the world. When students, faculty, or others shout down perspectives different from their own in the name of safety, diversity, or whatever, they are destroying exactly the benefits that diversity of campus is intended to achieve. Students should feel safe, but not from worldviews or opinions that differ from their own. On the contrary, exposure to differing worldviews is exactly what diversity is supposed to produce. This irony is lost on some of the most vocal protesters and, unfortunately, on some administrators as well.

The issue of diversity brings us to the question of how one creates an able and at the same time diverse student body. I deal with that question in the next chapter.

Part II

Who Gets In and Who Is Able to Go?

5

Admissions

How is college admissions done and how should it be done in an ACCEL university? Let's look first at how it is done and then consider how it could be done better.

Criteria for Undergraduate Admissions

Universities differ somewhat in how they admit students. Some admit all students who apply whereas others are selective. For those that are at least somewhat selective, what kinds of criteria are used to distinguish among applicants? And how good are these criteria? I argue below that many of the criteria that universities use are, in the words of Stephen Crane's poem, balls of clay disguised as balls of gold.

This chapter draws and expands on Sternberg 2010a.

High School Grade-Point Average

Grade-point average (GPA) is the most important factor in admission to most colleges and universities. There are several reasons why it is so heavily used.

First, the best predictor of future behavior is past behavior of the same kind. This applies to pretty much anything. For example, if someone has tended to overeat during holidays in the past, he or she will probably overeat during future holidays. If someone has been charitable in the past, he or she will probably be charitable in the future. And if someone has gotten good grades in the past, he or she will probably get good grades again in the future. Because academic work forms a cornerstone of college education, and because failing academic work can result in early dropout from college, it makes sense that college admissions offices would rely on high school GPA as a fundamental basis for making their decisions.

Second, high school GPA, although a single number, is actually quite complex in its origins. It reflects a student's academic ability, of course: getting good grades requires students to acquire a knowledge base and then to reason with it. It further reflects the student's practical ability: Can the student understand what is expected of him or her, devise strategies for studying for different types of tests such as multiple choice and essay, figure out what the teacher is likely to test, and budget his or her time in a way that allows him or her to excel not just in one subject but in several?

Third, GPAs are readily available for students in the large majority of high schools. Therefore the admissions office need not require anything extra of the student in order to get the information, except, perhaps, the permission of the student for the school to release the information. But students themselves typically arrange to send transcripts, so universities need do nothing but file the transcripts away correctly when they arrive.

As a criterion for university admission, GPA also has its challenges. Its interpretation is by no means straightforward, for a variety of reasons.

First, high schools differ in their quality and in the quality of the students who attend them. When my own children Seth and Sara were considering a private high school (which, in the end, they did attend), I warned them that just attending the preparatory private school would not necessarily improve their chances of college admission, because the higher qualifications of the students attending the school meant it would be much more competitive to attain a high GPA.

Second, high schools differ in their rigor, both between and within schools. In some high schools, having a 3.8 average may mean that the student has completed a highly rigorous selection of courses and has done extremely well in them. In other high schools, courses may be much weaker and the grades in them mean much less. Even within high schools, courses differ widely in how academically rigorous they are. A 3.8 for one student may indicate readiness for college work whereas for another student it may not indicate such readiness at all.

Third, high schools differ in what their grades mean. In former times—before most of us were born—the average grade was a C. In theory, roughly 8 percent of grades were As, 24 percent were Bs, 36 percent were Cs, 24 percent were Ds, and 8 percent were Fs. Schools may have differed in the exact percentage, but the term "gentleman's C" referred to the grade received by a student who did not work particularly hard and who made no effort to achieve at a level above the average. When I was in college, from 1968 to 1972, a C was the expected grade and a B was considered truly above average. Today a C is often considered a disgrace. For some students, it is much worse than that. I have had any number of students complain about grades of A–. They want to be the best, and anything less will just not do.

Fourth, the desire for high grades is partly a function of high motivation, but it is also a function of grade inflation. An A just does not mean as much anymore. Neither does a 4.0 average. With corrections introduced by schools for course difficulty and other factors, a 4.0 average may place a student in the upper portion of a high school class but, in many schools today, nowhere near the top. Efforts are made every now and then to hold grade inflation in check, but they have not been particularly successful. It is hard to believe that we have reached a point where a high school GPA of 4.0 may be considered above the ordinary but not exceptional. Because inflation differs from one high school to another, it is not always readily apparent whether a high grade means something for a given school.

Fifth, high schools differ in what courses even count toward the GPA. In one school, a course such as woodworking may not count at all; in another school, it may count but be weighted only weakly; in another school, it may count the same as any other course. The school may indicate what courses count, but not all admissions officers are prepared to recompute the whole GPA based on the courses they in particular would value.

Sixth, grades represent in some degree a skill in knowing what teachers want and giving it to them. Of course, students will have to perform the same act in college—figuring out what teachers want and how to give it to them. The question is how different high school versus college expectations are. In a rigorous high school, the expectations of the teachers may correspond to those of college instructors. But in a less rigorous school, an A may mean that the student was well behaved, did what he or she was told, and did it the way he or she was supposed to do it.

Finally, high school GPA will tell you little about the qualities that underlie active concerned citizenship and ethical leadership. Rather, it will tell you about how well people can meet a set of academic objectives that are assigned to them and that they are told they are expected to accomplish.

When I went to college, I did poorly my first semester. Even though I had taken Advanced Placement (AP) courses, I was unprepared for the demands of college work. In contrast, Seth and Sara were completely ready because they went to a highly competitive preparatory school. A risk with preparatory schools, in my experience as an admissions officer and a professor, is burnout. The students from private preparatory schools are at an advantage when they start college, but sometimes they burn out early because they just tire of the demands of highly rigorous academic work.

Some schools, public or private, will be known quantities to admissions officers. When I worked in admissions at Yale, more years ago than I care to count, I felt I could interpret quite well the grades and GPAs from schools with which I was familiar, usually ones that consistently sent a number of students to Yale over the years. But I also realized that my knowledge had the potential of creating a bias toward those schools.

After I was admitted to Yale, I went to work in the Office of Institutional Research under a psychologist who computed predicted grade-point averages. He was someone who, even then (in 1968), represented a past generation of psychologists. He had predicted GPAs using a hand calculator, and when computers came into use and he found himself without a job, he took to checking the calculations of the computer by hand! I discovered that he used a correction factor that took into account the high school the prospective student had attended. Yale had been using (right up to that time) percentage grades, and the psychologist in charge was converting high school grades to expected percentage grades at Yale. I discovered that because I went to a public high school that was largely unknown to him, he automatically subtracted 9 points. That meant that the highest predicted GPA I could attain was a 91.

The psychologist in charge of Institutional Research was trying to do his job in a manner suited perhaps to a mentality from earlier decades. But the problem that he was addressing is still not totally solved. When an admissions officer sees a GPA from an unknown school in rural Appalachia, or an inner-city high school known more for its disciplinary problems than for the academic achievement of its students, the officer may do in his or her head, perhaps not even quite consciously, what the psychologist did explicitly. Schools that seek diversity may end up admitting some of the students from the unknown high schools. But they represent a very small fraction of the students from those high schools, most of whom have little chance of being admitted to, or even applying to, any selective colleges at all. For these students, college may not even seem like a viable option, and a selective college may not be something they even consider. This is, in part, a problem of resources available to the high schools. Guidance counselors in some remote schools may not even be aware that their students have chances of attending colleges that, to them, may seem out of reach.

The irony is that going to a more selective university does not necessarily mean that one will have lower grades. For example, Harvard, among the most selective colleges in the United States, has been wracked by grade inflation, much more so than many of the community colleges with which it would never view itself as competing. Grade inflation has affected many high schools and private preparatory schools as well, including some of the most selective ones. But the general point is that grades are hard to interpret, for a wide variety of reasons. Fortunately, admissions officers look for more.

Class Rank

Most high schools provide a measure of a student's rank in class—that is, how far he or she is from the top of the class. The information in class rank is partially but not wholly duplicative of the information in GPA. This is because class rank controls for the severity of the grading in the school. In one school, a B (3.0) average may place a student in the upper third of the class, whereas in another school, it may place a student well into the bottom half. The class rank partially adjusts for these differences in grading. Some schools weight courses or make adjustments for honors courses, so that two students in a given school may have the same GPA but widely differing class ranks.

Class rank is always interpreted in the context of how many students are in the class, and is usually interpreted in the context of the school one attends. A class rank of 1 means a different thing at a large, highly competitive school from what it means in a small, not very competitive school with much less academically well-equipped students. But school quality is not always factored in: for example, as noted earlier, being in the top 10 percent of your high school class guarantees admission to the University of Texas, regardless of the school you attend.

Some public high schools and private preparatory schools prefer not to rank their students. The advantage of such a decision is that it takes some pressure off students during their high school careers. For some schools, it also makes an honest statement about their priorities and philosophy. The disadvantage is that the decision makes it harder for college admissions officers to evaluate applicants from such schools. Withholding class rank potentially could put the students from these schools at a disadvantage in their applications. If admissions officers are familiar with a high school, they may calculate, even implicitly, a rough class rank based on what they know about the school. But parents, in deciding where to send their children to school, need to trade off the costs and benefits of having versus not having class rank available to colleges.

Course Load and Profile

College admissions officers look not just at the GPA but also at the courses that the student has taken that enter into the computation of the GPA. The course load and profile can tell the admissions officer quite a bit about the student's academic skills and motivation. Is the student taking very challenging courses or relatively easy ones? If a college expects students to have studied a foreign language, how many years of foreign language has the student taken and how many languages has she or he studied? (In my experience, colleges generally prefer more years of one language than fewer years of each of two languages.) Has the student taken the requisite mathematics courses needed for college success? Are there special courses on the transcript, such as honors, International Baccalaureate (IB), or Advanced Placement (AP) courses, as available in the secondary school? What kinds of electives has the student chosen? Information about the course load and profile can reveal facts about students not available in their composite GPAs.

At the same time, admissions officers need to factor in extenuating circumstances. Not all schools offer Advanced Placement courses or the International Baccalaureate program; or even if they do offer AP, their selections may be relatively limited. Schools may also have different restrictions on who can take such courses. For example, in one school, AP courses may be available to virtually anyone, whereas in another school the courses may be available only to the very best students. So admissions officers need to factor in not just which courses were taken but which were available to be taken by the students in the high school.

The admissions officer also needs to see the course profile in the context of other activities in which the student is engaged. For example, a student who is heavily involved in high school sports may choose courses that will allow him or her to succeed despite spending a great deal of time on the playing field. The officer may or may not choose to view such activities as compensatory.

Home schooling is becoming more and more popular among parents. The advantage of home schooling is that parents get to teach their children exactly what they think is important at the same time they are able to bypass what they do not think is important. From the standpoint of college admissions, the greatest disadvantage is that parental grades and comments are not likely to be taken very seriously. Hence, standardized test scores, considered next, are all the more important in the cases of applicants who were home-schooled.

Class rank, like high school GPA, tells you next to nothing about the qualities of creativity, common sense, wisdom, judgment, ethics, and passion that underlie active concerned citizenship and ethical leadership. Again, we must look elsewhere.

Standardized Test Scores

Two standardized tests have a monopoly in the college-admissions market—the SAT and the ACT. They are among the best examples of Stephen Crane's balls of clay in the university business today.

Consider some of the history. The College Board was created in 1901, and the first of its tests was given in that year. At that point, the tests were essays measuring achievement in school subjects such as history, Latin, and physics. But the enterprise as we know it today did not get under way until June 23, 1926, when the first Scholastic Aptitude Test (SAT) was administered. Carl Brigham, a Princeton University psychologist, created the original version of the test. The test had sections measuring antonyms, arithmetic, analogies, and reading of paragraphs, among other things. It was administered to roughly eight thousand students. The test lasted only an hour and a half, despite having more than three hundred questions.

The kinds of questions used then did not differ much from the kinds of questions used today. Although particular item types have changed over time, the underlying skills that the tests measure have scarcely changed at all. All tests such as the SAT and ACT are somewhat thinly disguised measures of general intelligence, or g. They correlate about as highly with intelligence (IQ) tests as IQ tests correlate with each other. That said, intelligence tests measure only a small part of intelligence.

The name "Scholastic Aptitude Test" was later dropped in favor of "Scholastic Assessment Test," and this name in turn was later dropped in favor of simply using the acronym "SAT" without its meaning anything in particular. Different reasons might be given as to why, but the most obvious one is that neither the College Board nor anyone else is quite sure what the test measures, because it is based not on any particular scientific theory of a psychological construct but rather on a pragmatic assessment of what will predict scholastic success in college. There is nothing in principle wrong with this, but it does mean that, in practice, the test measures a construct that is undefined.

The SAT Reasoning Test has two parts, called Critical Reading (formerly called the "Verbal" section) and Mathematics. The test's composition has recently (as of March 2016) been changed, with emphasis on measuring vocabulary for use rather than abstruse vocabulary. The exact item types vary from time to time. The SAT Critical Reading test is scored on a scale of 200 to 800.

The SAT Mathematics section has three parts that measure numerical operations, algebra, geometry, probability and statistics, and data analysis (e.g., understanding and interpreting a graph). The level of question is up to the third year of college-preparatory mathematics, and the test has both multiple-choice and free-response items. It is not intended to measure re-call of basic formulas, and indeed, these basic formulas are provided. The test is scored on a scale of 200 to 800.

The second of the major college-admissions tests, which has now over-taken the SAT in terms of number of test-takers, is the ACT, which tra-ditionally stood for American College Test but, like the SAT, now goes just by its acronym. It was created as competitor to the SAT by Everett Lindquist and was first used in the fall of 1959. The test was designed to more directly measure achievement than the SAT, but the SAT also has subject-matter tests that are even more direct measures of achievement than the ACT. The ACT, traditionally, has consisted of four subtests: English, Mathematics, Reading, and Science Reasoning. It also includes at this time an optional Writing test. Scores range from 1 to 36 on each of the subtests and for an overall composite, which is an average of the four subtests. If the test-taker takes the Writing test, it is not included in the composite.

It is easy to see why the SAT and the ACT are popular among college admissions officers and other administrators and faculty. The tests have several positive features.

First, the tests measure skills that are relevant to college success. Stu-dents will need to read a tremendous amount of material in college, and they will need to understand and analyze it. Moreover, the material they will read will be in a variety of fields, the kinds of fields sampled on both the SAT and ACT. College students will also have to know high school mathematics in order to succeed in college math and science courses. They will need to be able to write well in order to complete essays on examina-tions as well as term papers and the like.

Second, the tests seem to provide a common metric across different stu-dents and schools. An SAT score of, say, 600, refers to the same number of correctly answered questions in one school as in another. (In the past, the College Board introduced a correction for guessing, subtracting a propor-tion of wrong answers from right answers, but this correction has been removed.) In contrast, the GPA may mean very different things in differ-ent places.

I say standardized tests "seem" to provide a common metric because a given score does not really mean exactly the same thing for each stu-dent who achieves it. One student may have grown up as a native English speaker with a lot of books in the home and highly educated parents.

Another student may have grown up with a foreign language as a native language, even with parents who do not speak English at all or, at least, well. That student may have had few books in the home and parents who were not able to provide an enriched educational experience. Admissions officers are trained, at least in theory, to take such differences into account, but no one can do so perfectly because no one knows exactly what the effects of different upbringings are. Moreover, the first student will likely be at an advantage in college with respect to having mastered the skills to achieve high grades. So the admissions officer must decide to just what extent he or she wants to take the background differences into account.

Third, the college does not have to pay for the test—the students taking the test do. This payment system creates a substantial incentive for universities to continue to use the tests, because their use is essentially free to the universities. High school students, in contract, must pay a substantial amount of money to take the tests. Moreover, many students take the tests multiple times, increasing the financial burden on them and their parents. So testing is really a pretty good deal—for universities.

Fourth, the tests give the appearance of being objective, so that colleges do not have to worry that the results are a reflection of who happens to be scoring them. The possible exceptions to this are the Writing tests, but even those have been parsed so that they can be scored in a somewhat objective way.

With all these advantages, why would anyone in his or her right mind not heavily (although certainly not exclusively) weigh the SAT or ACT in admissions decisions? There are several reasons.

First, although the tests measure skills relevant to college success, they do not measure all such skills. Despite differences in qualities of high schools and grading systems in those high schools, high school grades are nevertheless still the best predictors of college success. Why would this be? One reason, mentioned earlier, is that the best predictor of future success of a given kind is past success of the same kind, and so if one wishes to predict grades, the best way to predict them normally will be through other grades. On a related note, no one is claiming that the standardized tests measure all the skills that are relevant for college success. Students need practical, common-sense skills to know how to study and organize their time. They need metacognitive or self-understanding skills to recognize their own strengths and weaknesses and how they might improve. They need motivational skills and attitudes to get them to work hard. They need creative skills to generate novel ideas that are nevertheless high in quality. Most of all, they need to have a purpose for being in college. Some students who are generally motivated in their lives drop out of college because they cannot figure out why they are there.

Second, exactly how common is the metric? I mentioned above that scores can mean different things for different individuals. Does a given score mean the same thing for different groups as well?

As I mentioned earlier, Lynn Okagaki and I studied various ethnic groups in San Jose, California. We found that the different ethnic groups had rather different conceptions of what it means to be intelligent. Teachers tended to reward those children who were socialized into a view of intelligence that happened to correspond to the teachers' own. So a standardized-test score will have different meanings depending on whether the way a child was socialized corresponds well or not so well to what the tests happen to measure.

In any culture, practical intellectual skills matter for predicting adaptation to everyday environments. In particular, different groups may emphasize different skills depending on the environments in which children are socialized. A child growing up in inner-city Detroit, a generally low-income part of Michigan, faces challenges different from those of a child growing up in Grosse Pointe Farms, a generally wealthy suburb of Detroit.

Parents socialize their children to develop the skills they need to face the challenges of their own environments. So the SAT may actually measure somewhat different skills for different children, depending on the skills the parents emphasized as the children were growing up. The skills may be ones that Grosse Pointe Farms students started practicing at an early age at home, but not ones that some inner-city Detroit students had, on average, as much practice in, perhaps even through their school environment. As an example, the SAT mathematical test measures different skills for someone who has learned in school the algebra and geometry the test assumes than for someone who has not yet acquired this algebra and geometry knowledge and needs to figure out the answers to the problems in the absence of that knowledge.

Third, although the college does not pay for standardized testing such as the SAT or ACT, students do. So using the tests makes a statement that the value of information gleaned from the test is a worthwhile investment on the part of those who actually pay for it. If we add up the costs not only of multiple administrations, discussed above, but also of books parents buy for their children to help them prepare for the test, and of courses or tutors that may be quite expensive, the costs become nontrivial. Moreover, some books and outside courses are not directly for test preparation but indirectly prepare students for the skills needed to succeed in multiple-choice testing. There is also the cost to students in high schools that integrate what amounts to SAT preparation into their curricula. For students, there are what are called "opportunity costs": the time the students are spending preparing for these tests is time they are not spending doing other things that might be more worthwhile, such as athletics, art projects, studying music, or even studying literature instead of memorizing vocabulary words.

The ACT and SAT offer students score choice—that is, they can choose which scores to send to colleges. Score choice poses a bit of a dilemma. Is a student who receives a 550 and a 650 on, say, the math SAT really better than a student who twice receives a 600? The student who received the disparate scores can report only the 650 and thus look somewhat more skilled mathematically than the student who received the 600 twice. But is the student really more skilled? The average scores of both students are the same. One interpretation, of course, would be that the 550 merely represented a "bad day." But error of measurement goes both ways—it can result in scores that are too low or scores that are too high, the latter, for example, when the questions chosen just happen to measure areas in which the student is particularly strong. So score choice may skew the information available to colleges. It also poses another dilemma. If students need only to report the highest scores, it encourages them to keep retaking the test—and paying for it—in the hope that they will hit the jackpot of a score that is appreciably higher than the other ones they have received. In my view, score choice was introduced in large part to make more money for the testing companies. It creates an incentive somewhat like gambling—one keeps hoping to hit the jackpot.

Fourth, we overvalue the supposed objectivity of standardized tests. There is a story that is told of a man who is frantically looking at night for his lost keys. A police officer sees him looking and offers to help. Fortunately, the area where the man is looking is well illuminated. The police officer and the man look for quite a while, after which the police officer queries, "Are you sure you lost the keys here?" To which the man responds, "Why, no, I lost them over there but it is pitch black there, so I'm looking here where the light is better."

In standardized testing, we have tended to measure what is easy to measure. Arguably, this was right and proper in the 1920s, because testing was just starting out and it was impressive, at that point, that the testers could measure anything in a standardized and useful way. But the years passed and little changed. In testing, we have looked where the light is best, but in doing so, we have ignored what may well be the most important keys.

The so-called objective tests serve a purpose in college admissions. But there is no need to limit ourselves to such tests. The best assessments use a variety of methods. In the ideal, we would combine the traditional objective assessments with other assessments that, although more subjective in their scoring, allow students to better show the range of skills they possess.

The Common Application

The Common Application is an application form used by many colleges to save applicants the bother of having to fill out a completely separate application for each of a number of different schools. Before the mid-1990s, each college had its own completely separate application. That's what I did: I applied to a bunch of colleges, and each application was a totally separate enterprise. Students had to do a lot of repetitive work, filling out the same information again and again on multiple applications. The Common Application provided a way to avoid this mindless repetition of information.

The Common Application asks for personal data, family information, future plans, basic demographic information about oneself and one's family, test scores, lists of honors and academic distinctions, principal extracurricular activities (including volunteer and family activities), hobbies, varsity letters earned in athletics, and paid work experience. The exact contents of the application vary over years. The topics that are offered for essays have been pretty standard fare and clearly do not entice students to think in creative ways. Arguably, the topics have to be somewhat standard fare, because the Common Application serves such diverse and heterogeneous applicants and colleges. Considering such diversity, the questions must be "one size fits all." The application also asks about disciplinary history and any additional information the applicant may wish to provide.

The application also includes forms that can be distributed to one's teachers and to the guidance counselor (or the equivalent). The teacher form asks about attributes such as academic achievement, intellectual promise, maturity, motivation, leadership, and integrity. It also asks for an overall rating. The guidance-counselor form asks about how class rank is computed and also requests academic, personal, and overall evaluations, among others.

The Common Application does a good job of organizing a wide variety of kinds of information about the applicant in a way that can be used by a heterogeneous array of colleges and universities. Moreover, it cuts down enormously on the work applicants need to do in order to apply to multiple schools. If we look at its elements, though, there are problematical aspects, as there probably would be for any application of its kind.

First, as mentioned earlier, the essays are fairly standard, and indeed, anyone can write anything he or she wishes. Because one can write anything in any year, there is an opportunity for unscrupulous merchants to build up banks of essays that have been successful and, for a fee, make these available to students applying to colleges. There is little one cannot buy on the Internet these days. At best, students may use such essays as models. At worst, they may recycle old essays. The extent to which this happens is unknown.

A second feature of the Common Application is that the essay topics themselves do not particularly encourage creative responses (nor is this particularly the intent of the essays). Rather, they encourage students to spend years "building up records" that can then translate into college-admissions success. In essence, the high school experience and even earlier educational experiences can become largely about building a record for college. In some cities, such as New York, the competition starts early, with children vying for places in kindergartens that have good records of winning acceptances for their graduates in the more prestigious private schools of the city. What has happened, at least in some circles, is that the college-admissions game begins before students even enter elementary school.

A third feature of the Common Application is that recommendations, like grades, have become inflated over the years. Top-notch ratings have become more common, and thus it becomes harder for the colleges to distinguish among applicants. This difficulty is not limited to the Common Application, but neither does this application provide a remedy to this vexing problem.

A fourth feature is that although teachers are asked to give a number of distinct ratings, the ratings often form what is often known as a "halo effect." This simply means that if the teacher has a generally positive impression, most of the ratings turn out to be quite positive, and if the teacher has a generally negative impression, most of the ratings turn out to be less favorable, at least for a very selective college. Thus, although it would be nice to get distinct ratings for each of the rated elements, one rarely does. Rather, they reflect a general glow that the applicant emits in varying degrees. In the end, the written comments are often more helpful than the summary ratings.

A fifth feature is that the ratings can mean very different things in very different schools. The top student in Podunkville may indeed be the best that the town has seen in the past ten years, but he or she may be competing with students who are just not very competitive. The result, as discussed elsewhere, is that admissions officers may take more seriously recommendations from schools and particular guidance counselors whom they know and trust.

These concerns do not apply uniquely to the Common Application. They would apply to any application form at all. But taken together, they present challenges for applicants and admissions officers alike. They also present challenges for those who want to discover the qualities of active concerned citizenship and ethical leadership that underlie the ACCEL approach to education.

Interviews

Interviewing practices differ widely from school to school. Some schools do not give interviews. Some give interviews, but through alumni groups only. Others do on-campus interviews, but they may or may not do the interviews evaluatively. Some years ago, when I worked in admissions at Yale, I did a cost-benefit analysis of the Yale Admissions Office interview (Sternberg 1973). Somewhat to my surprise, I found that the interview did not count very much in admissions decisions. The admissions officers realized that the interview has limited value. It can help spot a few outstanding candidates and some real duds. But as I found when I did interviewing, most of the applicants looked good but were not terribly well distinguished from the rest. A curious finding, however, was that when applicants were asked to evaluate how well they had done, they thought they did much better than they actually did. And perhaps because they thought they presented themselves so well, they had a very positive impression, overall, of the interview experience. As a result, I recommended retaining the interview, primarily for public-relations purposes.

Alumni interviewers enable colleges to reach out to large numbers of applicants in ways that in-house interviews do not, but the range of talent among the interviewers is great, as is the range of standards to which they hold the applicants. It is often hard to know just what to make of the reports. Indeed, when I applied to Yale, my alumnus interviewer was from another generation in which the values of the university had been very different. It was unlikely that he would have even known what the school was looking for in 1967!

Interviews sometimes feel more valid than they are, because it is often difficult to separate self-presentational skills from the more basic attributes of the person. Self-presentational skills do matter in life, so having the interview may predict the kind of impression a person will make on others, at least within a short amount of time. However, they will disadvantage people who may be slow to warm up or who feel intimidated by the interview setting. Like everything else, the interview has its strengths and its drawbacks and can be useful when combined with other means for assessing an applicant's characteristics.

Interviews should tell us something about the qualities needed for active concerned citizenship and ethical leadership. Done well, they will tell us something. Done poorly or without systematic thought, they tell us primarily how much the interviewer "likes" a candidate, which sometimes means how similar the interviewer perceives the candidate to be to himself or herself.

Extracurricular Activities

Extracurricular activities form an important part of the application for many universities. They are considered important because they potentially reveal aspects of the applicant's personality and character that cannot be revealed in other ways. Admissions officers are often interested in seeking future leaders and productive citizens, and they know that test scores and grades tell one only so much. Extracurricular activities might speak directly to other qualities.

Not all schools count extracurricular activities. Some schools, especially state ones, are much more interested in class rank or a combination of class rank and test scores. In most of Europe, extracurricular activities do not count at all. Whether to count them depends as much on one's philosophy of admissions as anything else.

Even in the United States, colleges generally do not weigh extracurricular activities as much as they value test scores and grades. Why should this be the case, if such activities are among the few indicants of character? There are several reasons.

Will the student succeed academically? The first priority of the college or university is to ensure that the student can do the academic work at the institution. It is of no use to admit someone with a stellar extracurricular record who will flunk out after one semester. And in selective colleges, admissions officers will seek out not merely students who can pass their courses but rather students who can do quite well in them. Extracurricular activities generally do not say much about an applicant's ability to do the academic work of the school.

Just how good was the participation? It is hard to quantify extracurricular participation. Although admissions officers can assign ratings, there is a feeling that such ratings are subjective in comparison with the objective information provided by test scores and grades. Indeed, much of what admissions officers do is subjective. Their training is, in part, in how to evaluate and weigh subjective factors.

Is it for real? It is often hard to verify either that the extracurricular activity is properly stated or that participation in it was meaningful rather than empty. Suppose, for example, the applicant reports having been president of the debating club. Three questions arise: First, was he or she really president of the club? Second, how big a job was it? For example, how many members were there on the team, how much time did the student invest, and how many events were there? Third, what did the student actually do in the activity? Was he or she an active president who moved the club forward, or was the activity largely passive, serving to fill up a college application but little else? Ideally, the combination of sources of information will answer these questions, but not always.

How many opportunities did the school provide? At some schools, there may be room for everyone to be president of a club, whereas at others, there may be limited offerings that leave little opportunity for a student to shine in extracurricular activities, whether clubs or other kinds of activities.

Who wrote the description of activities? There is always the risk that the description of activities was written by someone other than the applicant.

Letters of Recommendation

Letters of recommendation offer an opportunity for teachers, guidance counselors, and occasionally others to provide information that may be gotten at in no other way. The assumption is that the letter writer knows the student well. In some cases, the recommender does not know the student well, or may not even know him or her at all. Every admissions officer encounters letters from people who, while prominent, obviously do not know the student well or at all. Such letters are usually given little weight.

On the one hand, letters can provide insights about a student that are available nowhere else. They can tell the college about academic performance, abilities, initiative, curiosity, character, motivation, and the like. But occasionally they are not nearly as useful as they could be. Why?

- Just as grades have shown inflation, so have letters of recommendation.
- Letter writers, even if assured that the letters of recommendation are confidential, may worry that if they say less than positive things they will later be liable to a lawsuit. Their worry may or may not be justified. Although the confidentiality of letters is protected under the Buckley Amendment, there are no absolute guarantees if the student signs an access waiver. I was once burned myself when I wrote a supposedly confidential letter and then found out that the student about whom I had written had nevertheless been informed of the content of my letter. I had no idea who had leaked the contents of the letter, but leaks happen, rare though they may be.
- Some letter writers don't know the students as well as would be desired, especially if the writers are responsible for very large numbers of students. Even if the letter writers know the students, they may not know about all of the attributes on which they are being asked to comment.
- Although multiple ratings can often be given to students, there sometimes tends to be a halo effect in which all or almost all of the ratings are roughly at the same level. Halo effects are common not only in letters of recommendation but in many other kinds of ratings people make.
- Some letter writers are very experienced and know how to write letters to get the result they intend. They are experts at coded messages. Other letter writers

do not understand the system and do not write letters that effectively communicate what they wish to say. For example, a teacher in a high school in which relatively few students go on to selective colleges will typically have less experience in writing persuasive letters than a teacher in a highly selective preparatory school where virtually all the students go on to competitive colleges.

* Admissions officers are inclined to give more weight to letters from schools and counselors they know and respect. Thus, students who come from schools that in the past have sent multiple students to the college to which the student is applying may have an edge.

The bottom line is that letters, like all other indicators, have strengths and weaknesses and must be considered in the context of all available evidence.

Tacit Factors

Other factors that affect admission are not specifically part of the admissions application. They may weigh in a decision, even heavily, but are tacit rather than explicit. These factors may include things such as the applicant's (a) sex, (b) ethnic group, (c) geographic origin, (c) religion, (d) athletic skills, (e) other specialized skills, such as music, drama, and art, and (f) connections to the university, such as parents or other relatives who are alumni, parents or other relatives who are large donors, or parents who work at the university.

Many colleges and universities say they seek diversity but do not elaborate beyond that statement, and with good reason. If they become too specific, they risk legal entanglement. Diversity is genuinely a good thing: you can learn things from someone whose upbringing was very different from yours that you could never learn from someone who grew up next door. But seeking diversity is rarely straightforward.

At a university that is, say, a major Division I competitor in varsity athletics, everyone knows that athletes receive different consideration than do non-athletes. Schools differ in just how much extra consideration they will give applicants who are athletes, but most weigh athletic and other skills.

Different people give different justifications for these special categories. Usually they are grouped together under "diversity," although sometimes preferences have impeded diversity, as in the case of facilitated acceptance for children of people who are well connected. As I write, there has just been a nationally covered scandal at a major state university regarding a special list that existed for children of well-connected parents. What amazed me was not the scandal but the number of people who acted as though they did not realize what was going on. The truth is, what happened at this state university happens every spring, in one form or another, at many other colleges and universities as well. Such patronage risks perverting the whole purpose of college and university admissions, namely, to admit the best candidates.

In the case of special talents, one might argue that particular applicants were accepted because of their special talents. For example, a given athlete might not be a top academic performer, but he or she is good at something that matters to the college or university. That something happens to be perceived as increasing alumni interest and participation in the school and probably financial donations as well. University athletics are big business. Wins enhance donations, sometimes greatly, and also enhance interest and hence ticket sales, which in turn enhance university revenues. Is it right to admit students because they enhance university revenues? It depends on whom you ask. Personally, I think such policies, at least when taken to extremes, lead universities down paths they will come to regret. In Europe, athletic prowess counts for nothing in college admissions. But in the United States, where there are teams and the college or university has a stake in their success, it would be difficult to remove athletic considerations from the admissions procedure. Moreover, athletics can develop leadership, and I have argued that a reason for college athletics to exist, beyond the commercial one, is that it provides one route toward the building of leadership skills among those who are involved.

Pragmatically, the temptation to succumb to various pressures is enormous. At one point, at one of the universities in which I worked, the child of a major potential donor was being considered for admission. The admissions office was aware of the enormous potential, and it made a proactive effort to find reasons to admit the child. In the end, he was rejected. The university might be willing to bend its standards a bit; it wasn't willing to break them. Other universities routinely break their standards, if they have any. But in the aforementioned case, the donor was furious and said he would never donate again, and he hasn't. So the decision to reject was potentially costly to the school. There was only one justification for the negative decision, really—it was the right thing to do.

But most cases are not black and white but rather gray. Perhaps the first oboist has just graduated and the orchestra desperately needs an oboist. Or perhaps the quarterback on the football team has graduated and needs to be replaced. Perhaps students came from forty-nine states the past year and here is a chance to be able to say that the university has students from all fifty states. Or perhaps a valued faculty member who is supremely rational in his physics work threatens to find another job unless his daughter is admitted. In admissions, reality constantly comes into rough contact with ideals, and the chosen solution is often somewhere in a gray zone that satisfies no principle but ultimately is made because it is viewed as pragmatic. Admissions is probably not a good place for idealists who cannot compromise, nor for pragmatists who lack ideals. One needs to use consummate and wise judgment operating in what is often a gray area.

We now have reviewed the various factors used to evaluate applications in a variety of universities. One factor stands out for its power—standardized testing. Standardized testing does not differ much from what it was like a century ago. Why?

Why Testing Has Changed So Little over the Years

How has the testing game come to take over not only schooling but even much of society? The route to the "takeover" has been a series of unfortunate collateral consequences of testing that has entrenched it ever more firmly in society's psyche.

Pseudo-quantitative Precision

Tests yield quantified, seemingly precise measures of students' abilities. Consumers have been taken with their apparent precision of measurement. The problem is that the actual validity of the tests comes nowhere near their appearance of validity. From the standpoint of an admissions officer, it is much easier to make a decision based on numbers than to make one based on seemingly subjective data, such as teachers' letters of recommendation or lists of extracurricular activities. Skilled admissions officers, therefore, take into account the subjective as well as the objective factors, recognizing the need for a holistic evaluation of each applicant. They resist the temptation to do their job the easy way—by the numbers.

Anyone is susceptible to overinterpreting numbers. Some years ago I was giving a talk to an audience of people who drilled for oil. They were interested in selecting people who would be skilled in predicting where oil was to be found. As I was talking about our work, someone in the audience raised his hand and made a curious point. He said that his company had the same problem with clients that we had with admissions. Clients would often prefer that the companies drill for oil in places where there were quantitative indices showing the likelihood of oil, even if the indices were known to be of poor validity. They would favor quantitative rather than superior qualitative information, simply because it was associated with numbers. And they got a lot of dry holes.

Similarity

People are attracted to others who are like themselves. We tend to be more attracted to others who are similar to us in how good-looking they are, in what their interests are, in their ethnic group, and so forth. The tests that have been so highly valued since the 1960s have yielded a new generation of power-holders who look for others like themselves—that is, others who have high test scores.

During the era in which most people going to elite colleges were from socially elite families, admissions officers were themselves mostly from elite families. So they looked for people with similar backgrounds. Today, to be admitted to elite colleges, it helps to have high college-admission test scores. As a result, some admissions officers have relatively high scores or work for faculties who do. So some of these admissions officers may look for applicants who, like themselves and their faculties, will continue the legacy they have created. Increasing diversity in admissions staff can increase diversity in matriculated students when the diverse staff members seek to mirror their own diversity in an entering class.

Similarity is an extremely conservative principle for making decisions, because it tends to perpetuate whatever already exists. But it is perhaps the most widely used principle. In the end, people are most comfortable associating with people like themselves. The result is that systems of social stratification are hard to change.

Stratification applies not just to socioeconomic class but also to gender. When I started at Yale as an undergraduate, it was an all-men's school.

The first year women were admitted, there was widespread outrage about it among many alumni. Within a short time, women were, on average, outperforming men in their academic work.

Which system for selecting college students is better—test scores or social class/wealth? It depends on whom you ask. People in positions of power tend to value whatever attributes got them into those positions. If you ask a Harvard professor who is making $200,000 a year and has published two hundred articles in her career, she might wax enthusiastic about the advantages of the standardized tests that helped her get to where she is. If you instead ask an entrepreneur who dropped out of school and is making $200,000,000 a year, that individual might laugh in your face, asking you who you think is smarter—the Harvard professor making $200,000 a year or she, making $200,000,000 a year? She might well think that money, or the abilities required to earn large amounts of money, is a better basis for making decisions than test scores.

Someone else might question both test scores and wealth as bases for decision making. Mother Teresa and Mahatma Gandhi led lives of relative poverty but made an enormous positive difference to the world. They or those who admire them might argue that much more important than test scores or family wealth is the set of positive ethical principles one brings to one's life, and one's willingness to act on them.

There is no one clear set of criteria for admissions—family wealth or status, test scores, ethics all might form bases for people's implicit theories of what one should look for. Historically, criteria have varied all over the place. One of the most important criteria in the past was gender.

When I became president of the American Psychological Association (APA), I would go to Board of Directors meetings and look at the pictures of all past presidents of the APA. It was pretty obvious that they were overwhelmingly men. Some might take this to indicate that men were more fit for such an esteemed position than women. But given that graduate schools for most of the history of the country did not admit women, what is surprising is not that there are so few pictures of women on the wall, but that there are any such pictures at all.

Of course, other groups have experienced even more extreme discrimination than women during the history of the United States. During World War II, Japanese people were interned in concentration camps. Going further back in time, we find slavery rampant throughout the north and south of the country. If you were born in 1800 as a slave and had an IQ of 160, it bought you little: you still died a slave. If you were born the first son of a plantation owner and had an IQ of 60, it mattered little: you still inherited the plantation. The law of primogeniture guaranteed that the inheritance passed to the eldest son. And no doubt, eldest sons felt the law to be remarkably fair in its recognition of their special role in the family and society.

Research by Claude Steele shows that socially defined race still matters in our assessments of ability, independent of those assessments. Steele and his colleague Joshua Aronson did a series of studies in which both white students and black students were asked to take a test with difficult verbal-ability items. Either the socially defined race of the participants was made salient to the students or it was not. When it was, there was a greater difference in performance between whites and blacks than when it was not (Steele and Aronson 1995).

It is possible to show how variables such as test scores, parental wealth, sex, socially defined race, and caste can affect future outcomes by imagining a thought experiment. Suppose that instead of using variables such as these to determine an applicant's place in the society in general, and in the college sweepstakes in particular, we used a different variable—height. What then?

This experiment is less absurd than it might seem. First of all, our society does use height to determine social outcomes. Taller people are, on average, more successful than shorter ones, particularly among males. CEOs, army generals, and other successful people are more likely to be taller than average than they are to be shorter than average. People probably respond better to authority in tall people. Second, height actually has some advantages that, say, tests of abilities do not have. Consider what these are.

First, we know what height is. It is how tall a person or a thing is. For example, I personally am about 5 feet 11 inches tall. You know what that means, right? But do you really know what an IQ of 125 means, or an SAT score of 580? And are they really different, or are IQs and SATs largely the same thing? Research suggests that they are indeed largely the same thing.

Some years ago, a colleague, Douglas Detterman, and I edited a book in which two dozen experts in the field of intelligence were asked to define what intelligence is (Sternberg and Detterman 1986). How many different definitions of intelligence did we get? You guessed it: two dozen. Even experts cannot agree as to what intelligence is. But there is virtually no disagreement regarding the nature of height.

Second, height is the same regardless of the instrument with which it is measured. You could measure me with any of several tape measures, yardsticks, rulers, or whatever, and within a tiny margin of error, I would be 5 feet 11. If you measured me with a metric tape measure, it would come out at about 1.80 meters, but that still converts perfectly to 5 feet 11 inches, with no loss of information. With ability tests, things are more complicated. You can give me half a dozen different ability tests, and I most likely will end up with half a dozen different ability scores, some of which may not be very close to each other at all.

Third, height has a reassuring consistency that is lacking in ability-test scores. I am 5 feet 11 inches today, and will be the same height until I shrink in my later years. Maybe I have already started to shrink: I'm pretty sure I was 5 feet 11 and a half inches when I was younger! In contrast, one can take an ability test one day, and the same ability test a day, a week, or a month later, and there is much less guarantee of consistency. On tests like the SAT, variations of over 100 points from one testing to another are, while not common, far from rare, and 50-point variations are quite common.

Fourth, some students cheat! They write their answers on their hands or inside their shirt sleeves, store the answers in the bathroom and then seek permission to go there, bring in hidden smartphones, or whatever. With height, all of these temptations to cheat are reduced. Sure, students can cheat by wearing platform or elevator shoes, but such devices are easy to detect merely by asking people to take off their shoes. Airports do it all the time; why shouldn't testing centers?

Fifth, you can't buy height. Conventional test scores are susceptible to modification if parents can afford to buy books, courses, or just a sound education for their children. With height, you've got what you've got unless you have the misfortune to be severely and chronically malnourished. In that case, college probably won't be in the cards in any case, at least in the United States.

So there you have any number of reasons why it makes sense to use height for college admissions. Suppose that we do in fact adopt the simple, easy-to-use height test. Now, to get into Harvard, you might have to be about 6 feet 11 inches. To get into Yale, perhaps you would need to be only 6 feet 10 inches, and one goes down all the way to Squeedunk, for which admission requires one to be only 3 feet 1 inch, and Podunk, which requires a height of a mere 3 feet even. What would the result be?

Almost without doubt, twenty-five years later, most of the CEOs, army generals, and other people of high position would be tall, and most of the flunkeys of the society would be short. And what would this prove? Obviously, that nature favors tall people, in much the same way that it favors rich people over poor ones, men over women, whites over blacks (or, in some societies, blacks over whites), people of one religion over people of another, higher castes over lower castes, and so forth. That is to say, it would prove nothing at all other than that people can devise their own methods of social stratification and then the means to enforce the self-fulfilling prophecies they have created.

So current university admissions tests, like high school GPA and class rank, tell us little about the qualities necessary for broad success in an ACCEL university. Once again, we are looking for things that matter, but only a little.

Accountability

In some universities (thankfully, not mine!), admissions officers are reluctant to admit students who do not have high test scores. If the students are unsuccessful, the admissions officers are afraid that they, and not the students, will be blamed. After all, the admissions officers made the decision to admit them despite their weak test scores.

Every year, some students in any given freshman class are identified as being at risk for flunking out. At some schools, deans may look back to their admissions records for clues as to what has gone wrong. Why are these students failing whereas others are not? Suppose those examining the admissions records discovered that the students who were flunking out were all admitted because one particular admissions officer had given them high ratings whereas no one else had. That admissions officer would justifiably fear for his or her job. So people in positions of decision-making authority, whether in a college, graduate school, law firm, or anyplace else, worry about the decisions they make, because these decisions have high stakes. What can they do to protect their reputations in case the people they recommend end up flunking out?

One thing they can do is use criteria in making their decision that will help insulate them from criticism. Test scores are such criteria. If students flunk out or fail to adjust, the admissions officers or other decision-making personnel can blame the tests for leading them astray. But if they ignore the test scores, they may feel that others will see them as having only themselves to blame.

Because test scores correlate positively with academic success, the chances of someone's flunking out are, on average, greater if that person has low test scores than if he or she has high ones. So people who make admissions or hiring decisions are taking a risk when they admit or hire people with lower test scores. Afraid of their own perceived future culpability, they may decide that the potential costs of taking a risk are greater than the potential benefits.

Publication Mania

It would be hard to overestimate the effects that published ratings have on the behavior not only of colleges but also of elementary and secondary schools. Many, probably most, elementary and secondary schools are shamelessly teaching to the standardized tests their students will have to take. Given the rather insane pressure the federal government is placing on schools to show high levels of performance of their students on largely trivial tests that measure nothing in particular, and often vary across states in what particular trivialities they measure, it is understandable that the schools will cave in. Principals risk losing their jobs and school boards control over their schools if their students underperform. Because the test results of various districts are publicized, they become excellent predictors of real-estate values, which are driven up in districts where test scores are higher. When I was looking for a house in the Boston area, I learned this from firsthand experience. Test scores in a given community were a terrific proxy for real-estate prices. If you knew the test scores, you pretty much knew the house prices, and vice versa.

Given the minimal level of critical thinking in much of the government, it is scarcely surprising that it would support tests that require similarly trivial levels of critical thinking in students. While the government is busy diverting elementary and secondary schools from their responsibility of educating students, *U.S. News & World Report* and other magazines that publish ratings of colleges and graduate schools are busy diverting these schools from the business of educating their students, instead encouraging the schools to set goals that raise ratings rather than educate students.

Test scores matter a lot for these ratings, and moreover, they are more manageable than other criteria that are used to evaluate the schools, such as alleged national reputation, whatever that is. So schools work hard to increase their mean test scores, thereby giving more authority and power to the publishers of the tests. It is a very good time to be a test publisher, because if you can get your product entrenched in the market-place, it is likely to produce a lot of money, regardless of what it happens to measure.

One could argue that tests are a means toward accountability, and all the magazines and newspapers are doing is making indices of account-ability public. This argument is a good one, assuming that the measures of accountability are good ones. And presumably, the measures are not ter-rible. They do not require, for example, knowledge of techniques of black magic or voodoo. But, as I argue later in the book, the tests we use tend to be incomplete, and they often measure trivial levels of knowledge that will be of little use in the workplace or even in life in general.

Colleges are eager to improve their *U.S. News & World Report* ratings as well as ratings by other media. Higher test scores improve ratings whereas lower test scores risk lowering ratings and, possibly, risk the jobs of those responsible for the lower ratings.

Superstition

Every once in a while, I am invited to give a talk in a highly desirable loca-tion, perhaps Arizona or New Mexico. The problem is that after I give my talk, I am sent home and rarely invited again. I keep thinking it would be nice to get another invitation so I can spend more time in one of the more desirable vacation spots.

Suppose I open up a service that guarantees rain. Given the increasing scarcity of water resources, such a service is likely to have a bright future. I promise municipalities, states—really, anyone who will invite me—that if they contract with me to make it rain, I guarantee I will make it rain or I will give them double their money back. So I finally wangle that return invitation to visit Arizona.

When I get to Arizona, instead of giving a talk on college admissions or leadership or something about which I actually have some knowledge, I do a rain dance. The question is whether, later in the day, it will rain. Given that I am in Arizona, that is hardly likely. So the town that has invited me asks for double its money back. I explain that there has been a grave misunderstanding: this is Arizona; they can scarcely expect the rain dance to work in just one day. In an arid environment like this one, it may take weeks or even months for the rain to finally come. So, every day, I do the rain dance in the morning and do tourism the rest of the day. Eventually, it rains. I congratulate the people of the town on their good judgment in inviting me to make it rain, and I pack my bags and leave.

This little story may sound silly, but it is exactly how superstitions work. If you do a rain dance long enough, eventually it will rain. And if it never does, you won't be alive to tell the story much longer. You may reply that you don't believe in rain dances. I don't either. But chances are you have some superstition that is equally powerful. For example, approach the first-floor elevator in an apartment complex or a busy office building and wait by the elevator. Sooner or later, someone in a hurry will come and push the elevator button, even though it is already lit up, indicating that someone has already summoned the elevator. Why would anyone push the button when it has already been pushed? One reason is that elevators provide what psychologists call a 100 percent reinforcement schedule. If you press the button, the elevator always comes. So even though pressing an already lit button has no discernible effect, people keep pressing because they are always rewarded for doing so.

I may sound as though I am making fun of the superstitions of others, but I have my own. I wear a medal around my neck that my parents gave me many years ago. They told me it would bring me good luck. Does it bring me good luck? I have no idea. But I keep wearing it because I feel that, in general, I have had a good life, and the cost of wearing it is so small. Probably taking it off would have no effect, but what if it did? And that is precisely how superstitions maintain themselves, including in the academic realm.

Once admissions personnel, faculty, administrators, and others come to believe that elevated test scores are a necessary condition for student success, they continue in their beliefs in the absence of evidence. When I was a faculty member at Yale, colleagues used to tell me that students with scores below 650 would not succeed in our graduate program. They pointed out that, in fact, all successful students had scores above that level. They were right: we refused to admit students with lower scores, so we never found out how they might perform. In colleges and universities, we have our own superstitions, and over time we come to believe them, often thinking they are rational rather than fanciful.

Some superstitions are benign. For example, no one is hurt by my wearing a medal around my neck. But other superstitions are anything but benign. As a result of our overuse of testing, many students never get a chance to show what they could do if only they were given the opportunity. So students who do not fit the particular mold that the tests create suffer as a result of our certainty that the test results mean much more than they do.

Self-Fulfilling Prophecies

Standardized tests create self-fulfilling prophecies (Rosenthal and Jacobson 1992; Weinstein 2002). I have experienced the effects of such superstitions personally. When I was young, I did poorly on IQ tests. I would like to believe that this was because of test anxiety, but who can say for sure? In the 1950s, when I was growing up, the elementary school I attended gave group IQ tests every couple of years. As a result of my low scores, my teachers thought I was stupid and I thought I was stupid too. They never came out and told us our IQ scores, but one could tell from the way teachers acted. In first grade, I was a mediocre student, which made my teachers happy because they got what they expected. I in turn was happy that they were happy, and in the end, everyone was quite happy. By second grade, I was slightly worse as a student, and in third grade, still worse. This is a fairly typical pattern. It is sometimes referred to as cumulative deficit. Once low expectations set in, one performs a bit worse each year than the year before. Eventually, one is labeled a perennial loser.

Was I really a perennial loser? Who is to say? But to the extent that there was a superstition that the low IQ scores ensured my poor academic performance, the superstition created a self-fulfilling prophecy, of which I was the victim. So academic superstitions are not victimless. They affect those about whom the superstitions are held. They also affect schools and society, because they result in more poorly performing students, as well as talent lost to society.

I was lucky. In fourth grade, I had a teacher, Mrs. Alexa, who saw beyond the tests, in a way that some college admissions officers do as well. She had high expectations for me. And she conveyed her high expectations to me. Just as I wanted to please my teachers in Grades 1–3, I wanted to please her. I was extremely taken with her, and remember regretting only that she was so much older than I—and married. So in fourth grade, I became an A student. My entire future trajectory changed, as a result of just one teacher. And from then on, I was a very fine student. But many times, I have asked myself: What would I have done if I had not had her as a teacher? Where would I be today? And when I was in working college admissions, I wondered how many of the students applying might have had far stronger records, if only they had had, as I did, a teacher who believed in them.

If this were just a story about me, one might write it off as a unique incident. But it is far from a unique incident. I see it all the time. Consider the story of a child named Adam (a pseudonym).

When Adam was in elementary school, he changed from one school to another. Because the school officials needed to place him in a reading group, they gave him a reading test his first day in his new school, in much the same way many colleges give language or math or other placement tests just as students arrive. At the risk of stressing the obvious, the initial few days when students arrive in a new school or on a new campus are not ideal days for giving tests. The students tend to be overwhelmed by the newness and challenges of the unfamiliar environment, and their minds are elsewhere than on the tests they are about to be given.

In Adam's case, he predictably bombed the reading test. His school could either have gone with his placement in his former school, which was essentially identical in quality to his new school, and placed him in the top reading group. Or they could have gone with the superstition that a test tells all and put him in the bottom group. They put him in the bottom group, ignoring his former placement. He was being set up to fail.

After a few weeks, his teacher noticed that he was reading at a level better than that of his classmates, so the teacher recommended that Adam be placed in a higher reading group. The school, locked into the superstition that tests tell all, decided to ignore the recommendation. Instead, they re-tested him. His reading test score now came out at the level of the middle group, so they put him in the middle group. Soon the teacher noticed that his performance excelled that of the students in the middle reading group, so the school once again gave him the reading test. This time he scored at the level of the top group. Given the school's ardent belief in the superstition that the test tells all, one would expect them then to have placed Adam in the top reading group. They didn't. They left him in the middle reading group.

Adam's mother and father made an appointment with high-level per-sonnel in the school to discuss why he was being retained in the middle reading group. The teacher was there, and the principal, and the read-ing specialist, and a school psychologist. It was a heavyweight conference indeed. The school officials explained to the parents that although Adam had scored at the level of the top group, he was now a full book behind the students in the top group. If they were to move him to the top group, he would lack the skills that the other students had. The parents were incredulous. They told the school officials that he was behind because the school had initially placed him in the bottom group.

The parents offered to help Adam with his reading. If he brought the book home, they would work with him to help him catch up in his read-ing skills. The parents felt that they were in a position to help because they both had relevant skills to helping him improve. Both were PhDs and worked in the field of education. The school explained that their policy was not to allow reading books to go home, and that therefore they could not help. So they were determined to ensure that the self-fulfilling proph-ecy they created would come true.

One would like to believe that colleges and universities are above such superstitions, but they are not. Rather, superstitions are firmly entrenched in our entire educational system, from elementary school onward. Colleges and universities use SATs and related tests in much the same way elemen-tary and secondary schools use standardized achievement tests. Sometimes the logic is laughable.

At one point, when I was working for the Psychological Corporation, a case was brought to our attention as a result of a complaint. A student was applying to a graduate program that, at the time, required a score of 25 on the Miller Analogies Test. This in itself was strange, because the test had 100 items, each with four multiple-choice options, so 25 was the score one could expect to receive if one answered the questions at random. A student applied with a score that was below 25: she was unlucky in her responses. The school admitted her anyway because she had other credentials that were excellent. She went through the program and was about to graduate with honors, when she was handed an unwelcome surprise: she was told that, in order to graduate, she would have to retake the Miller Analogies Test and receive a score of at least 25 so she could meet the admissions requirement. Here the predictor—the test—was being given more weight than the criterion it was supposed to predict—university-level academic performance. Her complaint was that she should not have to retake the test. The complaint later became moot when she took the test and received a score of 26. She graduated with her honors. Such a practice is probably quite atypical, but I have heard similar stories more than once.

Academic superstitions do not have to be about test scores. When Eve (a pseudonym) finished kindergarten, her Montessori School teacher wanted to hold her back because the teacher was convinced that Eve had not yet developed the social skills she would need to succeed in first grade. Eve's parents persuaded the teacher that they really believed she could succeed in first grade. The teacher kindly promoted Eve, who went on to go to study at a top-tier Ivy League college.

Some readers might wonder what all the fuss is about. After all, test scores do, on average, predict academic achievement, so why shouldn't schools use the tests as predictors of academic achievement? I have no objection at all to tests used in this way. Indeed, testing can be useful in diagnosing students' strengths and weaknesses and in helping the students to capitalize on their strengths and to improve on their areas of weakness.

The problem is that tests are often not used in this way. Some schools have cutoffs. These cutoffs may be explicit, in which case they are publicized; or they may be implicit, in which case admissions officers know they exist but do not talk about them. For example, in some business schools, if one's GMAT score is below 600, one's chances of getting in are reduced to practically zero. Many undergraduate as well as graduate schools use formulas for determining admissions. The assumption is that such formulas will accurately predict, at some level, who will succeed and who will fail. And it is further assumed that using such formulas somehow makes the process "fair." Given the correlation of test scores with family income, it would be about as fair to plug family income into the equation instead of test scores. This may sound ridiculous, but in fact, many schools implicitly do so. Those schools that are not "need-blind"—that is, which admit students in part based on financial-aid considerations—take into account family income in making their decisions, whether formulaically or otherwise.

Unfortunately, the large majority of schools are not need-blind, so they do, in fact, take into account family income in their admissions decisions. For the most part, they would like to be need-blind: they just do not have the economic resources to reach their goal.

Jesse Rothstein, an economist at Princeton University, has suggested that test scores essentially "launder" students' socioeconomic background (Rothstein 2004; see also Hoover 2004). Much of the effect of SAT is derived from the quality of the high school that a student attends, which in turn is a function of socioeconomic class. So test scores essentially disguise the effect of one's family background and its resultant education on a student's record. At the same time, admissions officers try to take these factors into account, although neither they nor anyone else can ascertain the full extent to which socioeconomic class affects scores.

When I have talked to admissions officers and other administrators, including presidents, I have been surprised by a tacit admission about their use of standardized tests. The overwhelming majority of universities and colleges in this country are largely tuition-dependent. The SAT, as Rothstein pointed out, provides a slightly roundabout way of identifying those students who are most likely to be able to pay full tuition, or something close to it. Thus, rather than select students directly for parental wealth, institutions are enabled by the SAT to select students indirectly for parental wealth and call it merit. This is not to say that the SAT benefits only the well heeled. But the correlation of SAT with socioeconomic status is high enough that the test can become a tool for helping to sustain the financial viability of the college or university using it.

Closed Systems

Our present admissions system is not working as well as it should because of what one might call "closed systems." Standardized "aptitude" tests can create a closed society. They predict achievement because, to a large extent, they are achievement tests. The SAT Reasoning Test and the SAT Subject Tests are, in many cases, so similar that one cannot distinguish the items of the one from the items of the other. Indeed, Alfred Binet's intelligence tests (Binet and Simon 1916), created at the beginning of the twentieth century, were designed to predict school achievement, so they were created essentially as achievement tests for skills that students should have acquired a few years before. Thus, tests create a closed system: ability test scores predict achievement test scores because ability tests are achievement tests and vice versa. And users are happy with the allegedly high "validity" of the tests, essentially for predicting scores on other tests like themselves but labeled something else.

At different points in time, societies, including our own, have found different bases for social stratification. In earlier times, socioeconomic class was the primary criterion used to stratify students, for college admissions and earlier. Then test scores came to be used, and they seemed to be more "merit-based," except that they produced largely the same results as the socioeconomic class indicators. The results were just different enough to give the appearance of measures that are wholly different. At various times, admissions officers have used gender, socially defined race, and caste as bases for admissions. They have then found, to their satisfaction, that the criteria they used predicted future outcomes. This was not a kind of thinking particular to admissions officers. They were reflecting the societal context in which they lived. Not so long ago, very few white Americans would have even considered the possibility of an African American becoming president of the United States. In most countries around the world, the possibility of electing a member of a minority group to a position of national leadership still does not exist.

Imagine that we, as a society, were still using medical tests that were largely the same as those that were used at the beginning of the twentieth century. Would you be concerned? If you have ever had anything beyond a common cold, you would have reason to be, assuming you survived whatever illness caused you to need the tests in the first place. We, as a society, are using tests of abilities and achievements that are roughly the same as the scales Binet and Simon introduced about a century ago. Our achievement tests have not developed much either. There certainly are cosmetic, surface-structural differences, but the deep structure remains unchanged.

The Vicious Effects of Closed Systems

A narrow conception of intelligence seems to be prevalent in today's society because of what is referred to as a closed system. A closed system is self-contained, internally consistent, and difficult to escape. Once it is in place, it becomes self-perpetuating and difficult to change.

The vicious circle perpetuated by such a system gave rise to *The Bell Curve*, by Richard Herrnstein and Charles Murray (1994), a book that looks at the history of intelligence and class structure in the United States. (For alternative views, see Fraser 1995). According to Herrnstein and Murray's analysis, conventional tests of intelligence, on average, account for about 10 percent of the variation in various kinds of real-world outcomes. Although this percentage is not trivial, it is not particularly large either, and one might wonder what all the fuss is about in the use of the tests. Of course, one might argue that Herrnstein and Murray have underestimated the percentage, but given their enthusiastic support for conventional tests, it seems unlikely that they would underestimate the value of the tests.

In fact, they may overestimate the value of the tests for predictive purposes. Clearly the tests have some value. But how much? In their book, Herrnstein and Murray refer to an "invisible hand of nature" that guides events so that people with high IQs tend to rise toward the top socioeconomic stratum of a society and people with low IQs tend to fall toward the bottom stratum. They present data to support their argument, and indeed it seems likely that although many aspects of their data may be arguable, in US society their argument holds true. For example, on average, lawyers and doctors probably have higher IQs than do street cleaners.

The problem is that although the data are probably correct, the theory behind the data is probably not. US society is not as it is because of an invisible hand of nature but rather because a closed system has been created. The United States and some other societies have created cultures in which test scores matter profoundly. Elevated test scores are needed for placement in higher tracks in elementary and secondary schools. They are needed for admission to selective undergraduate programs. They are needed again for admission to selective graduate and professional programs. It is quite difficult to imagine how a person could gain access to many of the highest-paying and most prestigious jobs if he or she did not test well. Low scores exclude students from many selective colleges, and low Graduate Record Examination (GRE) scores tend to exclude students from selective graduate schools. Of course, test scores are not the only criterion used for admission to graduate and professional schools. But they count enough that if a person bombs one of the admissions tests, he or she can say good-bye to admission to many selective schools.

This system is in many ways tragic. Students spend years in primary and secondary school working hard (or not so hard!) to achieve their goals, and then do the same in college. Sometime during their career, they take a test that lasts three to four hours. Then that test score ends up counting roughly the same as the products of years of effort and dedication. If it were equally valid in predicting success, perhaps this system would make sense. But it's not.

The 10 percent figure cited by Herrnstein and Murray implies that IQ-like abilities matter some, but not much, for life success. Other abilities may be more important. Many able people are disenfranchised because although their abilities might be important for job performance, they are not important for test performance. For example, the creative and practical skills that matter to success on the job typically are not measured on tests used to get into school. Society may be overvaluing a fairly narrow range of skills, even if that range of skills may not serve individuals particularly well on the job.

In a reductio ad absurdum of the whole IQ testing mentality, the New London, Connecticut, police force rejected an applicant, Robert Jordan, for having too high an IQ. His score, 125, was well above average but far from stellar. The police force argued that someone with too high an IQ might get bored quickly and then decide to leave the police force, thereby wasting the city's money spent in training the officer. Some might find it disconcerting that a police force would value mediocrity, but apparently this one did. The potential policeman sued and lost.

It is scarcely surprising that ability tests predict school grades, because the tests were originally designed explicitly for this purpose. This makes more obvious how the United States and some other societies have created closed systems. Certain abilities are valued in instruction, such as memory and analytical abilities. Ability tests are then created that measure these abilities and, thus, predict school performance. Then assessments of achievement are designed that also assess these abilities. Thus, it's little wonder that ability tests are more predictive in school than in the workplace. Within the closed system of the school, a narrow range of abilities leads to success on ability tests, in instruction, and on achievement tests. But these same abilities are less important later in life in the workplace.

Opportunity Loss

In general, closed systems seal off individual options and distort society, depriving many individuals of opportunities they should have. Society is also deprived of their talents. Using conventional intelligence-based measures is probably better than using height or many other such measures, but society can likely do better by expanding the abilities for which it tests.

In many respects, it is odd that the tests we use are so narrow. An early intelligence theorist, Charles Spearman, operating in the first decades of the twentieth century, believed that almost all there is to intelligence is what he called general intelligence (Spearman 1927). Belief in this general factor remains entrenched among many psychologists, even today. Many contemporary theorists, however, believe that there is more to intelligence than just one general ability. For example, Howard Gardner (2011) has proposed eight "multiple intelligences"—linguistic (again, understanding what you read), logical-mathematical (balancing your checkbook), spatial (using a map to find your way around a new city), musical (keeping tune in singing a song), naturalist (observing and understanding patterns in the natural world), interpersonal (understanding other people), and intrapersonal (understanding yourself). A theory such as Gardner's suggests that the tests we use for college admissions are narrow, as they are based primarily on linguistic and logical-mathematical skills.

Attributes that have nothing to do with intelligence (at least, according to the present definition and most others) can end up becoming conflated with intelligence. For example, I observed classes in a number of one-room elementary schools in Jamaica. In a typical school, there was no barrier separating the many classes in the single room, so the noise level was constantly high. I found myself asking what Alfred Binet might have put on his intelligence test if he had formulated it for these schools. I concluded that he might have decided to include a battery of tests on hearing. A predecessor to Binet, Francis Galton, actually did include tests of hearing acuity on his intelligence tests (see Galton 1883). This skill seemed most important for hearing the instruction and the test items, both of which typically were delivered verbally. In this situation, the students who heard better fared better, and those who did not hear well fared worse, especially if they had the bad fortune not to be sitting in the front center of the classroom.

The importance of hearing as related to intelligence is not just hypothetical. When I mentioned my observation in a colloquium, an individual from Guyana commented that she had grown up in similar schools and had always wondered why the smartest students sat in the front of the class. In this case, sitting in the front of the class may well have made students appear smart. The teacher probably did not think that good auditory (sensory hearing) abilities were a component of intelligence, but he or she might have easily conflated the effects of such abilities with intelligence. Similarly, students with poor vision who do not have the benefit of corrective lenses may also appear to not be very bright.

The experience in Jamaica also points out one other important fact, namely, that the (false) assumption in much research on intelligence is that all students have an equal chance to succeed on ability tests and in school. In fact, they do not. For example, in a study done in Jamaica in 1997, my colleagues and I studied the effects of intestinal parasitic infections (most often, whipworm) on students' cognitive functioning (Sternberg et al. 1997). Students with moderate to high levels of intestinal parasites tended to perform more poorly in school, and the researchers were interested in why this was the case. The study revealed that infected students tended to do more poorly on tests of higher-order cognitive abilities, even after controlling for possible confounding variables such as socioeconomic class. The data also revealed that although antiparasitic medication improved physical health, it had no effect on cognitive ability test scores. Presumably, the deficits that were occurring had built up over many years and were not alleviated by a quick-fix pill. Students who are parasitically infected find it hard to concentrate on their schoolwork because they do not feel well. The data showed that the cumulative effect of missing much of what happens in school probably cannot be reversed quickly. Students in all societies with problems of health, poor nutrition, or questionable safety do not have equal chances to succeed.

The general conclusion is that societies can and do choose a variety of criteria to sort people. Some societies use caste systems, whether explicit, as in India, or implicit, as in the United States. Others use or have used race, religion, or wealth of parents as a basis for sorting. Many societies combine criteria. After a system is in place, those who gain access to the power structure, whether via their passage through elite education or otherwise, are likely to look for others similar to themselves to place in positions of power. The reason, quite simply, is that there probably is no more powerful basis of interpersonal attraction than similarity, so that people in a power structure look for others like themselves. The result is a potentially endlessly looping closed system.

Why have we reached a point of stultification in our closed system? First, the cart somehow came to be placed before the horse: commercial interests came into play before the science of assessment had much opportunity to develop. Second, a small number of commercial enterprises monopolize the testing business, and many of the researchers in the field (including myself) either have worked for or have been supported financially or otherwise by these organizations. Such organizations, like any others, continue doing what works for and is profitable for them. Third, we have been and continue to be entranced by the notion of accountability, while largely ignoring just how narrow our cognitive and educational measures of accountability are. Fourth, the tests seem roughly consistent with the notion of a general ability that pervades many psychological performances. And finally, in some measures, the tests work: they predict various kinds of success at some modest to moderate level, so the question is not whether they work but rather whether we can do better.

Testing companies such as ETS and ACT are moving ahead with several projects to measure some of these other skills, such as the ETS Personal Potential Index, which seeks to measure skills beyond what the Graduate Record Examination measures. One would hope that more and more assessments would move in this direction, and that they would become a more important part of admissions processes, for undergraduate as well as graduate admissions. But that hope has been around a long time, waiting for fulfillment. It is the only hope I currently see on the horizon for admissions criteria that truly zero in on the skills underlying active concerned citizenship and ethical leadership.

Modernizing Standardized Testing

How might assessments better reflect the kinds of skills that matter not just in school but also in life beyond school? During my years as dean of arts and sciences at Tufts and as provost at Oklahoma State, we introduced a model for admissions based on WICS, discussed earlier, which is an acronym for wisdom-intelligence-creativity synthesized (Sternberg 2003b).

In our society, a problem with teaching and assessing more broadly is that the kinds of standardized assessments used in US college admissions are useful but also quite narrow. For example, the SAT Reasoning and Subject tests assess primarily a remembered knowledge base and analytical skills applied to this knowledge. Creativity, practical thinking, and wisdom are assessed minimally or, more likely, not at all. Is there any hope that our society can bring a broader model to high-stakes assessments?

My collaborators at Yale and then at Tufts and I decided to find out. In one study, the Rainbow Project, funded by the College Board, we designed tests of creative and practical thinking that could be used to supplement tests such as the SAT Reasoning Test, which measures analytical skills in the verbal and mathematical domains (Sternberg and the Rainbow Project Collaborators 2006). The collaboration was practically unique in bringing together a large, national team of investigators with diverse points of view, including both supporters and detractors of conventional standardized college admissions tests. We tested 1,013 high school students and college freshmen from fifteen different high schools and colleges. We gave them analytical questions much like those that are traditionally found on standardized tests. But we also asked them to answer creative and practical questions.

The creative tests required the students to stretch their imaginations. For example, they might be asked to write a creative story with a title such as "The Octopus's Sneakers" or "3821." Or they might be shown a collage of pictures, such as of musicians or athletes, and be asked to orally tell a story based on the collage. Or they might be asked to caption an untitled cartoon. The practical tests required the students to solve everyday problems. Some of them were presented in verbal form, others through movies. For example, students might see a student entering a party where he does not know anyone and everyone is already engaged in conversations. The task would be to decide what the student should do. Or they might see a movie showing a male and female student on a couch, apparently about to engage in romantic behavior, being interrupted by a knock on the door by a student who shouts out that he needs help. The task would be to decide what the couple should do.

The results suggested that universities need not limit themselves to narrow assessments of critical reasoning skills. There were three critical findings of the study.

First, we discovered three factors underlying our tests. One was creative thinking, as predicted; a second factor we predicted was practical thinking. But the third factor, which we did not predict, was multiple-choice problem solving. In other words, multiple-choice tests, no matter what they were supposed to measure, clustered together: students who were better at one multiple-choice test tended to be better at others as well. This result suggested that merely using multiple choice consistently tends to benefit some students and not others.

Second, we discovered that using broader tests for college admissions can enhance academic excellence. We doubled prediction of freshman-year grades over SAT alone. Compared with SAT and high school GPA, we still increased prediction by about 50 percent. In other words, our assessments were not quixotic ventures into esoteric realms. On the contrary, they enhanced our ability to predict who would be more versus less successful in college, at least from an academic point of view.

Third, we discovered that we could substantially reduce ethnic-group differences on the tests. In other words, using such tests potentially would increase the proportion of ethnic minorities admitted to selective colleges. In doing so, the tests not only would not compromise academic excellence but would actually enhance it. The reason was that different ethnic and other groups have different conceptions of what intelligence is, and so socialize their children to be intelligent in different ways. For example, on our tests, American Indians, on average, performed lower than most other groups on analytical assessments. But on oral storytelling, they had the highest average scores. Different groups excel, on average, in different ways, and giving them a chance to show how they excel gives them the opportunity to show that they can succeed.

Tests such as the Rainbow Assessment do not benefit only members of ethnic minority groups. There are many students who come from the majority group, and even from well-off homes, who learn in ways that are different from those assessed by conventional standardized tests. These children may well have the abilities they need to succeed in life and even in school, but these abilities may not be reflected in scores on conventional tests. Our tests help identify such students.

It is one thing to have a successful research project, and another to actually implement the procedures in a high-stakes situation. We have had the opportunity to do so.

In 2005, I moved from Yale University, where I was the lead collaborator in the Rainbow Project, to Tufts University, where I became dean of the School of Arts and Sciences. Tufts University has strongly emphasized the role of active citizenship in education, so it seemed like an ideal setting to put into practice some of the ideas from the Rainbow Project. In collaboration with Dean of the School of Engineering Linda Abriola and Dean of Admissions Lee Coffin, we instituted Project Kaleidoscope, which represents an implementation of the ideas of Rainbow but goes beyond that project to include in its assessment the construct of wisdom (see Sternberg 2010a). The Kaleidoscope program still is being used at Tufts as of 2015.

For all of the more than fifteen thousand students applying to Arts, Sciences, and Engineering at Tufts for the 2006–2007 school year, we placed questions designed to assess WICS on the application. The questions were optional. Whereas the Rainbow Project was done as a separate high-stakes test administered with a proctor, the Kaleidoscope Project was done as a section of the Tufts-specific part of the college application. It was just not practical to administer a separate high-stakes test for admission to one university. Moreover, the advantage of Kaleidoscope is that it got us away from the high-stakes testing situation in which students must answer complex questions in very short amounts of time under incredible pressure. The section was optional this past year, and students were encouraged to answer just a single question. For example, a creative question asked students to write stories with titles such as "The End of MTV" or "Confessions of a Middle-School Bully." Another creative question asked students what the world would be like if some historical event had come out differently—for example, if Rosa Parks had given up her seat on the bus. Yet another creative question, a nonverbal one, gave students an opportunity to design a new product or an advertisement for a new product. A practical question queried how students had persuaded a friend of the merits of an unpopular idea they held. A wisdom question asked students how a passion they had could be applied toward a common good.

What were the results? Some stakeholders were afraid that the numbers of applications would go down; instead, they went up. What was more notable was that the quality of applicants rose substantially. There were far fewer students in what before had been the bottom third of the pool in terms of quality. Many of those students, seeing the new application, decided not to bother to apply. Many stronger applicants applied. Other stakeholders were concerned that average SATs would go down and perhaps even plummet. Instead, they went up. The reason is that the new assessments are not negatively correlated with SATs. Rather, they just are not much correlated at all, one way or another. So adopting these new methods does not result in the admission of less qualified applicants. Rather, the applicants who are admitted are more qualified, but in a broader way. Perhaps most rewarding were the positive comments from large numbers of applicants that they felt our application gave them a chance to show themselves for who they are.

After a number of years in which applications by underrepresented minorities were relatively flat in terms of numbers, in that year they went up substantially. In the end, we admitted roughly 30 percent more African American students than the year before, and 15 percent more Hispanic Americans. So our results, like those of the Rainbow Project, showed that it is possible to increase academic quality and diversity simultaneously, and to do so for an entire undergraduate class at a major university, not just for small samples of students at some scattered colleges. Most importantly, we sent a message to students, parents, high school guidance counselors, and others that we believe that there is a more to a person than the narrow spectrum of skills assessed by standardized tests, and that these broader skills can be assessed in a quantifiable way.

Such projects can be done at the graduate level as well. We designed an admissions test for a large, highly rated business school in the Midwest. We showed that we could increase prediction and decrease both sex and ethnic-group differences in admissions.

One might wonder how one assesses answers to questions that seem so subjective. The assessment is done through well-developed rubrics. For example, we assess analytical responses on the basis of the extent to which they are (a) analytically sound, (b) balanced, (c) logical, and (d) organized. We assess creative responses on the basis of how (a) original and (b) compelling they are, as well as on the basis of their (c) appropriateness to the task with which the students were presented. We assess practical responses on the basis of how feasible they are with respect to (a) time, (b) place, and (c) human and (d) material resources. We assess wisdom-based responses on the extent to which they (a) promote a common good by (b) balancing one's own with others' with larger interests, (c) over the long and short terms, through (d) the infusion of positive (prosocial) values.

In a related project, funded by the Educational Testing Service and the College Board, we asked whether the same principles could be applied to high-stakes achievement testing used for college admissions and placement (Stemler et al. 2006). We modified Advanced Placement tests in Psychology and Statistics to additionally assess analytical, creative, and practical skills. Here is an example in psychology:

A variety of explanations have been proposed to account for why people sleep.

1. Describe the Restorative Theory of sleep (memory).
2. An alternative theory is an evolutionary theory of sleep, sometimes referred to as the "Preservation and Protection" theory. Describe this theory and compare and contrast it with the Restorative Theory. State what you see as the two strong points and two weak points of this theory compared to the Restorative Theory (analytical).
3. How might you design an experiment to test the Restorative Theory of sleep? Briefly describe the experiment, including the participants, materials, procedures, and design (creative).
4. A friend informs you that she is having trouble sleeping. Based on your knowledge of sleep, what kinds of helpful (and health-promoting) suggestions might you give her to help her fall asleep at night (practical)?

We found that by asking such questions, as in the other studies, we were able to both increase the range of skills we tested and substantially reduce ethnic-group differences in test scores.

The ways in which we assess student knowledge and skills have not changed much from what they were a century ago. Perhaps such assessments met the cognitive demands placed on students one hundred years ago. They do not meet the cognitive demands of the world today. Active and engaged citizens must be able (a) to be flexible in creative ways, responding to rapid changes in the environment; (b) to think critically about what they are told in the media, whether by newscasters, politicians, advertisers, scientists, or anyone else; (c) to execute their ideas and persuade others of their value; and most of all (d) to display the wisdom to use their knowledge in ways that avoid the horrors of bad leadership, as we have seen in Enron, Arthur Anderson, Tyco, and innumerable other organizations. It is time to have assessments that reflect the demands of the current century. We have suggested how we might create and evaluate such assessments.

The assessments described here do not measure all of the skills required for success in everyday life. For example, although I assess teamwork in courses I teach, the assessments I have described do not measure this skill, at least not directly. Moreover, the assessments have not been scaled up to be used on a statewide or national basis. Doing so would no doubt present new challenges, some of which have yet to be anticipated. Moreover, expanded assessments cost more time and money. But when we consider the benefits of opening up possibilities and hope to diverse students—of whatever gender or ethnic background—who learn and think in a variety of different ways, the costs may actually be relatively small. Our society needs citizens and leaders who are creative, practical, and especially wise, not just those who are memorizers and who are analytically adept. One way to find and develop such citizens and leaders is to emphasize in college admissions the importance of the broad range of skills that leads to active concerned citizenship and ethical leadership. But after we admit future active concerned citizens and ethical leaders, the question then is whether they matriculate. And they can matriculate only if they have sufficient financial aid, a topic that is considered in the next chapter.

6

FINANCIAL AID AND COLLEGE COSTS

Financial aid and college costs are inextricably intertwined, because the level of financial aid needed depends on college costs. So let's consider each in turn.

Financial Aid

There are few aspects of higher education that are quite as broken as the system for awarding financial aid. Financial aid, generally, is of two types: need-based and merit-based. Neither system works terribly well. Financial aid, handled effectively, can be a ball of gold. Handled poorly, it becomes a ball of clay. In some cases, for example, it is given to students who neither have financial need nor show any serious merit. In these cases, one can feel the clay weighing heavily in the university's pockets.

Need-Based Aid

The greatest problem with need-based aid is that there just isn't enough money to go around to all who need it. As I write this book, as mentioned earlier, the total cost of a private four-year education can easily be in excess of $70,000 per year, way out of reach for most families in this country. That figure will have been exceeded by the time this book is published. (If you have the good fortune to have twins, or even triplets as we do, good luck!) So most students will need financial aid. This is where the problem starts.

Existing formulas tend to make generous estimates of what parents can afford to pay, or are willing to pay, for a student's education. Because the estimates are so high, the students who can afford expensive universities are those whose families (a) are very well off, (b) are so poor that their costs for college are almost all paid by the institution, (c) wisely saved up for college from very early in the students' lives, (d) are willing or able to mortgage their future, such as through large loans, or (e) are willing or able to fake their financial-aid forms to get more aid than their financial situation merits.

The problem is that the large majority of students fall into none of these categories. Their parents are middle class or, as our society becomes economically more polarized, lower middle class; and they just don't have the assets to pay what the colleges say they should be willing to pay. The upshot is that one's ability to go to college will depend in large part on whether parents have emphasized the importance of educational savings throughout their children's lives, thereby perpetuating a socioeconomic class structure that favors students who come from families that value education. A student who might do as well as or better than another, but whose parents needed to or preferred to spend money on things other than education, is out of luck.

Most European countries deal with this problem by making university education free or almost free. I am an honorary professor at a German university, Heidelberg, and when the university started charging fees for the first time, the uproar was so loud that the fee structure was dismantled—and here we are talking in the order of $1,000 to $1,500 per year, all told. The European system has the advantage of enabling students to attend excellent universities, despite their parents' particular attitude toward saving for education. The disadvantage is that European universities cannot all afford many of the luxuries today's students in the United States demand or even take for granted: well-funded university-sponsored athletic teams, gleaming (or, in many cases, any) dormitories, spiffy science labs, arts complexes, splashy student centers, and the like. Moreover, some of the European and other foreign universities pay so poorly that professors end up taking second and even third jobs, leaving them little time to devote to their students or their research.

Thus, there is no simple solution to the problem. The current system contributes to the economic polarization of the country by favoring the haves and disfavoring many of the have-nots, unless those have-nots have so few resources that they get a full or close to full ride. Those students then face the major adjustment, in some cases, of attending college in campuses with much more privileged classmates who have received stronger high school training and for whom a night on the town is no large burden.

The general question is why students' ability to go to college should depend so much on their parents' attitude toward saving and expending money. Those whose parents were unwilling or unable to save sufficiently have the option of loans—which generally are available—but the students then end up mortgaging much of their future to repay the loans, sometimes well into middle age. A fair number never pay off their loans, wreck their credit ratings, and find their lives not much easier than they would have been had they paid off the loans in the first place. A system that burdens graduates with insufferable amounts of debt is simply dysfunctional, as many of our politicians recognize. Recognition, unfortunately, is not tantamount to solution.

To the extent that there is a solution to this problem, I believe it is in state and federal government aid. A number of states have systems of aid, but the systems still do not meet the financial needs of the students who attend college. To meet the needs of all students, taxation would need to be higher—as it is in most of Europe—but that in turn proves not to be a politically palatable solution. At the same time, in an age in which knowledge and the skills associated with higher education are so closely tied to a country's productivity in a global marketplace, I believe the answer is obvious: we either pay to stay, as a country, at or near the top or we see our position begin to crumble, as is now happening.

Merit-Based Aid

Merit-based aid serves a purpose very different from need-based aid. Merit-based aid is basically a means to attract to a given university whatever students the university most wants to attract. Merit-based aid is fraught with problems.

A first problem is that the funds that are going to merit-based aid are generally being taken away from need-based aid, resulting in less money for those with the most financial need. In some cases, named (endowed) scholarships are based only on particular merit-based characteristics, but for the most part, money is fungible so that it goes either to need-based or to merit-based aid.

A second problem is that definitions of merit are extremely slippery. Merit could include excellence in athletics—nice but unrelated to any academic mission of the institution. Today athletics has become a major source of revenue for some universities—especially those that field Division I teams—so there is great pressure on administrators to attract great athletes, to whom money is given that thereby is not given to students who may excel in areas more central to the purpose of a university.

Merit may also be a euphemism for achieving diversity goals. Diversity, as discussed earlier, is extremely valuable to an institution, but it is questionable to say that merely being from a particular ethnic or socially defined racial group creates "merit" in one that is worthy of financial aid. Moreover, some groups, such as Asian Americans, are not viewed by federal definitions as "underrepresented" minorities, so the funds available for "merit"-based aid tied to demographics often do not go their way.

Merit further may be a way of supporting students who are legacy admits—their parents or other relatives attended the university, so they are given preference in admissions and sometimes in financial aid. Legacy admissions are one of the best ways to support perpetuation of the existing class structure—those whose parents had a lot, get more, and those whose parents had little, get less.

Finally, even when merit is defined in academic terms, it often ends up being characterized only in terms of standardized test scores and high school grades, which, as we have seen above, represent a truly narrow slice of what it means to be meritorious. Should we really decide on merit as a result of a three-to-four-hour standardized test that generally correlates very highly with parents' socioeconomic status?

So merit-based financial aid, designed to help create more mobility in society, often actually serves to create less. I believe that if merit is to be used, it should be defined broadly so that students who excel in various ways related to the mission of the university—academically, but also athletically, musically, artistically, scientifically, journalistically, or otherwise—get a shot at it, not just students who happen to test well, get good grades, be star athletes, or be members of particular ethnic groups.

In sum, there probably is room for both need-based and merit-based aid in an ACCEL university. But I believe that the emphasis should be on need-based aid in order to bring into future positions of leadership those who otherwise would never have the resources to attain them. If merit aid is to be used, merit should be defined in terms of the mission of the ACCEL university. It should be distributed to students who show potential to be active concerned citizens and ethical leaders. Simply using high school GPA or standardized test scores cheapens any notion of merit. Especially awful is when standardized test scores are used by themselves, so that a student who has little to show for his or her high school career may be given so-called merit aid on the basis of performance on a three-hour test strongly linked to socioeconomic status. I have seen what it is like at a university that has aspirations to be what I call an ACCEL university but that hands out merit aid on the basis of narrow test scores. Their actions belie their vision. If we want students to become active concerned citizens and ethical leaders, we have to role-model for them the behaviors that underlie these goals. Doling out aid solely for test scores, or ethnicity, or race, or gender does injustice, if not violence, to the fundamental premises of an ACCEL university. Merit cannot be determined exclusively on the basis of status variables or standardized test scores.

College Costs

The greatest problem our society faces in higher education is perhaps not the quality of education that our universities provide. The greatest problem is the ever-rising cost of university education (Archibald and Feldman 2014). The cost is rising far ahead of inflation, but more importantly, ahead of people's ability to pay the costs. The result is that many families are being squeezed out of providing their children with the kind of education the family wants for their children.

Of course, the large majority of universities provide at least some financial aid. Where this breaks down is that what the universities believe the parents can afford is often not what the parents believe they can afford. And many parents never even get to the point of having their children apply because they believe, often correctly, that their children will not be able to afford to go to the college of their choice, regardless of the aid package offered.

The cost of college is way beyond most parents' means. The average family annual income in the United States was $51,371 in 2012, the latest year for which figures are available as I write. That is less than the annual cost of many competitive private universities. In contrast, when I went to college, the annual cost of my expensive private university as I started my education was $3,300, a steep figure in 1968, but not at the level of the average family income (of $8,632). Put another way, even one of the most expensive schools was priced at less than half of average family income in 1968, but now that same university is far in excess of the average family income. So what solutions are there to the problem of spiraling costs, given that current financial-aid models cannot possibly keep up with the accelerating difference between college costs and people's incomes?

Option 1. Cut professional salaries. We can reduce college costs by reducing professional salaries. Many people believe that university personnel are overpaid anyway.

There are multiple layers to this problem. Some administrators probably are overpaid, some of those in two categories in particular.

The first is certain university presidents. Do we need university presidents making close to, or in excess of, a million dollars per year? When salaries go this high, something else has to give, and research suggests that in institutions with very high presidential salaries, there tend to be more poorly paid adjuncts and relatively fewer tenure-track professors (McKenna 2015).

The second is some coaches of athletic teams, especially football. Coaches of some of these teams receive salaries many multiples of presidential salaries. Do we need football coaches making several million dollars per year? What kind of statement do such salaries make about our educational priorities?

In my experience, other salaries are not as far off the beam as these. One could lower professorial salaries, but except at the very most prestigious institutions, university professors are not particularly well paid. And at the most prestigious institutions, professors are paid more in large part because they truly are the professionals at the top of their fields. Pay them less and they will move to other institutions. And, unfortunately, that becomes the problem with university presidents and coaches as well. As long as there are competitor institutions that are willing to pay extremely high salaries, cutting salaries will not be a terribly effective strategy because the best people then will go to the competition. In essence, salaries in universities, as in anything else, are largely set by competitive pressures.

The pressures are not just external. Although some of us might be taken aback by the salaries coaches are paid, others feel that universities simply have to pay what the market will bear. For many alumni, their connection with the university is driven by athletics, and for them, if the athletic program loses its coach to a competitor, that is much more serious than the university's losing some of its best professors or even, for that matter, its president. When I was provost at Oklahoma State, I found most Oklahomans far more concerned about the performance of the university's top athletic teams, for example, football and basketball, than about the journals in which top professors publish. And those are the alumni on whose financial and other support the university must rely. In this regard, Oklahoma State was no exception in its Big XII conference.

So salaries of very top administrators and coaches might be a place to start, but it is not clear that there would be support among those whose views matter most, namely, influential alumni and supporters. Moreover, losing top administrators or coaches to competitors adversely affects a university's reputation. And in the end, cutting one or two salaries is not going to have a dramatic impact on costs for students. So let's look at other possibilities for lowering costs or raising financial aid.

Option 2. Cut services. Another option, which universities have used, is to cut services. Cutting services has the advantage that it can quickly cut costs. Another advantage is that almost any university has services that have seen their better days—academic programs that once were strong but no longer are; extracurricular activities that no longer attract student interest; offices whose function in the university perhaps were never that clear anyway. Cutting services can actually sharpen the focus of a university and enhance its quality.

Unfortunately, that is not what usually happens. There are several problems with cutting services that make it an unpopular choice.

The first problem is that cutting services usually means loss of jobs, and firing people almost never enhances the functioning of a university because it causes so much turmoil that any good that might come of it quickly gets lost. The people who go may not go quietly, and others, afraid for their own jobs, may become vocal in support of those who have been fired. Also, if employees believe that their employer is under duress, some of them will try to leave, fearing that unless they leave before it is too late, they will be forced out. The employees who are best able to leave are the strong ones, so the risk is that the strong people will go. Moreover, others may stay but with reduced morale. And reduced morale saps the strength of any academic unit. The bottom line is that sometimes employees just have to be let go, but the outcomes are not usually pleasant.

Another problem with cutting services is that it generally reduces the quality, or at least the perceived quality, of the university's offerings. At best, the university will discontinue something that at one time it did not think it needed, only at another time to wonder what people were thinking when they discontinued the services. In my own career, for example, I saw the discontinuation of a department of petroleum engineering—in a state heavily dependent on the petroleum industry. At the time of the discontinuation of the unit, the decision probably seemed to make sense. The petroleum industry was going through hard times; there was a need to cut money; there was little interest on the part of students in this particular program. But once the program was cut—or strictly speaking, merged into another program—it was no mean feat to get it back. When the petroleum industry rose again, there was outrage among many business leaders in the state that petroleum engineering had been cut, and a number of the associated businesses began to look elsewhere for their new hires.

The more general problem is that it is hard, at any given time, to know what is going away for good and what is going away for just a short period of time. In my own lifetime, I have seen many elementary schools closed and repurposed in times of shortages of elementary school students. When the number of elementary school students bounced back again—as these numbers tend to do—the buildings were already being used for other purposes and it became necessary to build new schools, a proposition far more expensive than maintaining the schools through hard times so they would be ready for use when the situation turned around.

Of course, it is possible to cut extracurricular activities rather than academic ones. For example, some universities have cut certain sports. But such cuts rarely endear the university to the alumni population on whom the university is dependent for donations. This kind of cut also angers the fans of that sport as well as leaders in the state or university community who almost inevitably believe that the sport that was let go is the most important thing to the university—beyond, perhaps, sliced bread.

One can always cut certain services with a promise to bring them back once the financial or general resource situation of the university improves. The problem with this solution is that creating or re-creating any kind of program from scratch is almost certainly more expensive and resource-consuming than is keeping an existing program going. The risk is that the total cost of stopping and then restarting a program may be greater than the cost of never having stopped it in the first place.

If the need arises to cut programs, it usually makes sense to have consultations with stakeholders, especially faculty members. When I was president of the American Psychological Association, I found that no matter how useless I found a particular activity to be, there almost always were supporters who could not imagine the organization's existing without that particular activity. By consulting with stakeholders, one at least gets some buy-in for what is bound to be a difficult process.

Option 3. Issue bonds or otherwise borrow money. Forget about it. Borrowing money only makes sense, in the long term, to pay for one-time costs, such as a capital construction project. If a university is borrowing money to cover shortfalls from tuition payments, it needs to get more students, raise tuition, find another way to raise money, or prepare for the end.

Option 4. Invest money more aggressively. In recent years, universities have generally become more aggressive in their investments, at the same time that they have hedged their bets by diversifying investments. But the problem with aggressive investing was made clear by the financial maelstrom of 2008. Those universities that were most aggressively invested predictably lost the most. Nevertheless, their bills did not go away because the financial situation of the country was poor. Rather, the universities had to figure out how to survive in a flagging economy that few of them had anticipated.

Option 5. Increase donor contributions. Raising money from donors is almost always the preferred option for dealing with shortfalls. The problem is always the same: finding the donors and/or increasing contributions from an already existing donor base. Usually, increasing donor contributions requires having excellent research to locate potential donors and then having a strong fund-raising (development) operation for raising the money. In my view, this is one of the best ways of raising money, but a university has to spend money to make money. You can't raise money if you don't have skilled development officers, and you can't hire skilled development officers unless you are willing to pay them competitive salaries. Moreover, it takes a while to train them and for them to form relationships with existing and new donors, so this is almost never a quick solution. In the short term, a university that is expanding its development staff will lose money in the hope of a long-term gain in assets.

A further issue is whether the increases in donor contributions will ever outstrip the money that can be earned merely by increasing tuition. It is so much easier for a university to increase tuition that this is what universities usually do, which gets us back to why universities are so expensive in the first place.

Option 6. Increase the size of the (full-paying) study body. When universities find their budgets falling short, they often consider increasing, or at least trying to increase, the size of the student body because additional students provide a quick way to increase revenue. There are several problems with this solution.

The first is finding the students. Of course, there are highly prestigious or otherwise popular universities where students are falling all over each other to get in. But a more common situation is for a college or university to actively recruit students to get them to come to the institution. Such recruiting costs money and does not always yield additional students.

The second problem is that having more students can lead to larger class sizes or to lack of access to classes. This situation compromises the quality of the education being offered. Moreover, it tends to anger instructors, who almost never feel that they are being underworked.

The third problem is ensuring that the resources are there to handle the additional students. Is there adequate dormitory space or other living space near the university? Are classrooms large enough? Can student-services professionals handle the additional students? And will the additional students be as well prepared as the already existing student body, or will they actually need extra student services?

The bottom line is that what can look like a quick source of revenue can be an added cost burden unless the existing university resources are being underutilized and thus are ready for more intensive use.

Option 7. Increase research and development support. Universities earn money from overhead (indirect costs) on grants. That is, for every grant dollar received, say, from the government, the university gets a certain amount of additional money for the cost of doing the research. The additional money pays for space, heating, air conditioning, maintenance, and so forth. The problem with grant overhead is that it usually does not even cover the true cost of the research being done. Costs are negotiated with a government agency, and unsurprisingly, government agencies are not eager to spend lots of money paying overhead to universities. So even if more research dollars are brought in, they are not likely to help the bottom line of the university a great deal.

More and more universities are turning to partnerships with industry, and this makes sense in these times. Few of those partnerships make universities tons of money (one hears a lot about Gatorade, which has made a huge amount of money for the University of Florida, but the fact that one so often hears about this single phenomenon bespeaks the difficulty of ventures reaching anywhere near that level of success). Moreover, universities need to take care in their partnerships with private concerns that their academic freedom is maintained. Sometimes industry does not wish publication of results that put their products in a potentially unfavorable light, and so it is essential that agreements with private concerns take into account the need to protect academic freedom to publish.

Another issue is that patentable inventions usually take a fair amount of time to go from the stage of being a dream to the stage of being a patentable reality. In my experience working with start-up operations that will potentially produce patents, the large majority of them never end up making much serious money. A university helps to fund these operations to support its faculty's research and development activities, and in the hope that a small number of the resultant inventions will make good money for the university.

Option 8. Seek out additional state funds. For public universities, at least, the first and last hope is increases in state funds. But many public universities are in the exigent situations they are in because of cuts in state funding. Although some of the funding lost around 2008 and thereabouts has been restored, there has been no consistent upward trend in funding for state universities. The general trend in state support has been in the downward direction, to the extent that some universities or parts of universities either have become "state-affiliated" or have continued to be state institutions in name only. I interviewed at one state university where the level of state support was a meager 3 percent, hardly enough to consider the university to be closely tied to the state in terms of its funding needs.

Option 9. Consolidate colleges and universities within a state. In one of the states in which I have lived, there is what could only be called a plethora of state-supported institutions of higher learning. In general, of course, it is good to have more institutions rather than fewer. But if a state is going to have more of them, then it needs to commit to supporting them at a high enough level that they can thrive. This is not happening in that state, and in many other states as well.

If there are too many institutions of higher education, given the state budget for supporting colleges and universities, why doesn't the state just consolidate these institutions? In the particular state I have in mind, almost everyone, including politicians, supports such consolidation—just so long as the institution to be closed is not in their own district. That is, the problem is in large part a political one. Even though the system of higher education would be enhanced by having fewer but better-endowed institutions, politicians don't want to risk sticking their necks out for a battle that is likely to make them unpopular and will likely be lost in any event. Having the courage to consolidate in a reflective way would help state education, but it is not likely to happen any time soon.

Option 10. Tinkering with allocation of college credits. What number of credits should be required for graduation? There is no conceptually "right" answer to this question, although universities or state systems may have legally prescribed answers. One way to reduce college costs is to reduce the number of credits required for college graduation. As a former dean and provost, I can say why this idea is unpopular, at least among faculty. First, it seems to cheapen the degree. Faculty often feel that degrees have already been cheapened—that if anything, we need as a society to move in the opposite direction. Second, this solution potentially cuts the number of credit hours for a given department and therefore may reduce allocations to the department. Third, cutting credits may reduce the already disappearing number of credit hours allocated to general-education courses, raising questions as to whether colleges are to become even more pre-vocational than they already are.

In the early days of advanced placement, universities tended rather freely to allocate credit for Advanced Placement courses taken in high school, especially if students received a score of 3 (out of 5) or above on the corresponding Advanced Placement examination. But some university professors began, over time, to question whether the high school courses really are equivalent. A further problem is that whereas Advanced Placement courses were once taken by only the best students, today they are much more widely available, and some students who take the courses do not always perform at the levels one would hope for from high school, much less college, students.

A different but related solution is to make it easier to transfer credits from another institution, especially a community college within the state, or to count life experience as deserving credit toward the degree. In my judgment, the first solution is generally a good one. The problem is that the bureaucracies for transferring credits are often quite complex and resistant to change. The second solution—counting life experience—comes close to being a nonstarter in competitive institutions. It tends to smack of manipulation and, in some cases, of outright fraud. Who is going to decide what life-experience credits to transfer, how many credits any given life experience is worth, and what kinds of credit they should count toward? The institutions that pursue the life-experience option tend to be less competitive ones that need to worry less about appearances, although they still need to worry about accreditation.

Option 11. Enhancing online learning options. Online instruction tends to cost an institution less than face-to-face instruction, so it is definitely an option for reducing costs. What is not clear at this juncture is whether students receiving an online education get the same value as those receiving an in-class education. The onliners may actually be getting more; we just don't know. What we do know is that some of the class discussion and networking options that are available in person are more challenging, although not impossible, in an online environment.

Option 12. Doing nothing. For a long time, universities have been tinkering with the problem of college costs around the edges, without confronting them head-on. I do not see this as a viable long-term option. Between 1985 and 2011, the cost of living rose 115 percent; college costs rose just short of 500 percent (Wadsworth 2012). That is not a sustainable difference. Either universities or state governments will find a way to bring increases in colleges costs in line with increases in cost of living, or else the whole system of paying for college will implode. Some would argue that it already has, given unsustainably rising levels of student debt (Lorin 2014).

If we put together the information on options discussed above, we can see why it is hard to control university tuition and associated costs. In most cases, there just are not alternative sources of revenue that can be collected as easily as tuition payments. Tuition can be increased by administrators just sitting around a table and making it so (assuming they can get trustee or regent approval). All of the other solutions are uncertain at best and require a large investment to yield any significant revenue. In the end, colleges and universities will need to utilize some combination of the options above (excepting number 12) in order to contain costs.

One might well ask why the costs of attending universities have skyrocketed in the first place. As someone who has spent a significant amount of time in university administration, I find that question easy to answer in one word: competition. Your competitor puts up a new stadium; there is pressure on you to do the same. Your competitor constructs new shiny dormitories with greater student appeal; there is pressure on you to do the same. Your competitor hires better faculty and goes up in the ratings; there is pressure on you to do the same. In many respects, universities compete with each other in much the same way as soft-drink manufacturers or soap manufacturers or software companies. You never can let your competitor get an edge on you, and certainly not a large edge, lest you be left behind in the dust. And as the "arms race" accelerates, so does the cost of running the university. Unilateral disarmament is hardly an answer. You can decide not to compete at the level at which you have competed before, but no administrator worth his or her salt wants to preside over the sinking of a university's reputation. That's a sure way of being labeled a failure. So the arms race continues, and universities become more expensive propositions for the students who attend them.

Universities in Europe and many other parts of the world can charge less or even nothing, but they operate under different systems. For example, my wife received an excellent education at Heidelberg University in Germany. But Heidelberg does not provide dormitories, meal services, extended library hours, athletic facilities, other extracurricular facilities, or numerous other kinds of amenities that many US universities provide. It does not have to, because its arms race is with other German universities that also do not provide those services. It is competing in a different market so it can afford to act differently. That said, German universities recently lowered their faculty pay scales, and such a move hardly motivates top students to decide to go into the professoriate as a career.

There is no magic bullet for stopping the rapid and, some might say, crazy increases in college costs our country has seen over recent years. The current US president, Barack Obama, has expressed on multiple occasions his concerns about the escalation of costs but has not made clear what he is going to do about them. The government, of course, provides student loans to help students meet the cost of college, but a large issue facing our society today is the level of student debt that graduates incur, which may last for decades. Moreover, default rates are higher than anyone would like. Loans do not appear to be a compelling solution, especially when students today are likely to have a lower living standard than their parents.

I wish, as an author of this book, I had that magic-bullet solution for the problem of college costs, but I don't and I know of no one who does. What I know for sure is that raising tuition while paying astronomical salaries to administrators or spending fortunes to build elaborate athletic stadiums or soaring student centers sends the wrong message to students, parents, and society. If we want students to become wise, we need to start role-modeling wisdom for them.

Models for Financing Higher Education

Models for financing higher education do not, as of 2015, appear to be working terribly well (Sternberg 2014b). In many other countries, universities are federally financed, but federal financing does not ensure any better results than state financing. In most of Europe, Latin America, Africa, and Asia, where financing of public universities is federal, funding levels are well below what would be needed to provide for top-quality teaching and research.

To put it another way, no financing model yet in operation seems ideal. An alternative, of course, is for universities to go the for-profit route, which many institutions in the United States and elsewhere have done, but this model has produced some questionable results and any number of federal investigations into whether some for-profit universities are recruiting students primarily as a means to obtain their federal financial aid. The for-profit model may make headway in terms of offering high-quality education—the Minerva group is trying to do so, for example—but the country is definitely not there yet.

Universities are, increasingly, seeking to rely on private donations to support their activities. Almost all top-level administrators spend a good proportion of their time fund-raising in the hope of finding private (or corporate) funds that will enable them to better fulfill their missions. But the fact that many private universities are charging in excess of $70,000 a year suggests that these efforts have been less than fully successful.

Given that no existing funding model is working as smoothly as anyone would hope for, the question is whether there is some alternative model that will provide the funding universities need without resorting to extremely high rates of tuition accompanied by steeply discounted tuition for those found not to be able to afford the full freight. Although such a model has obvious appeal, it basically amounts to wealthier students subsidizing less wealthy ones. In effect, full college tuition contains a built-in tax whereby the haves help pay for the have-nots. So one individual may pay $70,000, another nothing, to attend the same college. This system creates a perverse incentive for some parents to shed or even hide financial or other assets as their children approach college age so that they can be on the receiving end rather than the subsidizing end of the college-tuition continuum.

Purchasing a college education is unlike purchasing an automobile and most other products because the price of the product is not necessarily highly correlated with the educational quality of the institution. It is easier to understand why top private colleges would charge extremely high tuition but harder to understand how this works for colleges low in almost any pecking order. Some low-ranking small liberal-arts colleges are having trouble making ends meet these days because parents are grasping the notion that if they pay a lot of money, they should expect a very high level of quality in return, and they are not always getting that.

There is probably no perfect model for dealing with the financing problem, but one model that is being explored more and more is that of different-priced degrees from the same institution. For example, in Texas, former governor Rick Perry pressured state universities to create a $10,000 bachelor's degree, and some proceeded to do so. One will not get the same education for $10,000 that one gets for a larger amount, but one will get an education leading to the degree. For example, there are likely to be more online courses in the lineup than would be the case for the more expensive education. The diploma will be the same as that for the more expensive education.

I have less enthusiasm for this model than does former governor Perry and some other people because it creates a system in which one receives not the education from which one can most profit but rather the education for which one can pay. Students with lower socioeconomic status will end up, in some cases, with a lesser education. At least with automobiles, all of them will get you from Point A to Point Z, whether they are inexpensive Chevys or expensive Ferraris. What is not clear yet is whether the cheaper education will really get graduates from Point A to Point Z in terms of having the knowledge and skills they need to succeed in life.

The best solution to the problem of higher education in the United States is, I believe, also one that will be difficult to sell politically. The future of America will be decided not by our children's competition with each other but by their competition with workers in China, Singapore, Japan, Germany, Finland, and any of a number of technologically advanced countries. In order for our children to compete, they need to go to universities that are well financed but also that are well resourced. Therefore, we either pay now—whether in taxes and tuitions—or pay later in terms of decreased international competitiveness. The choice, I believe, is clear.

The sky is not falling on higher education (Sternberg 2013a). Doomsayers believe that purveyors of massive open online courses, or for-profit companies, or shadowy entrepreneurs will make higher education so cheap that any number of existing colleges and universities may soon find themselves out of business. Those arguments are off track because they make two false assumptions: that participants in higher education have homogeneous goals, and that students are consumers and not producers, or constructors, of their own personalized product of higher education.

First, the doomsayers assume that every potential college student is looking for more or less the same thing in a college education. This means that if push comes to shove, the student will choose the cheapest version of higher education that provides a degree that employers will accept. But when we look at students as consumers, we find that the marketplace of consumers of higher education is no more undifferentiated than any other marketplace.

If you want lip moisturizer, you can go online and buy it for $2 or $22. Both products moisturize lips. Some people pay more than $400,000 for a new car; others, less than $10,000. Both cars get you from one point to another. Watches range in price from a few dollars to over a million. They all tell time.

The higher-education marketplace, like the marketplaces for lip moisturizers, cars, and watches, is differentiated. Some people want the cheapest education possible that will get them the job they want. Others want much more—nice dormitories, diverse student activities, world-famous professors, top-flight institutional reputation—and are willing to pay for it. An advantage of the higher-education market is that financial aid is often available to help students reach beyond what they normally could afford.

Second, students are not merely consumers of higher education; they also actively construct their college careers. They develop a plan for their coursework, their project work, their extracurricular activities, and their social network.

Two consumers buying a particular model of car get essentially the same car (except perhaps for unfortunate production errors). But two students going to the same college may produce entirely different educations. Indeed, students may choose their college in large part on the basis of their projection as to whether they can construct the entire educational experience they wish to create. So there is great variation in students not only as consumers but also as producers of an educational product—their college careers.

This is important because those two roles interact with costs. For example, a degree from a top-rated German university costs a small fraction of what a comparable degree would cost in the United States. But typically, as noted earlier, the German institution would have no university-sponsored athletic teams or facilities, fraternities, sororities, student clubs, dormitories, meal plans, or other accouterments that many students take for granted in the United States. If students in Germany want activities, they organize them and bear the costs themselves. More of the burden of students as producers is placed on them—for better or worse. As producers they are basically on their own, without the supports that most American colleges provide.

American universities can reduce costs by greatly lowering their overhead (as do the German universities) or by having professors do some or even all of their teaching online (Selingo 2013). What students may lose, however, is much, or even most, of the informal curriculum of college—the networking and the face-to-face personal interactions that many people feel are so important to the college experience.

So less expensive degrees can be had. The only question is: What does one want to give up to reduce costs? This question is playing itself out on a much larger stage in the United States as local, state, and federal levels of government struggle to balance services and costs.

The problem with the Chicken Little view of higher education is that it can create self-fulfilling prophecies. If decision makers in higher education believe the sky is falling, they may find themselves taking actions that are value-destroying rather than value-enhancing. For example, institutions may start to teach courses online not because that is the optimal way to teach them (and there may be some courses that are optimally taught online) but merely to cut costs; or valuable student activities may be discontinued in order to anticipate the falling of the sky.

Framing the debate about the costs of higher education solely in terms of what it costs students to go to college is the wrong way to go about fixing the problem. The debate instead should be framed in terms of value received. How much value do students, as producers and as consumers, receive for the dollars spent? Is education at a prestigious private college worth several times the cost of education at a not-very-prestigious public college? Let the student (and his or her parents) decide the costs and benefits, much as they do with lip balm, cars, and watches. As long as an institution appeals to some marketplace segment, provides value, and watches its finances, it will do just fine. I believe that, ultimately, the greatest value is to be found in the ACCEL university, where expenses can be justified in terms of their development in students, faculty, and staff alike, the fundamental building blocks of active concerned citizenship and ethical leadership.

The problems of financing higher education are so serious in the United States that they can easily crowd out consideration of the problems in the instructional models underlying higher education. Whatever its financial model, a university cannot succeed if it does not have a strong instructional model. We turn to instructional questions in the next chapter.

PART III

STUDENT LEARNING AND LIFE

7

Teaching and Learning

Instruction and assessment are, or at least should be, the heart of any university. There is no one right way of teaching and learning. Different students learn and think in different ways. Some students may learn better from lectures, others from class discussions. Some may learn better via oral presentation, others by reading. Some may prefer verbal presentation of material, others pictorial representation. Some may love to delve into details; others may prefer to concentrate on the big picture. By varying teaching techniques, one is likely to reach more students more successfully.

There is no one formula for developing active concerned citizens and ethical leaders, any more than there is one formula for actually being an active concerned citizen or an ethical leader. If we wish to develop maximally productive future citizens, we need to take into account their individual teaching and learning needs. If teachers always teach the same way to all students, merely because they are teaching in a way that is easy for them or that represents their own preferred learning style, they are presenting students with Crane's ball of clay. However the instructors teach, they need fundamentally to develop in students the principal skills underlying active concerned citizenship and ethical leadership: creative, analytical, practical, and wisdom-based thinking skills as well as passion.

Similarly, there is no one right way of assessing students' achievement. Experience suggests that some students excel in multiple-choice tests, others in essays. Some students do well so long as the questions are limited to factual recall, whereas others do better if they are allowed to show their deeper understanding, perhaps of fewer facts. Unidimensional assessments (e.g., tests that are all multiple-choice, all short-answer, or all essay) often fail to enable students to capitalize on strengths (Sternberg 1997a). The same students may repeatedly excel and others repeatedly do poorly not for lack of ability or even achievement, but for lack of variety in the way the students' knowledge and skills are assessed.

Teaching to Strengths and Weaknesses

Leaders are effective to the extent that they capitalize on their strengths as leaders and find ways to correct or compensate for their weaknesses. Typically, they delegate tasks that are outside their realm of expertise. Similarly, instructors should teach to and assess strengths, but to weaknesses as well (Sternberg and Grigorenko 2007). Some teachers might misunderstand the message here as a plea for extreme individualization—an individualized program for each student. Such a program is usually impractical, especially at the introductory level, and often is counterproductive. Students need to learn to correct or compensate for weaknesses as well as capitalize on strengths. Thus it is important that students be intellectually uncomfortable some of the time, just as it is important for them to be intellectually comfortable and secure some of the time. The students need to learn to deal with more challenging methods of instruction and assessment as well as with those that challenge them less. By varying methods of instruction and assessment for all students, we automatically provide an environment in which, at a given time, some students will be more and others less comfortable. Fortunately, different students will be at different comfort levels at different times.

Students need to learn to balance adaptation to, shaping of, and selection of environments. The balance of these three responses to the environment has certain implications for teaching:

1. *Students, like teachers, need to develop flexibility*. A rigid classroom or institutional environment is likely to foster rigidity in the thinking of the students in it. Given the amazingly rapid rate of development today—the initiation and rapidly changing environment of the Internet, the changing nature of jobs and the requirements of those jobs, the rapidly changing social structures that render behavior that is socially acceptable one year socially unacceptable the next—schools are obliged to develop flexibility in their students. The rapid accumulation of knowledge may render much of the knowledge students acquire in school obsolete, but it will never render obsolete the facility they acquire in coping with novel environments. As a result, teachers need to not only encourage students by challenging them but also encourage students to challenge themselves. For example, the school environment should be structured in a way that encourages students to take difficult courses or those that challenge the boundaries students may have previously set for themselves.

The environment should also encourage students to understand and be able to represent points of view other than their own. At the same time, students need to learn to critique in a thoughtful and systematic manner beliefs that they may have held dear throughout their lives, whatever these beliefs may be.

2. *Students need to be allowed and even encouraged to take risks and to make mistakes*. People often learn more from their mistakes and failures than from their successes. An environment that does not allow students to make mistakes or ever to fail in their endeavors deprives the students of important learning opportunities. Environmental selection means choosing a new environment over an old one. It can apply to changing one's term-paper topic after discovering that one's first choice did not work out, or changing one's course schedule after deciding that the selection of a particular course was a mistake. Students often view the decisions to make such changes as implying that they have wasted time in their former choices (e.g., of paper topics or courses). Quite on the contrary, the students have learned a lesson they will need in life—to have a sense of when and how to cut losses and to recognize that there is a need to change one's direction or even one's goals. Put succinctly, they need to learn that nothing ventured, nothing gained.

3. *Students need to learn how to overcome obstacles.* When the environment of the classroom, the institution, or even the society is less than ideal, it often requires guts to try to change it. Outmoded and counterproductive practices continue in all institutions and even classroom settings simply because no one, including the faculty, wants to challenge authority and cut through the red tape needed to improve the learning or working environment. Often when students or faculty try to make changes, they encounter opposition and even outright defiance. Yet the world would be a much worse place to live if no one had the courage to stand up to opposition and fight for change—to shape the environment.

At the same time, students need to learn to balance adaptation with shaping. Someone who initiates and then fights one battle after another is likely to lose considerable time, as well as credibility, in the resulting skirmishes. Students and faculty alike need to learn to pick their battles carefully, and then to stand up for the causes that are truly meaningful to them. As teachers, we might find numerous aspects of our institutions in need of change. We cannot change them all. We, just like our students, therefore need to develop a taste for which battles are worth fighting and which are not. But when we choose, we must then be willing to stand up for our beliefs and show persuasively why others should adopt them.

Teaching and assessment should balance use of analytical, creative, and practical thinking skills. At the same time, as teachers, we need to put behind us the false dichotomy between "teaching for thinking" and "teaching for the facts," or between emphases on thinking and emphases on memory.

Thinking always requires memory and the knowledge base that is accessed through the use of our memories. One cannot analyze what one knows if one knows nothing. One cannot creatively go beyond the existing boundaries of knowledge if one does not know what those boundaries are. And one cannot apply what one knows in a practical manner if one does not know anything to apply.

At the same time, memory for facts without the ability to use those facts is useless. A story recently appeared in the news about a man who entered a truck on which an electrical wire had fallen during a continuing storm. A second man, observing the first man's imminent entrance into the truck, shouted at him to stop, but too late. The first man was electrocuted. The first man had master's degrees in physics and engineering; the second man had no such degrees. Without doubt, the first man's educational achievements gave him the declarative (factual) knowledge that he could have used to save his life. But he was unable to apply this knowledge (turn it into procedures) in a way that would have ensured his survival.

It is for this reason that we encourage teachers to teach and assess achievement in ways that enable students to analyze, create with, and apply their knowledge—some of the key skills ACCEL universities develop. When students think to learn, they also learn to think. And there is an added benefit: students who are taught analytically, creatively, and practically perform better on assessments, apparently without regard to the form the assessments take. That is, they outperform students instructed in conventional ways, even if the assessments are for straight factual memory (Sternberg, Torff, and Grigorenko 1998). Moreover, our research shows that these techniques succeed, regardless of subject-matter area. But what, exactly, are the techniques used to teach analytically, creatively, and practically?

1. *Teaching analytically means encouraging students to (a) analyze, (b) critique, (c) judge, (d) compare and contrast, (e) evaluate, and (f) assess.* When teachers refer to teaching for "critical thinking," they typically mean teaching for analytical thinking. But there is more to critical thinking than just analysis.

2. *Teaching creatively means encouraging students to (a) create, (b) invent, (c) discover, (d) imagine if . . . , (e) suppose that . . . , and (f) predict.* Teaching for creativity requires teachers not only to support and encourage creativity but also to role-model it and to reward it when it is displayed. In other words, teachers need to not only talk the talk but also walk the walk.

3. *Teaching practically means encouraging students to (a) apply, (b) use, (c) put into practice, (d) implement, (e) employ, and (f) render practical what they know.* Such teaching must relate to the real practical needs of the students, not just to what would be practical for individuals other than the students.

When I received my first test score—a 3 out of 10—in college introductory psychology, I realized that I had some hard slogging ahead, especially after the professor told me that "there is a famous Sternberg in psychology and it is obvious there won't be another one." I eventually pulled a C in the course, which the professor referred to as a "gift." That professor was probably as surprised as I was when I earned an A in his upper-level course, and I certainly was grateful to him when, as chair of the search committee, he hired me back to my alma mater (Yale University) as an assistant professor, where I would remain as a professor for thirty years. My instructor probably wondered, as did I, how I could have done so poorly in the introductory course and so much better in the upper-level course.

Multiple causes may have contributed to the difference in performance, but one was almost certainly a difference in the styles of learning and thinking that were rewarded in the two courses. The lower-level course was pretty much a straight, memorize-the-book kind of course, whereas the upper-level course was one that encouraged students to formulate their own research studies and to analyze the research studies of others.

Psychologists and educators differ as to whether they believe in the existence of different styles of learning and thinking. Harold Pashler and his colleagues (2008) have claimed that the evidence for their existence is weak, but a number of scholars, including Li-fang Zhang and me (Zhang and Sternberg 2006; Zhang et al. 2012; see also Kozhevnikov et al. 2014), have provided what we believe to be compelling evidence for the existence and importance of diverse styles of learning and thinking. I have often felt that anyone who has raised two or more children will be aware, at an experiential level, that children learn and think in different ways.

My own thinking about styles of learning and thinking has been driven by my "theory of mental self-government" (Sternberg 1997b). According to this theory, the ways of governments in the world are external reflections of what goes on in people's minds. There are thirteen different styles in the theory, but consider now just three of them. People with a legislative style like to come up with their own ideas and do things in their own way; people with an executive style prefer to be given more structure and guidance or even be told what to do; people with a judicial style like to evaluate and judge things, especially the work of others.

From this point of view, the introductory psychology course I took, like many introductory courses, particularly rewarded students with an executive style—students who liked to memorize what they read in books or heard in lectures. In contrast, the advanced psychology lab course rewarded students with a legislative or judicial style, in that students came up with ideas for their own experiments and evaluated the research of others.

In a series of studies I conducted with Elena Grigorenko of Yale University and later with Li-fang Zhang of the University of Hong Kong (see Sternberg et al. 2008), we had both teachers and students fill out questionnaires based on my theory of mental self-government (see Zhang et al. 2012 for a review of this literature). In one set of studies, Grigorenko and I then computed a measure of the similarity of the profile of each student to his or her teacher. We also evaluated the styles preferred by the diverse educational institutions on the basis of their mission statements and descriptive literature. There are three findings from that study of particular importance to college classrooms.

First, institutions differ widely in the styles of thinking that they reward. For example, in the study, one tended to reward a conservative style (characterizing people who like things to remain more or less the way they are) and tended to penalize a liberal style (characterizing people who like things to change), whereas another rewarded exactly the opposite pattern. The correlations of styles with academic success were statistically significant in both schools, but in opposite directions. Teachers also value different styles. Hence it is important for students to select a college or university and, to the extent possible, professors who value at least to some degree the kinds of learning and thinking that best characterize a particular student. Similarly, it is important for professors to select a school at which to work that values the ways in which the professors prefer to think and to teach.

Second, teachers tend to overestimate the extent to which students match their own profile of learning and thinking styles. Teachers often teach in a way that reflects their own preferred styles of learning and thinking, not fully realizing that the styles that they prefer may not correspond to the styles that many of their students prefer. They believe they are teaching in ways that meet the needs of diverse students, when in fact they often are not. In essence, we are at risk for teaching to ourselves rather than to our students.

Third, teachers tended to grade more highly those students whose profiles of learning and thinking better matched their own. In showing this pattern, the teachers were not purposely favoring people like themselves, nor were they probably even aware of favoring those students. But the fundamental principle of interpersonal attraction is that we are more attracted to people who are like ourselves, and so it is not surprising that teachers would value more highly students who think in the same ways they do. Ideally, teachers will be flexible, both within and between courses. (The psychology professor to whom I referred earlier was flexible between courses but not within each course.)

These preferences become a problem if the styles that lead to success in a particular course do not match the styles that will be needed for success either in more advanced courses in the same discipline or, worse, in the occupation for which the course prepares students. For example, in most occupations, one does not sit around taking short-answer or multiple-choice tests on the material one needs to succeed in the job. The risk, then, is that schools will reward students whose styles match the way they are taught but not the requirements of the work for which the teaching prepares them. As an example, thirty-five years after receiving the C in introductory psychology, I was president of the American Psychological Association—the largest association of psychologists in the world—and did not once have to sit down and take fact-based quizzes on the material I needed to succeed on the job. Indeed, the factual content that would be taught in an introductory psychology course, and in many other courses, had changed radically in those thirty-five years.

In my own teaching, I have had run-ins with the importance of styles. For example, when I first started teaching introductory psychology, I taught it the way I ideally would have liked the course, with lots of emphasis on "legislative" activities—students coming up with their own ideas for structuring their learning. It became obvious to me within a couple of weeks that the course was failing to meet the learning needs of the students. I later realized it was for the same reason that the introductory psychology course I had taken had not worked for me. I was teaching to my own style of learning, not to the diversity of students' styles of learning. I now try to teach in ways that encourage a mix of legislative, executive, and judicial activities. For example, students come up with their own ideas for papers but also have to answer some short-answer questions on tests and analyze the theories and research of various investigators.

Similarly, in teaching an advanced statistics course, I had pretty much pegged some of the students as "stronger learners" and other students as "weaker learners." One day, I read about how to teach one of the techniques geometrically rather than in the algebraic way I had been teaching that and other material in the course. When I started teaching the material geometrically, I found that many of the students I had identified as "strong learners" were having difficulty, whereas many of the students I had identified as "weak learners" were easily absorbing the material. I had confounded strength of students' learning skills with matches of their learning styles to the way I happened to be teaching.

In sum, styles of learning and thinking matter in the classroom. If we want to develop active concerned citizens and ethical leaders, we best serve our students when we teach in a way that enables all students to capitalize on their preferred styles at least some of the time, but that recognizes that students must acquire flexibility in their use of styles and so cannot always learn in their preferred way. My own former institution, Oklahoma State University (OSU), has a Learning and Student Success Opportunity Center that intervenes with students in ways specifically oriented toward meeting the needs of their diverse learning and thinking styles. Likewise, the OSU Institute for Teaching and Learning Excellence teaches teachers how to meet the stylistic needs of students. Educators' goal in higher education should be to prepare students for the diverse demands that later courses and careers will make on their learning and thinking styles so they can be successful not just in one course but in their later studies and work. Educators also need to teach students how to think in an interdisciplinary way.

Interdisciplinary Problem-Based Learning: An Alternative to Traditional Majors and Minors

The teaching-learning process needs to not only emphasize the development of analytical, creative, and practical skills, and diverse styles of thinking and learning. It needs to develop these skills and styles in the context of interdisciplinary and problem-based learning (Sternberg 2008a). Consider four distinct problems confronting society in recent times, today, and perhaps in the future: (1) finding a way to manage—or ideally eradicate—epidemics (e.g., AIDS, SARS, Ebola, perhaps avian flu); (2) achieving ways to manage or eliminate terrorism and terrorist attacks; (3) finding ways to combat global warming and related changes in the atmosphere before it is too late to keep the earth habitable for humans; and (4) developing positive, effective, ethical leaders who will have at heart the best interests of all their stakeholders, rather than primarily their own interests or those of groups to which they feel they owe allegiance. These four major problems, in common with virtually all problems facing the world, can be solved only through multidisciplinary thinking. They very well could form the foundations for problem-based majors and minors in university settings.

Consider, for example, the management of epidemics. Successful management of epidemics may well require biologists to understand the cellular mechanisms by which diseases cause harm, medical researchers to study potential cures, epidemiologists to understand how the diseases spread, psychologists to understand how people can be persuaded to behave in ways to minimize spread of the diseases, political scientists to weigh in on how to work with governments to adopt national and international policies that promote disease prevention, economists to study the costs of and funding mechanisms for managing epidemics, sociologists to understand how societies perceive health threats and react to them, historians to see whether we can learn from the past so as not to repeat mistakes, and perhaps others as well. Ideally, a single individual would have some background in each of the areas so that he or she could understand the issues from a variety of disciplinary standpoints rather than just his or her own. In the absence of such background, the individual is like the blind person feeling one part of an elephant but not understanding that it is an elephant he or she is feeling.

Similarly, the problem of confronting global warming is an interdisciplinary one. In his 2006 movie *An Inconvenient Truth*, Al Gore drew on a wide variety of integrated disciplines to discuss the problem of combating global warming, including film studies, meteorology, political science, psychology, economics, graphic design (in the creation of effective charts), and history.

Responding to the four major problems mentioned above—and indeed, almost any serious problem at a global or even national or local level—requires problem-based, interdisciplinary thinking. If this is the case, then is it time to think seriously about alternatives to the traditional undergraduate "major," which, in most cases, tends to be focused on just a single field of inquiry?

The current idea of a major (or minor) subject may have made more sense in a less complex and interconnected world, in which the perspectives and methods of one discipline could be applied to a fairly confined and narrow problem. In today's world, however, few problems of any significance are either confined or narrow. Rather, they aggressively cross boundaries that render the perspectives and methods of single disciplines incomplete and inefficacious. In effect, then, we are teaching undergraduates to think in ways that may prepare them less than adequately for the problems they will confront once they leave the college environment and face the outside world.

Of course, a liberal arts education teaches students course content from a variety of disciplines, with most of the general education occurring during the first two years of the college experience. The problem is that students learn to think in terms of silos of learning but do not learn how to connect them. It is rare that students are taught how to integrate what they learn in the various subjects they study, despite the fact that this integration is, arguably, the most important element in solving real-world problems.

The current system poses three problems. First, as noted, in the first two years of college, students learn to think in silos rather than in an interconnected, multidisciplinary way. A problem-based major or minor provides a way for students to see beyond such silos. Second, when they major (and possibly minor), students learn to think more deeply in one or perhaps, in the case of double majors, two of these silos, still without learning what is most important: how to integrate the knowledge across silos. A problem-based approach teaches such integration of knowledge. Third, students may not realize how limited their thinking is. Like the carpenter desperately looking for some task in which to use a hammer, the student may come to believe that his or her field provides the answers and that practitioners in other fields have less to offer in the solution of complex problems. A problem-based approach puts the problems before the tools.

As an example, the economist may come to view the world in terms of idealized economic models, paying too little attention to the psychological factors that may contribute to the solution of complex problems. Conversely, the psychologist may not fully appreciate the economic problems inhering, say, in the management of mental health care.

In order to prepare students for today's complex world, some schools engage them in problem-based learning, trying to hone the students' skills in applying what they learn to the kinds of problems they are likely to face. But more often than not, problem-based learning is employed within the silo of a single discipline rather than across multiple disciplines. The result may be a false sense of security created by approaching problems from a unidisciplinary perspective.

Many colleges and universities have started at least some interdisciplinary majors (and minors). For example, at Tufts University, there are majors such as community health, peace and justice studies, and international relations, and a minor in leadership. Such interdisciplinary majors are often popular with students but may be viewed by faculty with some suspicion because they are not conducted under the auspices of any one department. Moreover, even these majors may consist of sequences of isolated courses, and it is left to the student to draw the connections among the various disciplines and how they approach problems. That is asking a lot of students, since drawing such connections challenges even the faculty who teach the students.

Perhaps it is time to think not only about problem-based learning within disciplines but also about problem-based major and minor subjects. Clearly, the problem a student might study in such a major or minor—for example, the four significant problems identified above—is not the only problem a student will ever confront. But what a problem-based major or minor can do is teach students the knowledge and skills needed to think in an interdisciplinary way, so that such thinking is seen as a model for the kind of thinking needed to solve any serious problem. Such majors and minors need not replace traditional ones, but might supplement them as a viable option for many students.

An assumption of the kind of program I sketch is that learning approaches to the acquisition and utilization of knowledge are, in the long run, more important, at least to most people, than is the particular subject matter at a fixed point in time of any one discipline. For example, it is more important to acquire the perspectives of psychologists, economists, historians, chemists, musicians, or philosophers than it is to learn all of the knowledge that currently is taught within the context of a single-disciplinary undergraduate major.

I would argue that there are three reasons why approaches to and modes of thinking are of primary importance in undergraduate education. First, for those who truly want to specialize in great depth, they have the option of going to graduate or professional school and becoming deeply steeped in a discipline. Often, however, students specialize by virtue of the jobs they hold, not necessarily only by virtue of the formal education they receive. Second, no matter how much material one puts in a single silo, the absence of a connection to other silos is what will prevent the problem solver from being fully able to grasp the essence of a problem and how to solve it in a multidisciplinary way. Third, the knowledge one learns today often quickly becomes outdated or limited in terms of its applicability to real-world problems. For example, in my own field of psychology, there is precious little overlap between the precise content being taught in today's introductory courses and in the courses as they were taught in 1968, when I studied introductory psychology. Much of the specific knowledge one acquires will quickly become dated in any case.

How might one go about forming a problem-based major or minor? I suggest six principles for the construction of such courses of study. First, the problems constituting the majors or minors must be truly complex, engaging, and relevant to the concerns facing the world—yesterday, today, and tomorrow. Students will learn best if they are facing large, real problems in their full contexts rather than small, artificial, or context-limited problems. The problems can be expected to be different across time and space.

Second, the course of study must be truly interdisciplinary. It needs to recognize that complex problems are not solved in a unidisciplinary or even dual-disciplinary way. The program must include instruction that crosses a variety of disciplines, likely bridging aspects of the humanities, arts, social sciences, and natural sciences.

Third, the instruction must be truly transdisciplinary, bridging silos rather than merely teaching an amalgam of courses across different disciplines. In all likelihood, such instruction would involve faculty members working together across disciplinary boundaries to teach students to think across disciplines in solving problems. An advantage of this kind of teaching is that the instructors may learn just as much as, or more than, their students.

Fourth, assessment of performance must go beyond traditional disciplinary boundaries, involving projects and other forms of performance that encourage students to apply the full range of what they have learned to the solution of problems. Assessment of progress is likely to involve the efforts of faculty across and not just within disciplines.

Fifth, students must be shown the benefits of the new approach. Students and their parents are often among the more conservative elements in a college or university environment. They often want the traditional rewards of a college education, such as a better job or better admission prospects for future study. Changes in curriculum need to be linked, for them, to enhanced future outcomes. At the same time, employers and graduate/professional schools need to be sold on the idea that the problem-solving skills and attitudes acquired in a problem-based major or minor will be highly useful in the world. The students will learn better tools for thinking, and to useful ends.

Sixth, faculty members need to be rewarded for participating in such problem-based ventures. The form of reward will depend on the particular situation of the college or university. But if faculty are expected to take on more than they have done in the past, there needs to be, at the very least, recognition of service and, in all likelihood, a temporary reduction of other responsibilities as they construct new courses based on interdisciplinary, problem-based learning.

When I was at Tufts, we created a program along these lines. It is an interdisciplinary, problem-based leadership minor designed to enable all interested students to learn the skills and attitudes that are essential to positive, effective, ethical leadership. The minor consists of three tiers. The first tier involves courses across the disciplines that teach directly about leadership—theories of leadership, research on leadership, case studies of leadership, ethics, and so forth. The second tier involves courses in the entire range of the liberal arts that pertain to leadership but do not directly teach it. Students might learn about leadership through literature (the foibles of Othello or King Lear), philosophy (Plato's or Aristotle's views of leadership), the history of art (how great artists have depicted leaders at different times and what these depictions show about their views of leadership), political science (theories of leadership as it applies in different forms of government), history (studies of successful and failed leaders throughout history), psychology (interactions between persons and situations that lead to successful leadership), sociology (leadership of social movements), anthropology (conceptions of leadership in diverse cultures), the sciences (the role of good taste in problems in scientific leadership, the interaction between theory and data in scientific advances), and so forth. The third tier involves a substantial leadership experience and a reflective paper written about it that shows how what the student learned in the first two more academic tiers can be applied in the third, more practical tier. The paper is be interdisciplinary, cutting across the various disciplines that contribute to a comprehensive understanding of what constitutes good and effective leadership, from local to global levels. It provides students a chance to put together all they have learned in the various courses they have taken.

Some might argue that what constitutes good leadership—or addressing problems of epidemics or global warming—cannot be directly taught, as no one is sure of the answers. This is probably true. But it is the nature of real-world problems that they are ill-defined and ill-structured, and the sooner students learn to deal with such problems, the better. What one can do is to create the kinds of experiences that enable students to learn about leadership, global warming, or anything else.

In my own undergraduate course on the nature of leadership, I design a series of experiences for students that enable them to learn what it means to be a leader. As in most other courses, I use books, articles, and some lectures. But the course also contains more distinctive features. Every class except the first and the last features a leader from industry, finance, government, religion, education, consulting, or some other field who talks to students for a quarter of an hour about his or her own practice of leadership and then engages the students for the rest of the hour in a dialogue on how they can apply the individual's ideas to their own lives. In this way, students learn from diverse leaders in the everyday world how principles can be transformed into practices. This is the most popular part of the course, as it exposes students to the thoughts and actions of people confronting real problems in real jobs.

Almost all of the classes also include active learning about leadership. For example, in the first class of the semester, I would begin by reviewing the syllabus, after which an individual in the class would speak up, loudly and obnoxiously complaining about the syllabus and how unreasonable it was. Other students would be flabbergasted until I thanked and dismissed the individual, who was a shill I had planted in the classroom. I would then point out to the students that in leadership roles, the question is not whether someone will publicly challenge your authority but rather how you, as a leader, will deal with such challenges. I would then divide the class into three groups, each of which would simulate how it would handle public challenges of this kind. In another exercise, I taught in a blatantly incompetent way for five minutes. I then pointed out that leaders always encounter, sooner or later, incompetent team members who drag down their team but who the leader is unable, for one reason or another, to remove from the team. Three teams then had to simulate how they would handle an incompetent superior, coordinate, or subordinate member of their work team. In yet another class, students had to hire a team member (a dean), going through the steps of choosing the team member—from vision statement to job interview to the interview in which the team attempts to persuade the selected candidate to take the position.

Students were also actively involved in interviewing a leader and analyzing his or her leadership, and then evaluating their own leadership. They further analyzed, as a team, the leadership of a well-known leader. Groups selected leaders as diverse as Bill Clinton, Bill Gates, and Kenneth Lay.

How to create positive leaders is only one example of the kinds of problems students might confront in a problem-based major or minor. Other topics, such as how to deal with epidemics or other catastrophes, how to deal with global warming, or how to deal with human conflicts, also form bases for such academic programs. In the end, problems are interrelated. For example, there are many elements of crises that are the same, regardless of their particular content—whether it is the battle against an epidemic, global warming, terrorism, or corruption in leadership. Problem-based major and minor subjects will enable students to learn the wide variety of knowledge, skills, perspectives, and attitudes needed to solve the wide variety of problems they will face in their lives. Most importantly, students will learn to think across rather than merely within silos—to see problems in their full complexity rather than in the limited ways any single discipline can bring to bear.

One question that arises is how transdisciplinary learning best is done—residentially, online, or through some combination of the two. Let us consider that question next.

The Roles of Residential and Online Learning

Why go to class when you can do your entire education online, possibly at a fraction of the cost of learning on a bricks-and-mortar campus? This question is challenging students and universities alike as online learning increases its already substantial footprint. What are some of the advantages and disadvantages of online learning?

Online education has some distinct advantages. First, you can attend online classes and study anywhere. This is particularly important in a state like Wyoming, where the population centers tend to be small and the distances large. Second, online education provides great flexibility with regard to when you study. You can study during the day or night, wearing a suit, pajamas, or, for that matter, nothing at all! Third, you can often save money through online courses because they reduce the costs associated with construction and maintenance of bricks-and-mortar campuses.

There are also some disadvantages to online study. First, course-completion rates are lower; for free massive open online courses (MOOCs), they often are less than 10 percent. Second, online courses, if they have very large numbers of students, sometimes permit exclusively multiple-choice or short-answer exams and so do not assess learning in more meaningful ways. In MOOCs, grading sometimes ends up being done by other students. In smaller-enrollment courses, grading is usually not an issue. Third, online courses seem to work best for students who have reasonably good preparation for the subject matter; they work less well for students who are not as well prepared. Standard online courses that are integral parts of degree programs seem at the present time to be more effective, on average, than are MOOCs.

I do not believe that online education is likely to completely replace bricks-and-mortar education, at least in the foreseeable future. There are benefits to being on campus that online education simply cannot match.

First, the main goal of a college education, as I have said before, is to instill ethical-leadership skills. The development of these skills is just not likely to be optimized through online instruction. You learn active concerned-citizenship and ethical-leadership skills through interaction with others and through watching firsthand what they—and you—do right and wrong.

Second, a major goal of college is to establish lifelong networks of colleagues and friends. Especially in a small state like Wyoming, where personal connections are so close, knowing people who can later be helpful to you is much more likely to occur in person than online. Many of us find that the networks we establish through personal and professional relationships in college last us a lifetime.

Third, college is one of the best places to develop high-level social, practical, and emotional-intelligence skills, as well as the most important skills of all—those of learning to learn. One learns what works with other people and what doesn't; what gets a job done and what doesn't; and how people react—often in surprising ways—to things we say and do. One also learns how to learn across a lifetime. Online instruction does not really allow us to fully learn the kinds of skills that only face-to-face interactions develop.

Fourth, much of what we learn in college is through extracurricular activities—athletics, student government, band, art, journalism, service projects, fraternities and sororities, and the like. These activities do not lend themselves as well to Internet-based instruction.

Finally, most college students benefit from the close one-on-one mentorship they can have in bricks-and-mortar campuses with advisers, counselors, teachers, and more advanced students. Such relationships often form spontaneously but can change the way in which we live our lives, in college and afterward. You can have an online adviser, but the relationship is, literally, remote.

In conclusion, online learning provides a valuable supplement to the learning one can attain in a bricks-and-mortar college. For students who cannot come to a college campus because of distance, family ties, job responsibilities, and the like, online learning is invaluable. But for other students, an on-campus experience, perhaps including some online courses, will provide the optimal college education to last a lifetime. There is no one solution that works for everyone.

My proposal for problem-based learning is not without challenges. Colleges and universities, and the stakeholders within them, are used to traditional majors and minors, and have based their instruction for many years on this traditional system. Problem-based study would cause some dislocation for those used to the traditional system. But I view problem-based majors and minors as a supplement to traditional offerings, rather than a replacement. Undoubtedly, most students would continue to major in traditional fields of study, which have served as useful bases for undergraduate education in the past and will continue to do so in the future. Students should have the option of choosing what they want to learn, and teachers the option of choosing what they want to teach.

The kind of system proposed here is not altogether new. Many colleges already have problem-based offerings. Tufts University is one. Wheaton College in Norton, Massachusetts, is another. At Wheaton, there is a program that enables students to explore different areas of knowledge and different approaches to problems in an integrated way. At Hollins University, one can study a concept such as human freedom from multidisciplinary standpoints, including philosophy, psychology, sociology, and political science. At the University of Virginia, there are multidisciplinary majors such as medical ethics. So the seeds of the kind of system described here already exist.

Such a system would probably have to be phased in over a period of years, but it would not replace more traditional offerings. Phasing it in would have one great advantage: it would prepare students to think in an interdisciplinary way so that when they are confronted with the problems of tomorrow, they start with the problem rather than with their toolbox, and then work with others to choose the set of toolboxes that will best address the problem at hand.

Once interdisciplinary or any other form of learning is well integrated into the curriculum, one has to plan how to assess it. When I was in seventh grade, I had a social-studies teacher, Mr. Ast, who was a master of transdisciplinary teaching and learning in the classroom but who then proceeded to give tests that had nothing to do with the way the classroom was run. The tests were traditional memorize-the-facts tests. Students quickly learned that the rewards were not what they appeared to be in the classroom instruction. So let's consider in the next chapter how assessment can be integrated with modern modes of instruction.

8

Assessing Student Learning

Decisions about how college administrators measure, report, and respond to data on student learning have substantial repercussions for how faculty members teach, how they organize their classes, and how they are perceived by the broader public. Yet too often faculty members base their selection of assessment instruments and methods on pragmatic reasons of cost, reputation, ease of administration, and tradition, while ignoring critical issues of institutional purpose, mission, and identity. Both sets of considerations need to be taken into account.

In measuring collegiate learning, it is important to focus first and foremost on the specific qualities the college or university wishes to measure and then secondarily on assessment instruments and methods—not the other way around. In other words, it is essential to identify the learning outcomes that are valued by the institution before selecting a tool to

This chapter draws and expands on Sternberg, Penn, and Hawkins et al. 2011.

assess learning. Students, their parents, and donors of scholarships spend enormous amounts of money on college education, and they are entitled to institutional accountability for learning outcomes. Yet, regrettably, assessment decisions are frequently made without serious consideration of what the various assessment methods actually measure. All assessments, even those presented as atheoretical, have an underlying theory of skills measured. It is important to bring these theories out into the open rather than to leave them obscured.

The tendency to put the cart before the horse has plagued educational assessment since the early IQ tests (Sternberg 1990). As a result, many widely used tests do not measure all the characteristics their adopters may expect an intelligence test to measure—the creative or practical thinking included in my theory of successful intelligence (Sternberg 1997a), for example, or the musical, interpersonal, or naturalist intelligence included in Howard Gardner's (2011) theory of multiple intelligences. For assessment to be most effective, it must be based on a clear conception of what is to be assessed.

The goal here is not to survey trends but rather to examine the available options for assessing student learning at the college level as well as the psychological theories of learning and achievement that underlie them. In other words, we seek to understand better what we are "eating" when we choose one of these options. The examination is organized according to the assessment taxonomy developed by Peggy Maki (2010), which groups assessment methods into four categories: (1) standardized instruments and inventories, (2) indirect methods that focus on students' perceptions of learning and engagement, (3) authentic performance-based methods, such as portfolios, and (4) locally designed tests and inventories.

Standardized Instruments and Inventories

The first option is to use a standardized test. The main ones at this time are the Collegiate Learning Assessment (CLA), the ETS Proficiency Profile (ETS-PP, formerly the MAPP), and the Collegiate Assessment of Academic Proficiency (CAAP). These measures have the strengths of standardized tests—reputations of established publishers, norms, and validation information. They also have the weaknesses of standardized tests, in that they are not tailored to individual programs but rather are one-size-fits-all. Although there are many standardized tests available, these three have received particular attention as a result of their inclusion in the Voluntary System of Accountability (VSA), which provides information on the undergraduate experience (see http://www.voluntarysystem.org/).

The CLA was created with the intention of measuring critical-thinking skills in an authentic way. The assessment presents what are supposed to be realistic problems. Students are then expected to analyze these complex problems and solve them in ways that allow assessment of their abilities to think critically and write cogently. The ETS-PP measures skills in critical thinking, reading, writing, and mathematics in the context of the humanities, social sciences, and natural sciences. The CAAP measures reading, writing, mathematics, science, and critical thinking.

Tests such as the CAAP are similar in spirit to tests like the ACT (from the same publisher) and the SAT. What do they measure? As an example, "SAT" was once an acronym for "Scholastic Aptitude Test" but in recent years has been used as an independent term in which the letters do not stand for anything. Loosely, tests such as the SAT, ACT, CLA, and CAAP are based on a notion of intelligence as involving, largely, analytical or critical thinking applied to a knowledge base. Test publishers are not eager to make the association, but the roots of these kinds of tests can be traced back to the Binet-Simon Intelligence Scales, which were first presented in 1905 as measures of the ability to succeed in school (see Binet and Simon 1916). These tests measure verbal, quantitative, and spatial reasoning skills as well as one's level of general information.

Among some educators, these tests have acquired a dubious reputation in part because they are (incorrectly) believed to measure fixed innate traits and in part because they show somewhat notable ethnic-group disparities (as would the other standardized tests considered in this section, since they measure roughly the same constructs). Although the cosmetic appearance of such tests has changed somewhat over the years, the constructs measured have not. The tests largely measure so-called general ability, or g, and all tests of this kind correlate very highly with one another. For example, in one study, correlations of the CLA with the SAT had a median of 0.50 when the student was used as the unit of analysis and a total correlation of 0.88 when the college was used as the unit of analysis (Klein et al. 2009). These correlations indicate that whatever it is that the CLA measures, it is similar to what the SAT measures.

Tests such as the CLA, ETS-PP, and CAAP are highly correlated with the SAT and ACT (Klein et al. 2009). Data collected through the VSA also show that the CLA, ETS-PP, and CAAP are very highly correlated with each other. So in the end, it does not matter greatly which test is used, because they all measure roughly the same thing: aspects of general intelligence. Where the choice of test may matter, however, is in comparing results from different colleges. The placement of a given college relative to others will depend on which schools used the same assessment.

Underlying all these tests is the assumption that the same learning outcomes are relevant, regardless of what the student has studied in college. The tests measure the same outcomes for engineers as for artists.

One major advantage of tests such as the CLA or CAAP is that they are standardized. This means that it is possible to compare the performance of one's own students to that of other students; the tests provide a uniform basis of assessment for all students. And because the CLA also contains items that require the application of critical-thinking skills to authentic problems, the items presented to students are somewhat more engaging than those in other, more typical standardized tests.

Standardized tests are often pitched as measuring the "value added" by a college education, but whether they actually do this, and whether they do it in an appropriate way, is debatable. The question an administrator has to ask is whether this model of assessment is appropriate for college seniors who are going out into the world—perhaps to further schooling, perhaps to jobs. The model of measurement seems appropriate for assessing the analytical aspect of undergraduate education, but is it as appropriate for assessing other skills that may matter more later in life—expertise in one's major, creative skills, practical skills, wisdom-based skills, motivation, conscientiousness, or passion for a particular career?

The abilities demonstrated by a highly successful music major, or engineering major, or even liberal-arts student may not be reflected on a test like the CLA, ETS-PP, or CAAP. The risk is that, while such a system might have been useful in predicting first-year grades in college from the SAT or ACT, this model of measurement may be less useful later in predicting from tests such as the CLA, ETS-PP, or CAAP. For those students who go into careers where verbal reasoning is of only secondary or even tertiary importance, this model of measurement may seem to be lacking. Overemphasis on standardized measures such as the CLA, ETS-PP, and CAAP risks focusing our institutions on a narrow set of analytical and written communication skills that, while important, represent only a small subset of the skills and abilities we need to be developing in our students to prepare them fully for later life.

Indirect Measures and Engagement Measures

The second option for gathering data on student achievement is to use an indirect measure, such as a student survey, focus group, or exit interview. One indirect measure that has received much attention in recent years—and is included in the VSA—is the National Survey of Student Engagement (NSSE), which is intended to assess the extent to which students are engaged in the college experience. Although "engagement" is not a well-defined term, it generally refers to how much a student is involved with or even immersed in the college experience, including both academic and nonacademic components.

Although indirect measures are not explicitly theory-based, they seem to derive from motivational rather than ability-based theories. On this view, a student is successful in college to the extent that he or she is involved in the life of the college, both academically and nonacademically. Motivation is not totally unrelated to abilities, however. A typical Japanese view of ability is that it is, in fact, motivational at its core, and some psychologists studying intelligence, such as Carol Dweck (2007), have emphasized the importance of motivational elements underlying conceptions of intelligence, such as whether or not it is modifiable through hard work. In a similar vein, John Cacioppo and Richard Petty (1982) have emphasized the importance of the "need for cognition," or the impetus to think and learn.

There are volumes of data on NSSE, so it is possible to compare data from one's own college to data from other colleges. It is also possible to measure students' level of involvement in college. Many conventional types of measures are based on a model in which all that seems to matter are the academic aspects of a student's career. Academics are not the major focus of all students, however, and a measure based on a motivational model will recognize outstanding efforts in a wide variety of areas that may matter to college students.

NSSE is a typical rather than maximal performance measure. In other words, it measures a person's performance in a situation that does not require one to put forth one's best effort. This situation presents a possible challenge to interpreting NSSE data. Ability tests are usually maximal performance measures: they measure how well one does when working as hard as possible. In contrast, personality tests are usually typical performance measures: the person indicates an answer, often on a Likert-type scale (as in a rating from 1 to 5). Such typical performance measures are "fakable" in that one can give an answer that one believes the examiner wants to hear, whether or not the answer truly characterizes one's own thoughts or behaviors.

NSSE is based on a model of measurement that values engagement, broadly defined, which presents a larger problem than faking. Students have very different career trajectories, both during and after college. One student may have been extremely engaged, but in only one activity—say, chorus. Another may have been extremely engaged in a project emanating from his or her studies. Yet another may have done lots of things but may not really have any core knowledge about an academic discipline. Overemphasis on indirect measures like NSSE risks rewarding students and institutions that are very broad but not necessarily very deep in their engagement, and it can inadvertently encourage manipulation of scores for the sake of appearances. In addition, indirect measures like NSSE do not directly measure any of the creative, critical, practical, or wisdom-based skills that are important outcomes of a college education. Instead, they provide only a glimpse of students' own perceptions of their level of performance—perceptions that may or may not be veridical.

Portfolios and Other Performance-Based Assessments

The third option for measuring student learning is to use portfolios or other performance-based assessments. This option best represents the ACCEL mission, because it best allows students to express their individuality and their potential active concerned-citizenship and ethical-leadership skills. Such skills are simply not going to come out in a standardized test or even a measure of engagement. Unlike the options described above, performance measures and portfolios—including electronic portfolios—do not measure the same outcomes for all students assessed. They measure the skills most relevant to each individual. The idea here is that students have studied different things, have pursued individual trajectories, and hence have different strengths and weaknesses after their college studies. Each portfolio is thus an idiosyncratic product, allowing a student to highlight his or her strengths and, perhaps inadvertently, weaknesses.

Because portfolios allow students to essentially construct their own assessments, they measure motivational elements as well as many of the broad cognitive skills in my (Sternberg 2003b) and Gardner's (2011) cognitive theories. Portfolios thus combine aspects of the first and second options discussed above, and theoretically speaking, they are more broad-based than either. For example, the theory of "successful intelligence" (Sternberg 1997a), as described earlier, holds that people are successfully intelligent to the extent that they recognize and capitalize on strengths at the same time as they acknowledge and correct or compensate for weaknesses. This requires creativity in generating new ideas, analytical ability in ascertaining whether the new ideas are good ones, practicality in implementing the ideas and persuading others of their value, and wisdom in ensuring that the ideas help achieve a common good over the short and long terms through the infusion of positive ethical values. Portfolio measurements have the potential to assess such a broad range of skills.

Although the products may be entirely different across students, it is still possible to create rubrics for scoring portfolios. The theory of successful intelligence would suggest that the portfolios be scored, at the very least, in terms of four attributes: creative thinking, analytical thinking, practical thinking, and wisdom-based thinking. Through its Valid Assessment of Learning in Undergraduate Education (VALUE) project, the Association of American Colleges and Universities (AAC&U) has provided fifteen rubrics that measure diverse aspects of performance, including ones that are similar or identical to what I have referred to as creative, analytical, practical, and wise thinking (see http://www.aacu.org/value). For example, acquiring competencies, taking risks, solving problems, embracing contradictions, and thinking innovatively, as well as connecting, synthesizing, and transforming, can all be assessed using the VALUE rubric for creative thinking.

A major advantage of portfolios is that they allow students to highlight their own idiosyncratic strengths and to demonstrate their own understanding of what they have accomplished. A student who has done one or more major science or engineering projects, or who has composed a sonata, or who has written significant poetry or journalistic works will have an opportunity to demonstrate his or her achievements in a way that would not be possible through a conventional standardized test.

A drawback to portfolios is that they take a great deal of time to create, score, and code into a database. Moreover, some courses of study may lend themselves better to the assessments than others. A student majoring in English or philosophy may have a number of essays, papers, creative pieces, or other items that fit naturally into a portfolio. By contrast, a student majoring in engineering or agriculture may have many artifacts—such as models, seeds, or animals—that would be challenging to include in a paper-based or electronic portfolio. There may even be differences within a given broad field. Civil engineers may have designed bridges or tunnels, whereas chemical engineers may have comparable knowledge bases but fewer physical products to show for their studies. In brief, the measures may conflate opportunity to create products with quality of learning in the college years. Unless portfolios are carefully designed to incorporate a wide range of paper-based and non-paper-based achievements, overemphasis on portfolio measurement risks limiting the skills and abilities we emphasize in our institutions. Further, if instructors do not give students opportunities to create materials that can go into the portfolios, student portfolios may look thin—not because the students lack value-added skills but rather because they were not given the opportunity to create products that would fit nicely into a portfolio.

Finally, portfolios can be very challenging to score, and scoring them requires considerable expertise. Although there are rubrics available, it is not clear that they capture all or even most of the elements that make for a distinguished portfolio, especially because those elements may differ from one portfolio to another. Measurement will probably not be as reliable as that obtained from a standardized test such as the CLA or CAAP.

Locally Designed Tests and Inventories

The fourth option for measuring student learning is to use locally designed tests and inventories. Colleges and universities may choose not to use any of the standardized assessments and to create their own assessments instead. Such assessments may be constant across the entire institution, or they may vary from one department or program to another.

With local assessments, there are potentially as many underlying theories of skills as there are instructors who create the assessments. The strength in this is that the assessments are not narrowly circumscribed by a particular theory. The weakness is that it may not be clear what the assessments are actually measuring, at least in psychological terms.

The most obvious advantage of locally designed assessments is their flexibility, which enables them to meet the perceived needs of the academic unit. It is not clear that there is any one measurement that is relevant across all disciplines, and professors in different institutions have different goals for their students and serve different student populations. In one university, for example, the application of knowledge to the real world may be viewed as very important; in another, it may be viewed as strictly optional. Even within specific programs, faculty may have differing opinions on what is important to assess. Locally designed assessments can reflect all the different emphases of colleges, units, or programs, and if faculty members' diverse perspectives are incorporated during the process of creating the assessments, this approach can increase faculty engagement in assessment.

One significant disadvantage of these "homemade" assessments is their lack of standardization, which makes it difficult to compare results across academic units and to establish when "good enough" is "good enough." Another potential drawback is that academic units may not enforce rigorous standards for the assessments or for their scoring, either because of a lack of expertise in measurement and assessment or because of a lack of resources to fully support this complex work. Strong leadership from the unit head is essential for ensuring the quality of locally developed assessments, but this too can be problematic if the unit head is uninterested or if there has been significant turnover in the unit-head position. Although locally developed measures allow for the incorporation of skills and abilities that are emphasized in each institution's mission, an overemphasis on them risks creating the perception of sidestepping full accountability.

Which Assessment Method to Choose?

There is no single "best" approach to student-learning assessment. All the methods considered here have strengths and weaknesses. If the goal is to measure an institution's success in educating college seniors, then ideally several different methods would be used. However, it is far more difficult to measure an individual student's learning or the "value added" by college education for an individual student; no currently available assessment method even comes close to achieving either of these goals. But ultimately, the first question to ask is not which measure to use but rather what is to be measured. Since no college or university has the time or resources to measure all possible learning outcomes, a selection must be made. Overall, the individualized portfolio approach best represents the ACCEL mission.

If a measure based largely on somewhat narrow cognitive theory is required, then one of the standardized assessments would be the best choice. If a motivationally based measure is needed, then a typical-performance assessment of engagement would be best. If a measure representing a mix of broad cognitive and motivational factors is appropriate, then portfolio assessments would be best. Locally designed assessments vary widely, and what they measure depends on how they are constructed.

At first, it may appear to be a sad state of affairs that the existing measures are so limited in what they can accomplish. But the outcomes of a college education are multifarious, and it is unlikely that there will ever be one perfect measure—because of the diversity of students as well as the diversity of skills, abilities, and disciplines. As is always true in measurement, using several different methods of assessment can compensate for the inadequacies of each. Using a variety of methods almost always helps to reduce error of measurement and, thus, to focus on the constructs of greatest interest. An overemphasis on any one method risks distorting the assessment process itself, because no single measure can capture all the learning outcomes of a college education.

Unfortunately, college learning assessment has become a bit like ability assessment—the cart has come before the horse. College administrators often pay more attention to the various measures than to the more fundamental question of what qualities they want to assess by using the measures. If there is a lesson to be learned from over a century of ability measurement, it is that we need first to decide what we want to measure, and only then to select among existing measures or create new ones. It is not very reassuring that some tests are now named by acronyms that stand for nothing; the danger is that no one knows quite what the tests measure—and worse, no one cares. This is the legacy of a history of measurement that is atheoretical and, hence, unclear in its intellectual grounding. One may argue that the advantage of an atheoretical test is that it does not favor any particular point of view, but in the end, tests always favor some point of view, whether or not their creators acknowledge it. Test developers may not specify the theory behind their tests, but implicitly there always is one (or more).

Although cost is not inherent to any assessment method, which is why I do not discuss the issue above, any selection of measures will inevitably involve cost-benefit considerations. Portfolio measures are almost certainly the most expensive to design, administer, score, and process, simply because of the quantity of information they produce and the need to evaluate it subjectively. Locally designed measures are typically the least expensive, and the cost of standardized testing falls somewhere in between. The ratio of cost to benefit is something each institution has to compute for itself, depending in large part on how highly it values what is measured by a given assessment method.

In the absence of a perfect measure, some might wonder whether it is worthwhile even to assess college learning at all. I would argue that it most certainly is. It is true that no test given at any institution is ever perfect. Psychological and educational measures are, by their very nature, flawed and imprecise. However, college administrators owe it to themselves, and certainly to their students, to assess the value of the education they provide. Imperfect though they are, the existing methods described above are nonetheless useful ways of conducting such assessments.

Assessments help instructors and administrators weigh who has the academic heft to continue with a university education and who does not. Ultimately, such a consideration leads to issues of who will be retained and who will be graduated. I consider these questions in the next chapter.

9

Retention and Graduation

One of the most serious problems facing colleges and universities today is that many students leave before finishing their studies. When students drop out, it is bad for them because they lose huge future career and income potential; bad for the institution they leave because of lost reputation, revenue, and opportunity to make a difference in the students' lives; and bad for society because of the need for an educated workforce that is able to compete in the global marketplace.

Risk Factors for Dropout

Although there are many reasons students drop out, twelve research-validated risk factors, often in various combinations, help account for why most students drop out. These risk factors apply at a wide variety of institutions of higher education. Here are the risk factors and how to mitigate them (Sternberg 2013c).

1. *Uneven formal academic knowledge and skills.* The most obvious and frequently addressed issue behind dropout is academic background. At many institutions, large numbers of students enter with spotty academic backgrounds, especially in science and mathematics (STEM) disciplines and in writing. Institutions of higher learning need counselors and tutors who will remediate deficiencies but also enrich areas of strength. To pinpoint deficiencies and ensure proper placement, institutions need to move toward tests measuring specific skills and content knowledge and away from reliance on general aptitude tests, which are not very helpful in identifying specific strengths and deficiencies in knowledge and skills. Tests of general academic aptitudes account, at most, for only 25 percent of the variation in academic success in college. It therefore is a mistake to rely on them heavily for placement (or even admissions) decisions in college. In work my collaborators and I did while I was at Yale University and then at Tufts University, studying diverse students around the country, we found that tests of broader aptitudes (creative and practical as well as analytical) could as much as double prediction of first-year college success (Sternberg 2010a).

Neal Schmitt and his colleagues at Michigan State University have found that biographical data significantly enhance prediction of college success (Schmitt et al. 2007). If colleges rely too heavily on general academic aptitude scores in making placement decisions, they risk creating self-fulfilling prophecies dooming students to lesser success.

2. *Lack of informal knowledge about being a college student.* In any new environment, whether an academic environment or a work environment, one needs to acquire "tacit" knowledge—the informal and often unspoken keys for achieving success in that environment. For example, which courses and advisers should one gravitate toward or avoid? Which kinds of student activities become unrewarding time sinks that interfere with studying? How does one decide who to hang out with? How does one study for a multiple-choice versus an essay test? In research on college students, Wendy Williams and I found that acquiring informal knowledge—"learning the ropes"—is at least as important for success in college as learning specific formal content knowledge. Rick Wagner and I found that those with high academic abilities are not necessarily the ones with high levels of informal knowledge, and vice versa (see Sternberg et al. 2000). Put another way,

academic skills are no guarantee of common sense. Unfortunately, in many cases, the informal knowledge with which one enters college from high school actually transfers negatively to the college environment: for example, a student may believe that the meager amount of studying he did in high school will be adequate in college, when in fact it is not.

3. *Inadequate development of self-regulation skills.* In high school, one often has a support network to help regulate one's time and energy. Most important for many students is close supervision by parents or concerned individuals at one's high school. In college, students often find themselves largely "on their own" for the first time in their lives. Some are able to channel their newly found freedom effectively, but others are not. They may spend too much time on extracurricular activities and too little time on studying, or they simply may use their study time ineffectively. Edward Deci and Richard Ryan (2012) have found that those who lack an autonomous style of self-regulation—who have trouble managing themselves independently—are at risk for lack of success in a number of different kinds of environments. Moreover, Teresa Amabile (1996) has found that students and others who have been pushed hard by their parents, teachers, or employers, and who have become used to extrinsic rewards for success, may have trouble motivating themselves intrinsically when immediate extrinsic rewards (parental approval, reward money, extra praise) are no longer readily available. A sufficient intervention should include a detailed analysis of how students spend (and do not spend) their time in order to determine whether their self-regulation is adequate to their needs as a college student. As an example, a tendency toward procrastination can lead students to underperform simply because they did not allow themselves enough time to adequately carry out the assignments at hand.

4. *Self-efficacy beliefs.* Some students come to college uncertain as to whether they have the ability to succeed in their college work. Other students come expecting to succeed and then receive one or more low marks on college assignments or tests that lead them to question whether they are able to compete after all. As their self-efficacy fails, their drive to succeed in college goes with it. Studies by Albert Bandura (1997) and his colleagues at Stanford University have found that self-efficacy is one of the best positive predictors of success in any working environment. Counselors thus need to ensure that students have not only the knowledge and skills to succeed

but also a belief in their own potential to succeed. The students need to further understand that many of their peers who have an initial failure end up successful in their fields.

In my own case, as noted earlier, I ignominiously failed my first psychology test freshman year; nevertheless, thirty-five years later I served as president of the American Psychological Association. The resilience to get beyond disappointing setbacks is key not only in college but also in work and in life in general. In my long career as a psychology professor, dean, and provost, I have noticed that many of my graduate-school classmates and later colleagues who never achieved the success for which they hoped lacked not the ability to achieve but rather the resilience to believe in their ability to succeed in the face of disappointing setbacks.

5. *A mindset believing in fixed rather than flexible abilities.* Carol Dweck (2007) of Stanford University has found that students (and others) typically have one of two mindsets—or folk conceptions—regarding their abilities. What she calls "entity theorists" believe that abilities are largely fixed; on this view, when a student makes a mistake, he or she shows a lack of abilities that is potentially very embarrassing. What Dweck calls "incremental theorists," in contrast, believe that abilities are modifiable and flexible and that making mistakes is useful because it helps one to learn and, in general, to grow. Dweck has found that although both kinds of students perform roughly equally well in easy or modestly difficult courses, incremental theorists excel in challenging courses because they are unafraid of extending their skills and making mistakes along the way. Students therefore need to understand that abilities are modifiable, that people learn through their mistakes, and that difficult but manageable challenges are good because they enable one to move ahead in one's learning.

6. *Inability to delay gratification.* In many college courses, students do not find out until the end whether they have achieved their hoped-for level of success. And they do not find out for four or even more years whether they will indeed get the diploma they hope for. Often, success in a particular course or in college seems far off, whereas there are many gratifications to be had instantly, especially in the social domain.

Some students just cannot wait that long. Walter Mischel (2014) performed experiments with young children on their ability to delay gratification—to wait for a larger reward instead of receiving an immediate smaller reward. He found that those individuals who were able to delay gratification performed better academically, many years later when they were of college age, than did children who were unable to delay gratification. In other words, parents and teachers need to work with students to help them realize that many of the best rewards in life are not immediate.

7. *Impaired ethical judgment.* Many students today do not have the ethical judgment that we who teach in institutions of higher learning take for granted. In my own work on ethical reasoning (Sternberg 2010b), as mentioned earlier, I have found that many of today's students do not view behaviors such as cheating on tests or plagiarizing papers even to be ethical issues. For many students, it just has become too easy to take the low road, and given the temptation, they do so. They get caught, with disastrous results for their success and sometimes longevity in college. It therefore is essential that students learn, as soon as they arrive in college, the ethical expectations of the institution. It should not be assumed that they have been taught, or at least have learned, these expectations.

8. *Disengagement from the university environment.* For many students, a precursor to dropping out is a progressive disengagement from, or failure ever to become engaged in, the university environment. The students simply never connect with, or become disconnected from, the environment, and hence become more and more psychologically distant and even alienated from it. Disengagement, or a failure to engage in the first place, may result from what the French sociologist Emile Durkheim and later the Harvard sociologist David Reisman (1963) referred to as anomie, or a breakdown in the social bonds between the individual and the community. Anomie can be a particular challenge for students whose sociocultural background is far removed from that of many others in the college or university. When anomie develops, students may become more and more withdrawn until they literally withdraw from the college or university. Students should be strongly urged to actively engage in at least one extracurricular activity in order to enhance engagement with the university at large. Advisers also need to try to make sure that students stay "connected" and do not start to withdraw from the life of the university.

9. *Lack of interest in courses.* When students enter college, they are often eager to get on with their required courses. They may load up on distribution requirements or other courses that they need to get out of their way. But Richard Light (personal communication) of Harvard University has found

that one of the best predictors of academic adjustment is taking at least one course during the freshman year solely because it is interesting, regardless of whether it is required. Students who load up too much on courses that are required but that do not interest them are at greater risk of dropping out simply because they are bored and find no relief.

10. *Issues in academic trajectory.* Issues in academic trajectory include either an uncertain trajectory or a trajectory that is ill-matched to one's interests or skills. Paul Pintrich (2000) argued that students are likely to perform at a higher level when they feel they have some kind of academic "destination" in mind—or at least when they feel that what they are doing will lead to such a trajectory. In some cases, students simply made a poor choice, perhaps because their interests do not match their skills, or perhaps because parents or other authority figures pushed them in a direction that does not well fit them.

11. *Psychological issues.* Psychological issues include a diverse range of challenges, such as substance-abuse problems, interpersonal problems with important others, and untreated or nonaccommodated psychological problems, such as learning disabilities, attentional/hyperactivity disorders, autism-spectrum disorders, and so forth. Students entering with such problems should immediately be referred to appropriate counselors and programs. Appropriate programs work, but waiting can be fatal.

12. *Financial concerns.* I have saved for last the most challenging of the risk factors for nonretention, namely, financial concerns or anxieties about financial concerns. In the end, some students drop out just because they cannot make college work for themselves financially. The financial needs of students make it imperative that colleges and universities calculate aid needs correctly. Although we know that student debt is a major problem in our society, students who graduate from college will earn, on average, a million dollars more than students who do not graduate. Sometimes avoiding debt is penny-wise but pound-foolish.

Project DEEP

Project DEEP (Documenting Effective Educational Practice) was undertaken by the NSSE (National Survey of Student Engagement) Institute to try to better understand the educational practices that would lead to success in college and thereby to enhanced retention and graduation. The project is probably the most exhaustive study to date seeking to understand factors leading to success or failure among students advancing through their college education. The resulting book (Kuh et al. 2010) summarizes much of what was learned through the extensive project, which is based in part on a study of twenty high-performing colleges and universities.

It is impossible to adequately summarize such an extensive study in a short review. Here are examples, however, of key findings (Chickering and Kuh 2005). Six conditions that matter to student success are:

1. "Living" Mission and "Lived" Educational Philosophy
2. Unshakeable Focus on Student Learning
3. Environments Adapted for Educational Enrichment
4. Clear Pathways to Student Success
5. Improvement-Oriented Ethos
6. Shared Responsibility for Educational Quality and Student Success (Chickering and Kuh 2005, 1)

The real strength of the whole of Project DEEP is the focus on what can and should be done to improve student success. A problem in some past research has been an excessive focus on generalities, such as "Be student-centered." Project DEEP not only gets quite specific but addresses different practice professionals, such as top-level administrators, student-affairs professionals, and professors.

LASSO

When I was at Oklahoma State University, in pursuit of an ACCEL mission, we attempted to systematically address the problem of dropping out, especially after the first year of college, and to devise solutions that would keep students on track to earn their degrees. We created a new center—the Learning and Student Success Opportunity (LASSO) Center—which targets students who are at risk for dropping out. All students are eligible for LASSO services, although our particular focus was on students in the first year, when the risk of nonretention is greatest.

Students are identified for LASSO services in one of several ways: self-referral, referral by a professor (easily done through electronic means), or automatic referral through low GPA, uncertainty about career trajectory, or an at-risk admissions profile. OSU also has other resources, such as a Mathematics Learning Success Center, a Writing Center, and college-based student-success centers, which seek to help students reach their maximum potential. Such research-based efforts can help large numbers of students stay in college who might otherwise drop out.

For the most part, colleges do and should try to retain students rather than usher them out. But there truly are some students who are better counseled out. It may be that college is not, in the end, a good match for them, or that their particular college does not offer them the academic or extracurricular programs they need in order to be a good fit. In my "theory of successful intelligence" (Sternberg 1997a), I argue that people who are successfully intelligent in their lives often first try to adapt to the environments in which they find themselves; that failing, they may try to shape the environments better to meet their needs; but if that fails as well, they may find that their best option is to select another environment that is a better fit to their interests, skills, values, or needs. In the end, whatever our goals as an institution of higher learning, we ought always to be serving the students who entrust their academic careers to us.

Student retention, of course, is a function not only of what occurs in the classroom but also of what occurs in the entirety of students' lives. The Project DEEP analysis shows that the entire college context, not just the context of the classroom, can lead to either better or worse student retention. One factor that can tilt either way is college athletics, which are considered in the next chapter.

10

The Role of Athletics

Never a varsity or even junior varsity athlete, I have no vested interest whatsoever in athletics. In the tradition of Groucho Marx, I would have refused to be a member of any serious team that would have been willing to have me on it. That said, I've come to view college athletics as playing an important, perhaps even necessary, role in a well-rounded college education.

Collegiate athletics truly can be a ball of gold, in the sense of Stephen Crane. As discussed below, done right, athletics develop active concerned-citizenship and ethical-leadership skills such as teamwork, good sportsmanship, knowing how to win and lose battles, and a sense of responsibility toward not just teammates but also fans and sponsors. But done poorly, athletics can undermine and even destroy the values underlying the ACCEL university.

True, there are few things that college and university faculty and business officers complain about more than college athletics (though parking may be one). As a faculty member, I was at the front of that grievance line.

I saw all the downsides: the time that athletics take away from academics, a sense of entitlement on the part of some athletes, the cost of constructing and maintaining facilities, and the doubt about what athletics had to do with college education anyway. With budget shortfalls and declining revenues, faculty members and others may especially resent the resources they see as going into college athletics.

As an administrator, I had an opportunity to view college athletics from a more positive angle. I've concluded that college athletics provide great value on the field and off. I have also concluded that, at least in Division I, athletics in many instances have gone seriously off track. Following are a baker's dozen reasons why, along with some cautionary notes.

The Value of Athletics

1. *Leadership development.* College stakeholders have different views of the ultimate goal of higher education. My opinion is that a college education produces tomorrow's leaders—people who make a positive, meaningful, and enduring difference to the world. Ideally, college graduates will become the people who will make the world a better place. For me, this ought to be the purpose of college education in any institution, but it is especially true in an ACCEL institution, where the expectation is that the university will give back to the community, the state, the nation, and the world.

We might then ask, what leadership characteristics are important for an undergraduate education to develop? These might include traits and skills such as strategic and tactical planning, persistence, sensible risk-taking, resilience, self-discipline, time management, a sense of fairness, teamwork, an understanding of one's adversaries, and sportsmanship (being both a good winner and a good loser). If we now consider which characteristics competitive athletics help develop, the lists would track pretty well. That is, done right, participation in competitive athletics is leadership development.

Then, too, coaches, if properly trained, can be tremendous leadership mentors. Carmen Cozza, the head football coach at Yale for more than thirty years, was a role model to generations of college students. Students can learn as many lessons about leadership and life from a great coach as they can from any great professor.

Obviously, such development can also be done badly, as when a team adopts an attitude, say, of winning at any cost. But all aspects of college education run the risk of being done badly. Professors, for example, may require students to memorize content without first ascertaining whether or not all of them understand the material they are memorizing. On the other hand, students can allow themselves to become so distracted with technology gadgets and tools that homework and learning are neglected.

Many employers I have talked with have said they prefer to hire college graduates who have participated in competitive sports. Hiring organizations recognize, even if implicitly, that college athletes have developed leadership skills that other students did not have or take the opportunity to engage. Of course, participation in competitive athletics is not the only way to develop leadership skills. For example, I teach an undergraduate course on the psychology of leadership; among my goals for the course is the development of leadership skills. Nonetheless, competitive athletics can complement other aspects of college life in developing valuable skills as well as attitudes of leadership.

2. *Spirit*. During more than four decades in university teaching, I have been on campuses that are alive with enthusiasm and vibrancy and on others that have appeared to be spiritually dead. School spirit can come from many sources, but college athletics are near the top of the list.

I never imagined the excitement and enthusiasm that college teams could generate until I arrived at Oklahoma State. Come game day, thousands of people dress up in orange and crowd into the athletic stadium to cheer on their team. The spirit carries over to nongame days as well. Some might feel that such an attitude is hardly becoming of an institution dedicated to developing the life of the mind, but I would take the excitement and passion of the schools with spirit any day. It makes life on the campus much more fun and boosts morale and a feeling of identification with the institution. It also provides a sense of positive competitive spirit that can unify diverse stakeholders who may otherwise have rather different or conflicting agendas.

3. *Pride and loyalty*. While other activities can inspire institutional connection, pride in athletic teams can inspire high levels of loyalty to a university. It is just nicer and more energizing to work or study in an institution where people feel a connection that competitive athletics can instill.

4. *Memories*. Students typically spend only four to six years in undergraduate study, a period that quickly becomes a distant memory. For many alumni, competitive athletics provide some of the most salient memories. The recollections are not always pleasant; my most indelible memory from my undergraduate years at Yale is the football disaster "Harvard Beats Yale 29–29," in which the two Ivy League schools tied for the Ivy crown, although the Harvard Crimson claimed otherwise in its headline. Nevertheless, such events become a part of the joy we have in recalling our college days, which are often some of the best days of our lives.

5. *Lifetime fitness*. Lifetime fitness leads to better adult health and longevity. Mental decline, not just physical deterioration, has been tied to lack of physical exercise and healthy nutrition. Many of the habits we acquire in college become the behaviors we maintain over a lifetime. Physical fitness should be one of them.

Even for those who argue that a college education should primarily develop the life of the mind, athletics are important because of the ties between mental awareness and physical health. Thus, even college faculty and staff would be well advised to make use of athletic facilities.

6. *Recruitment*. In general, applications climb when teams have winning seasons. For example, even after the Butler University basketball team narrowly lost the 2010 national championship to Duke University, Butler saw its popularity skyrocket. Some faculty members might ask whether the school really wants those extra applicants, but it is almost always better to be able to select from a larger applicant pool. And the reason applications increase is not only that students want to attend a school with great teams. It is also relates to what psychologists call the "availability heuristic." That is, winning championships, or even coming close, gives colleges a regional or national visibility they would not otherwise have. In that way, the colleges become "available" in applicants' minds.

It's true that most students will not play intramural sports, but many will engage in intramural athletics. Students who play want good facilities. They want regulation-size fields, courts, and swimming pools. They want attractive locker rooms and up-to-date exercise facilities. Providing such facilities also helps recruit students to the institution.

7. *Stress relief and prosocial behavior*. College students are experiencing a time of their lives when they need to blow off steam. They have what may seem to be boundless energy, and they need to channel it somewhere. They

also require outlets to help them relieve stress. Athletics and physical-fitness activities in general can provide effective ways to channel energy and relieve anxiety. And such activities are certainly better alternatives than drug and alcohol use.

8. *Well-roundedness and balance.* Obviously, students go to college to study and learn. Much of that knowledge is gained in experiences outside the classroom. Some would argue that most of what they learn is extracurricular—a tacit knowledge of how to accomplish a life well lived.

Although studying hard is important, it is not all there is to the higher education experience. One of the critical things we learn is that there is always something that drives us: achieving the best grades to qualify for a top-notch graduate or professional program; leveraging graduate work to land a great job; achieving and accepting one promotion after another; and ultimately continuing to climb the professional ladder—until somewhere along the line we feel that life has passed us by. To avoid such disappointment, it is essential to learn that life is constantly a balancing act and that people who find a balance tend to be happier and more fulfilled. The college experience—and participation in athletics—can help provide such balance and fulfillment.

9. *Town-gown relationships.* The interests of a town sometimes, but not always, coincide with those of a college or university. On the one hand, a university is a source of jobs and usually provides education and entertainment venues for local citizens. On the other hand, some townspeople may resent the fact that college properties are typically untaxed, and they may encounter unacceptable behavior from college students. College athletics, like college cultural events, can go a long way toward helping town-gown relations, if they are handled in a way that respects the interests of the surrounding community. By encouraging attendance at games and support of the college teams, the campus can draw in residents who might otherwise develop a somewhat antagonistic attitude toward the college or university. Athletic games create revenue for the town, and in cases such as varsity football, this is a substantial benefit.

10. *Alumni loyalty and involvement.* Every college and university wants to build a loyal and involved alumni base that can serve the institution in many ways. One of the most effective activities is to provide opportunities for alumni to serve as advocates and ambassadors, helping create a positive reputation. College athletics tend to keep alumni tied to and involved

in the college. An important by-product of these connections is the ability of alumni to hire graduates and otherwise assist them as they navigate through their careers.

11. *Advancement.* Perhaps the most controversial benefit of college athletics is in the area of advancement. Those of us who are active in fundraising learn quickly that alumni give for their own reasons, not those of the fund-raisers. And we all know that winning teams translate into more dollars for many colleges. While not every team will be a winning team every year, many alumni appreciate it when a team gives its best, regardless of whether it wins or loses.

While some faculty might worry that all the advancement benefits of college athletics will go back to athletics, this simply is not true. Obviously, some of the funds support athletics, but contributions go to many other uses. In fact, college athletics can help in all areas of advancement by building loyalty, connection, and lifelong relationships.

12. *Branding.* The quality of an institution's brand helps determine the kind of students and faculty a college can attract, the resources that can accrue to it, and the general reputation it experiences in the community, state, country—and even the world. For better or worse, college athletics typically form part of that brand. They will obviously be a more important part of the brand in some institutions than in others. But to those for whom it makes a difference, athletics can matter to the positive reputation of the school—and to the related licensing fees the brand can attract.

13. *Lifelong friendships.* Perhaps there is no other time in a person's life when he or she can make friendships in quite the way that is possible in the college years. Friendships often form best when people participate together in activities that are engaging and fun, and athletics can and should be fun for the players and fans involved. Whether we are fans or athletes, the friendships we make at the athletic field are often the ones that make a difference and the ones we call on during critical points in our lives.

Five Caveats for College Athletics

Although college athletics can be a ball of gold, they can also easily be a ball of clay, and too often are. College athletics face four serious challenges. Any one of them can destroy the value that athletics might otherwise bring to an institution. Today much of the value of college athletics is gone as a result of a culture driven largely by money.

1. *Disparate missions.* If college athletics become disconnected from the academic and leadership-development missions of an institution, the result can be a troubled relationship between the two entities. Administrators need to pay attention to integrating the athletic programs with the leadership-development functions of the college rather than allowing them to go on separate tracks.

Where the issue of disparate missions is shown most starkly is in the special treatment awarded to athletes in truly unfortunate circumstances: major violations of NCAA rules, special treatment for players accused of rape, creation of spurious classes that award high grades on the basis of little or no work, tutors who essentially do the students' work for them, extremely high dropout rates, or admission of students who without their athletic prowess would never even be considered. The special treatment does not apply only to athletes. Some coaches are now receiving pay at such high levels that they are leaving the NFL to coach college football. The worst of the problem is not that these things are happening but that the administrators, alumni, and sometimes professors seem to wink at them.

2. *Conflicting business models.* When the athletic program's business model is separate from that of the institution—or no model even exists—athletics can become a drain on the business side of the overall operation. In some cases, they become a source of structural deficit in the university budget. In other circumstances, while there is money to be made, the programs and related revenue do not serve to enhance the functioning of the university as a whole. If college athletics are to become a business in their own right, they should simply be separated from the college. We should not pretend that institutions are serving an educational function when they no longer are or, in some cases, never were.

3. *Reputational risk.* College athletics are fertile fields for high-profile ethical scandals. While nearly any aspect of a university can become enmeshed in serious misdealings, athletics violations and scandals tarnish college and university reputations in a way—and to a level—that few other kinds of malfeasance can reach.

4. *Takeover.* In some universities, college athletics have come close to taking over the institution. Alumni and others pay more attention to athletics than to the academic mission of the institution. The teams become

professionalized. And the original goal of athletics as harmony in a university gets lost as athletics become the melody—they control too much of the day-to-day functioning of what happens when and to whom. In these cases, the tail has come to wag the dog.

5. *Corruption.* As I mentioned earlier, some of the most important figures in FIFA, the worldwide soccer organization that brings us the World Cup, were indicted as I was writing this book (see Apuzzo 2015).

The soccer scandal, of course, did not occur in any college or university. But one does not have to look very far to find awful scandals of corruption in college athletics (Branch 2011). And the scandals extend to professional baseball (Tylicki 2011), football (SportsYeah 2015), and other sports. A culture of corruption has engulfed various sports, and some of this culture has reached to the top levels, as happened in soccer. For me, the largest challenge in collegiate athletics is that a culture of corruption can undermine all the positive values that characterize an ACCEL university. The solution is the same as that of the US government with FIFA: root it out aggressively. The overwhelming majority of people who are fans of athletics and athletic teams want athletics to be clean. As a society and world, we owe at least that much to the fans.

All that said, when athletics harmonize with the academic and business missions of a college or university, the effect can be hugely positive. Done right and managed properly, college athletics might even be seen as necessary, not just window dressing.

This chapter has pointed out the importance of constantly evaluating college athletic programs and the coaches and administrators who run them to ensure that they are acting in ways consistent with the values of the ACCEL university. But of course, the most central players in promoting the mission of the ACCEL university are the faculty. Although faculty may sometimes be quick to criticize the role athletics play, they too need to be evaluated in terms of the mission of the ACCEL university. How does one proceed to do that? We consider this question in the next chapter.

PART IV

STRUCTURAL ISSUES

11

Assessing Faculty

The main assessment points in the life of a faculty member are tenure and promotion. How should faculty members be assessed at these points?

Tenure and Promotion

Most colleges and universities in the United States award tenure—a career-long contract—after roughly seven years of service to the institution. The awarding of tenure seems odd to many people. But there are at least three reasons why colleges and universities award tenure.

1. *Market forces.* Any organization—whether nonprofit or for-profit—needs to remain competitive. Organizations that fail to compete, fail. The major colleges and universities in all fifty states award tenure. If one of them were to stop, that institution would immediately become noncompetitive, and within a short period of time would become mediocre, at best. Why? Because no good academic from the outside would want to come

to that institution, and no good one there would want to stay. Teaching, research, and outreach all would decline sharply and quickly in quality. In a similar case, a search-engine company might want to charge users each time they use the search engine on their computer. Doing so certainly would increase the company's bottom line. But the company cannot do so if major competitors don't follow suit because the company quickly would lose its customers to the competition.

2. *Academic freedom.* "Academic freedom" is a faculty member's freedom to publish ideas and research results. Before faculty members receive tenure, they may hesitate to report freely or otherwise express unpopular views. Suppose, for example, a researcher finds that a drug alleged by a manufacturer to be safe has potentially lethal side effects. She might hesitate to publish the results if she were afraid that, as a result of her findings, the politically powerful company that manufactures the drug might pressure the administration of her university to fire her from her job.

3. *Research and scholarship can take a long time to reach publication.* Some academics spend many years on a single problem. Moreover, the time needed to complete research projects varies greatly across academic disciplines. Without tenure, faculty members might be discharged because they seem to be unproductive. For example, a researcher seeking new treatments for complex diseases, such as heart disease or cancer, may not obtain conclusive results for many years. Moreover, treatments that have some degree of success are often those that seem initially to have a low probability of success. Tenure assures researchers that they can take the risks that may be needed to produce successful results.

Tenure does not always function as it should. There are academics who abuse the system. Some of them, through a lengthy process, do get fired. But the large majority of academics continue to merit the tenure they earn. In current times, without tenure, a major college or university would be unable to successfully compete in the academic marketplace. That could change.

I believe that permanent tenure is a mistake. It makes it, quite simply, too easy for a faculty member to retire on the job. Since the removal of a forced retirement age (which, for better or worse, generally used to be sixty-five, my age as I write these words), I have seen faculty members who stay on the job too long. When I was an administrator, I sometimes encountered the unconscionable situation in which a professor would demand a special deal to retire or else he or she would continue to be a do-nothing faculty member collecting a salary for doing a pedestrian and minimalist job of teaching and no research. Whether these professors once had moral scruples I don't know—what I do know is that they had them no longer.

Better than permanent tenure would be a long-term contract, for twenty, twenty-five, or at most, thirty years. At the end of the contract, the faculty member would still be eligible for shorter-term contracts, for example, the same kinds of three- or even five-year contracts often given to junior faculty members. In this way, faculty who remained productive would be able to stay in their jobs and those who had become unproductive would be required to leave.

I do not believe a fixed retirement age is the answer. Any number of faculty members I have known continued to do excellent work after the age of sixty-five, and their retirement would have been, and in some cases was, a loss to the universities at which they taught. But one cannot assume that everyone will stay productive forever, and universities should not, ideally, put themselves in the position of having faculty members who retain tenure but no longer work hard for a living.

As an administrator, I decided there was not much I could do about tenured faculty members who met the requirements of their jobs, however minimally. But I was not willing to put up with tenured faculty members who were not willing even to meet those minimal requirements, and there were some. So I instituted dismissal proceedings against a number of tenured faculty members. We sometimes forget that even tenured faculty members must meet certain requirements. They have to show up for class; they have to show up on time; they have to fill out annual reports; they have to do service requirements that are assigned to them. Although dismissing tenured faculty members is challenging and typically involves a complex, multi-step process, it is doable. I never lost a case. Administrators need to be understanding but also tough: they can't just let faculty members, or anyone else, run a show that has nothing to do with the priorities of the university.

Assessing Faculty Performance

Generally, three main factors enter into tenure and promotion decisions: research, teaching, and service. How does one assess each of these factors?

Assessing Research

ACCEL universities serve the academic world, but also their communities, their states, and the nation. They do so in part through their research.

First of all, it is important to realize that basic research and applied research are not two discrete categories but rather regions on a continuum. The US military, which funded me for almost my entire career as a researcher, recognizes this fact. The military historically has supported research from levels "6-1" to "6-4," from purely basic research (6-1) to basic research with clear practical applications (6-2), applied research arising out of basic research (6-3), and applied research with fairly immediate application (6-4).

Second, an ACCEL university needs all four levels of research because one can never tell what basic research will yield practical applications. Chances are, for example, that at some point in your life you have taken antibiotics. The discovery of the first major antibiotic, penicillin, arose strictly by chance out of basic research. Sir Alexander Fleming noticed that a mold had killed a bacterial culture he was growing. Fleming realized that the mold was of paramount importance. It was this penicillium mold that yielded penicillin, which has saved countless lives. Similarly, the development of the transistor, the basis for much of modern electronics, arose out of basic research.

Third, one often cannot even tell what research is basic and what research is applied. When I was a professor at Yale, I did research that was funded as "basic" to develop measures to assess creative, analytical, and practical cognitive skills. Within a few years, assessments arising out of this research were being used with tens of thousands of applicants for undergraduate admission to Tufts University (during my term as dean of arts and sciences there). Similarly, we were once funded for basic research on teaching students to their strengths in learning. Within a few years, thousands of students were receiving instruction that enabled them to learn better by helping them capitalize on their cognitive strengths. Research that I viewed as basic, and that was funded as basic, turned out to have relatively quick practical applications.

Fourth, one of the best ways to educate students is to have them engage in research, whether basic, applied, or anything in between. In this way students learn how to conduct research, a vital skill to learn for their future, when they will need to research important decisions in their lives, such as investment or purchasing decisions. Faculty members collaborate with students in research so that the students can become better-educated active citizens and ethical leaders.

Finally, most of the knowledge that scientists and many engineers need to acquire in learning their disciplines stems from basic research. They need to know the basic research findings—so they can then see how to apply them. Basic research forms the backbone of almost any intellectual discipline, in the sciences or, for that matter, in the humanities or other fields of endeavor.

Citizens may feel that when funding agencies such as the National Science Foundation or the National Institutes of Health spend money on basic research, the agency is wasting taxpayer dollars. But next time you are prescribed an antibiotic, or put on cotton permanent-press clothing, or turn on your computer, or make a call on your cell phone, or listen to the radio, remember that you are able to do what you are doing only because of its foundation in basic research.

There are many ways to evaluate research. Four of them, in ascending order of importance, should take precedence: quantity, quality, visibility, and impact.

Quantity   In my view, there is nothing more dreadful than universities that count publications. In my own career, when I interviewed at a university in which the chair told me they kept a count of publications, I withdrew. How do you compare a book to an article? How about an article in a top refereed journal versus an article in a weak journal? How about a refereed article versus a book chapter or a book review? Counting encourages a mindless attempt on the part of faculty members to produce publishable units of work, no matter how small or trivial they may be. When universities give tenure largely on the basis of counting publications, they are turning their tenure process into a ball of clay.

At the same time, though, ignoring quantity would be an equally large mistake. First, as research by Dean Simonton (2004) has shown, despite some scholars' intuitions to the contrary, quantity is associated with both quality and impact. The reason is that scholars throughout their career tend to have a fairly high consistency in hit rate—the proportion of their publications that get somewhat wide citation and visibility. Hence, the more a scholar publishes for a given hit rate, the more his or her work will be likely to have an impact simply because more publications will emerge as successful in terms of visibility and impact. Often, those who reject quantity totally are scholars who themselves have not been terribly productive and cling to their folk conception that although they have not published much, all that they have done is of sterling quality.

Second, the best predictor of any given kind of behavior in the future is that same kind of behavior in the past, as almost anyone who has been in an intimate relationship can tell you. As a result, past productivity is the best predictor of future productivity. No university wants to tenure someone who then stops producing on the official conferral of tenure. If someone has not been producing much or has produced only under pressure in the last few years before the decision, chances are they will not produce much in the future.

Third, students model faculty members' behavior, and if graduate students and postdoctoral researchers see a faculty member not producing much, the lesson they are likely to absorb is that a low rate of production is a good model to follow.

Finally, to judge quality, one needs enough quantity to ensure that the judgment of quality is reliable and valid. A scholar could have one great hit to his or her name, but as most of us have learned, there are any number of scholars for whom their one great work is also their last great work.

So quantity matters, but it needs to be assessed in a reflective and informed way, not just by counting publishable units. I have never seen a weighting system that adequately reflects the complexities of quantity. Quantity, although appearing to be one-dimensional (how many publishable units are there?), has too many nuances (units of what?). Quantity should be assessed mindfully rather than blindly.

Quality   Quality is largely a function of three factors: the importance of the problem studied, the degree of skill with which the problem is studied, the effectiveness with which the results of the research are communicated, and the extent to which the results can make a positive and meaningful difference, whether to the field or to society in general. These four qualities correspond roughly to the creative, analytical, practical, and wisdom-based skills that have been discussed earlier.

Investigators of creativity, including myself, have stressed the importance of problem finding for creativity. In our view, society often places a great deal of emphasis on problem solving without a corresponding emphasis on the extent to which the problem that was solved was worth solving in the first place. Those who review journal articles can become so focused on the extent to which the results of a study show what they are supposed to show that the reviewers lose sight of whether what was shown was actually worth showing. Mihalyi Csikszentmihalyi (2013), among others, has argued that the greatest artists and scientists are not necessarily those who do the most exacting work but rather those who tackle large, important, and often messy problems. Not all highly creative artists, scientists, and other scholars become great names in a field, but virtually all scholars who become great names are highly creative.

Standardized tests such as the Graduate Record Examination measure analytical abilities, the abilities needed to analyze research results, critique a poem or other work of art, analyze a historical document, or compare and contrast two economies. A major factor in evaluating the quality of research is simply the extent to which a scholarly work accomplishes what its author or authors say it is supposed to accomplish. A work can be analytically strong and creatively weak if it accomplishes its task well but the task is fairly trivial. Or it can be creatively strong and analytically weak if it tackles a big problem, perhaps in a nonobvious approach, but does so in a way that is not compelling.

Practical skills are involved in writing up a scholarly work or orally presenting it in a way that is clear, compelling, and persuasive to the audience intended to receive it. Some scholars believe that their work is done once the research is done, and they look at writing up the work as a chore. But in universities, scholarship does not really carry any value until it becomes public. And the way it becomes public matters a lot—where it is published, when it is published, and how it is published. For better or worse, departments in universities place higher value on articles and books that have undergone rigorous refereeing processes, and that is not likely to change, whether publications are in traditional paper format, online, or both.

Wisdom-based skills are involved in showing that the research one has done makes some kind of difference. That difference can be to the field, to society at some level, or, one hopes, both. ACCEL universities often put more emphasis on value of the research to local communities and to the state than do some other kinds of universities, but many other universities also welcome research that helps somehow to change the world. Unfortunately, in my view, there are also universities or at least departments within universities that view research that has societal value as being somehow contaminated and not truly scholarly. This is a warped value system that is not worthy of any serious university.

Visibility   Visibility refers to the extent to which a scholar's work becomes well known to people in the field and even, in some cases, to the general public. Visibility is important because a major function of research is heuristic—to guide future researchers along their own personal paths to finding and solving problems—and research cannot guide future scholars if they are unaware of it. Hence, universities often judge the visibility of the journals to which researchers submit work (are they widely distributed or seen by only a handful of people?) and also evaluate scholars' oral or poster presentations to assess whether the scholar is making a successful effort to help his or her work become known.

Visibility is like quantity in that it can be a double-edged sword. With quantity, the concern is that a "publish-or-perish" mentality can lead to publication of the smallest publishable unit. With visibility, the concern is that a scholar will become visible for the wrong reasons—essentially becoming notorious as well as visible. For example, in my own field, several scholars in recent years have become highly visible for all the wrong reasons—for mistakenly interpreting or even outright faking data, for taking extreme positions on social issues far afield from what they study, or even for using their research to foster unsupportable positions on such social issues. William Shockley, for example, was a Nobel Prize winner, but his views on race and intelligence were scientifically unsupported. Philippe Rushton was in the field of human intelligence but did what appeared to be ideologically motivated research whose interpretation he arguably stretched to support very strange racial views on intelligence. Linus Pauling, another Nobel Prize winner, was a great fan of vitamin C for preventing or curing the common cold—without the evidence to support his position. So visibility is important, but it needs to be the right kind of visibility.

That said, creative work is work that defies conventional paradigms and ways of thinking in a given field, and sometimes it initially is rejected vociferously by stalwarts of the old order (Sternberg 2015c, 2015d; Sternberg and Lubart 1995). Thus, one has to be careful not to simply reject work that gains visibility for attacking existing orders, because it may be the work that starts a new paradigm or shows that previous work was much more limited than people had realized. In physics, Nobel Prize winner Albert Einstein comes to mind, as does Nobel Prize winner Herbert Simon in the field of behavioral economics.

Impact   Finally, and most importantly, a tenure or promotion committee will want to assess the impact of a person's work—how much difference it makes to one's field or to society at large. In the end, impact is what matters most: How is the world different as a result of the work that was done? Impact typically can be measured most accurately over the long term, but tenure and promotion committees often do not have the luxury of waiting many years to determine what the impact of the work will be.

There are various measures of impact, none of them totally satisfactory. An example is H, the number of publications cited at least H times. So someone who has ten publications cited ten times would have an H value of 10. Although H is a reasonable measure, like any other single index it can be problematical. For example, a work could be cited repeatedly because it is methodologically flawed and other scholars want to point this out. Or it could be cited as a foil—as an example of a theory gone wrong. Moreover, one runs into the problem of cited by whom: Does one count citation by a prominent scholar versus an unknown scholar the same? How about a local newspaper versus a national newspaper? In all evaluations of research, there is no substitute for informed judgment.

In the ACCEL model, impact is measured broadly. It includes more traditional measures of scholarly impact, such as H, but it might also include impact on farming or ranching practices in a state, or impact on the economy of the state. Universities ought to measure impact in terms of their mission and their goals, not merely in some vague and generalized sense.

Assessing Teaching

Virtually all universities assess teaching as part of their tenure and promotion decisions, at least for those faculty members who teach. Some faculty may have no teaching assignment, such as those who have pure research or extension (outreach) appointments. But the overwhelming majority of faculty members teach, usually anywhere from two to eight courses per year. Teaching loads vary for a number of reasons.

First, on average, teaching loads are higher in the humanities than in the natural sciences. The social sciences usually fall somewhere in between. The reduced load in the natural sciences results from several factors. First, scientists often run labs, and a lot of the teaching occurs in the labs informally. So the scientists are teaching, just not in the classroom. The problem, in my experience, is that not all scientists run active labs or interact with students intensively, so for some scientists, the teaching load amounts to something close to a vacation dream job.

Second, in most institutions, professors can "buy out" of teaching by grants. That is, for a certain amount of money, they can receive a reduction of one course (or even more) in their teaching load. The idea is that they will spend more of their time on research funded by the grant or contract that buys out the teaching. This arrangement can make sense, as it leaves more of the teaching to faculty members who are less active in funded research.

Third, administrators typically have reduced teaching loads and, at the top, may not teach at all. Department chairs typically receive a one-course or two-course reduction. Other administrators, such as a director of undergraduate studies, also often receive a one-course reduction. I made a point of teaching as an administrator, because I enjoy teaching and because I felt that teaching kept me in closer touch with the most important constituency in a university, its students. But deans, provosts, and presidents often do not teach at all. On the one hand, reducing or eliminating the teaching load makes sense, because top administrators are very busy. On the other hand, eliminating teaching can result in an administrator's getting out of touch with students and failing to fully understand their needs.

In my view, it is a mistake in an ACCEL university to have fixed loads as a function of department. Rather, it makes sense to have a fixed workload policy. Different professorial activities are assigned different weights, and all professors are expected, in the end, to have the same total load. Some may spend more time on research, others on teaching, others on service, but they all have assignments that are equally challenging, at least in theory.

Having diverse assignments makes sense because different faculty members have different things to contribute to a university. If someone is an outstanding researcher but only a so-so teacher, the university is better off with the faculty member spending more of his or her time on research. Or if a faculty member excels in both teaching and research, then finding a sensible balance would help maximize the university's outcomes.

Assessing Service

Service is the hardest of the "three-legged" stool to assess, in part because it can take so many different forms. In particular, service can be to a field, a department, a college or school within a university, the university as a whole, the community in which the university is embedded, the state, the nation, and the world. As a dean, I was not really interested in just lists of service work. Rather, I looked for the same attributes in service as I did in research. In particular, I assessed quality, quantity, impact, and visibility of the service work. All of these contributions can be reduced by self-sabotage, as discussed below.

The Problem of Self-Sabotage

As an assistant professor, I came to realize that almost all faculty members have enemies. It may be people in the department with whom they do not get along, or people in their field who see things differently from the way they do. I hypothesized in those days—and still believe—that one's worst enemy is likely to be oneself. In an ACCEL university, or any other, one can fail to fulfill one's mission because of the stumbling blocks one sets up for oneself (Sternberg 2013d).

Pogo recognized long ago that we are often our own worst enemies. Sure, he was a cartoon character, but he had a point—especially in higher education, where self-sabotage seems to be a standard characteristic of academic careers. I have observed many academics harm their own careers, often without realizing it. Here are fifteen ways in which faculty members can be self-destructive (based on Sternberg 2013d).

1. *They don't seek out multiple mentors.* Too many faculty members sit back and wait for guidance and advice from their department heads or

promotion committees. Successful academics, early in their careers, look for several mentors, including from departments other than their own. No one person or committee can be relied on to give you definitive career advice. In the end, faculty members need to seek out multiple sources of advice, sort the good from the bad, and take responsibility for their own career development.

2. *They don't seek out external evaluations.* For some academics, the first time they get any sort of formal external feedback is during a tenure review. That's too late. Faculty members need to pursue multiple external evaluations of their work early in their careers—via reviews of their articles and grant proposals, colleagues in their field to whom they send their work for comments, and people who listen to them give talks. Sometimes the reviews are negative, and sometimes they are brutal. A prepublication review of my first scholarly book (Sternberg 1977) consisted of seventeen single-spaced pages of trenchant criticism on why the book should not be published. (The book was published and became a citation classic.) One needs a thick skin in this business. If faculty members wait until tenure time to seek external evaluations, they are setting themselves up to fail.

3. *They are either perfectionist or perfunctory in putting their work into print.* Everyone wants to write the perfect article or book, but no one ever does. The longer that faculty members wait to publish, the more likely someone else will beat them to press with the same idea, and the less likely they will be to find a publication outlet in time for gaining credit from a promotion committee. Moreover, many kinds of research go out of date quickly. If faculty members wait too long, they court their own doom. But if they rush materials into print, they will likely find themselves getting rejections and revise-and-resubmit notices, which also can hold up their bids to build their CVs in time for consideration by a promotion committee. They need to do their best on an article or book, but not wait for Godot (see Beckett 1982).

4. *They hold on to revisions too long.* Or rush them out. Very few articles are accepted on the first go-round with a publisher. Normally, academics can expect to do one or more revisions, whether for a book, article, or grant proposal. If they hold onto revisions too long, they end up stifling their careers. Editors and grant-review panels change, so academics may find that the people evaluating their work later are looking for different things than

were those who reviewed the work earlier. Many of their revisions may then end up being in vain.

5. *They pay too much attention to personal relationships—or too little.* Some early-career academics get so involved in their work that they ignore personal relationships with colleagues in their department. Or they act rudely toward others, believing that career success depends only on the quality of their work. Whether departments admit it or not, they prefer to promote people who fit in—who contribute to the life of the department and of the institution. The person who is seen as a good fit will always have an edge over the misfit. But it can also be a mistake to devote so much time to personal relationships that one's investment in those relationships is at the expense of one's work.

6. *They fail to understand the cultural norms of their institution.* What counts for promotion differs from one institution to another, and what is written in the promotion guidelines sometimes fails to capture what is most important for success. Academics need informal knowledge of the cultural norms of their institution, not just formal knowledge of the promotion requirements. It's important to be alert to the tacit, or unspoken, knowledge that only experience can teach (Sternberg et al. 2000), lest one come up for promotion and meet the formal guidelines while falling short on the informal ones.

7. *They aren't well known outside their institution.* Important people in a field who are external to one's own institution must know who the faculty member is, because they are the ones who will be asked to write about him or her at tenure or promotion time. Of course, a strong internal reputation is important, too. When tenure candidates are asked to recommend external letter writers but have no names to offer, that is a bad sign.

8. *They lack resilience in the face of failure.* In any academic career, the question is not whether one is going to have failures; the question is what one is going to do when one fails. One will have articles, book manuscripts, and grant proposals turned down; courses that are poorly received; talks for which audiences give one the cold shoulder. Academic careers are not for the faint of heart. In my experience, the people who are most successful in academe are reasonably smart and at least somewhat creative, but more importantly, they persist in the face of obstacles. Failed academics may be smart and creative but, when challenged, give up or become embittered.

9. *They have been involved in one too many intradepartmental squabbles.* It is best to stay out of them if at all possible, or at least wait until one has tenure.

10. *They are too selfish or too selfless.* Department members quickly pick up on selfishness in a new hire. Selfish colleagues are the ones who never have time for others, and when they do, hog credit or, worse, steal ideas. It is equally risky to be too selfless. Faculty members want a reputation as helpful, but they cannot afford to let their own work go undone while spending time helping others. Especially at risk are academics with technical skills. It is very hard to get promoted on the basis of the technical skills one used to help one's colleagues.

11. *They got stuck on their dissertation paradigm.* Academic careers falter if they resemble one-act plays. By the time one comes up for tenure, one needs to be, at the very least, starting a second act—a second book, a new research paradigm, a new topic for research, new course preparations. If the faculty member is seen as a one-idea kind of academic, he or she will be viewed as a bad tenure risk.

12. *They collaborate too much with colleagues from graduate school or their postdoctoral years.* Faculty members are expected, when they start out, to show increasing independence. Some make the mistake of getting sucked into extended, intense collaborations with graduate or postdoctoral mentors or collaborators. The message they send in doing so is that they never achieved the independence that will identify them as having embarked on their own career. Some collaboration with graduate or postdoctoral colleagues is fine, but it should be limited.

13. *They fail to have a coherent research program.* Faculty members need a certain quantity of published research, but they also need a rational and organized research program. If there is no consistent theme, or perhaps pair of themes, professors will wonder if the faculty members have a meaningful future as investigators, or if they are merely people who flit from project to project, aimlessly pursuing investigations.

14. *They are guilty of any form of academic dishonesty.* If a faculty member is caught in any form of academic cheating, there is a single word to describe his or her career: over. It is very difficult, although not impossible, to recover from verified academic dishonesty.

15. *They haven't figured out who they are.* As an academic, if one tries to please everyone, one ends up pleasing no one. So faculty members need to

figure out what they do best and capitalize on it. At the same time, they need to correct or compensate for the things they don't do well. No one is good at everything. They need to make sure they are good enough at everything on which they will be evaluated, and very good on some of those things.

In general, faculty members learn how to do research and may learn about teaching. Later in their careers, some of them go into leadership and governance positions. In the next chapter, we evaluate how they may fare in such positions, especially in the context of ACCEL universities.

12

GOVERNANCE

Once upon a time, there were university presidents who helped shape not only their universities but also the nation. Robert Maynard Hutchins at Chicago, James Bryant Conant at Harvard, and Kingman Brewster at Yale come to mind. We rarely see presidents of that stature and influence anymore because the job of a university president has changed so much.

Today's university president, and to a large extent the provost and deans, are locked into a situation in which their greatest challenge is keeping their jobs. As one university president put it to me, you can afford to antagonize one powerful constituency—faculty, alumni, powerful donors—at a time, but you cannot afford to antagonize more than one group at once. He was being conservative. You can hardly afford to tick off any group at any time. The result is that many top administrative jobs have become balancing acts in which the primary point of balance is not what is best for the university but rather what is best for maintaining one's job—which usually means raising a lot of money while saying as little as possible that might be offensive to anyone.

This perilous situation can be mitigated by a strong board of trustees that chooses a president with a mission and then supports the president in the attainment of that mission—so long as the mission continues to serve the university. But trustees themselves are under great pressure—from governors, legislators, donors, alumni, politically influential individuals who may have no connection to the university—and their appointment and continuation may depend on appeasing one or more of those constituencies. Some trustees may be more concerned about their own preservation on a board than about the future of the university, so governance becomes fraught with difficulties.

The result of these conflicting pressures is often a bizarre kind of conservatism in which the administration can become afraid to do almost anything that will result in constructive change because any change is bound to upset some powerful group of constituents. For-profit businesses, at least, have a clear measure of success—profit, or the bottom line. But for universities, there are many bottom lines and any change will help some and hurt others, inevitably resulting in distress to some group. Tenure-stream faculty members, in particular, have created environments that they believe serve them well, and are reluctant to give up the benefits they feel they have worked so hard to earn.

The best solution, I believe, is to hire administrators not because they are superannuated as scholars or teachers or businesspeople, as so often happens, but rather because they bring a particular vision to their institution that is compatible with its needs. Changing an institutional culture is difficult, as we have seen, but universities cannot keep up with the rapidly evolving competitive landscape unless they have a vision and seek to realize it. Few universities do that anymore, and it is a loss for those universities and for society. We need more administrators of the ilk of Hutchins, Conant, and Brewster, but we will not get them if the jobs of top administrators continue to be to stay in power rather than to optimally lead the university where it needs to go.

Styles of Leadership

Academic leaders bring different styles to their work.[1]

---

1. This section is based on and adapted in part from Sternberg 2013b.

What Works When?

Educators recognize that administrators lead in different ways. Styles of leadership for organizational leaders can be divided roughly into four categories, summarized in table 12.1.

Although I believe that one style of leadership is perhaps more effective, on average, than the other three, I have also found that leaders may have to display some flexibility in adopting different styles of leadership depending on the circumstances they face at a given time.

This model assumes that there are two distinct aspects of leadership style: problem formulation (or definition) and problem solving. Most leaders have received more education about how to solve problems than in how to define problems, which leads us to focus on the solutions to problems without taking the time to properly define the problem that is to be solved. In our eagerness to be proactive or innovative, we overlook the crucial step of correctly specifying the problem and the goal in solving it.

Although well-defined problems are easier to solve, most problems faced by organizations are ill-defined. Ill-defined problems can have multiple outcomes depending on how the underlying goals of the solution are framed. For instance, solutions utilizing short-term benefits may differ from those focusing on long-term benefits. Misdefining the problem may lead us to follow solutions that do not address the original problem or merely address the symptoms and not the underlying causes. Organizations that do not take the time to fully formulate problems and articulate associated issues are at risk of wasting resources. At the same time, correctly defining a problem is not of much use to an organization unless one can execute its solution. Therefore, as leaders, we need to focus both on how we solve problems and on how we ensure that we are solving the problems that truly need to be solved.

TABLE 12.1. Four styles of leadership for organizational leaders

Problem formulation and problem solving	Top-down	Bottom-up
Top-down	I Authoritarian	III Follower-based authoritative
Bottom-up	II Leader-based authoritative	IV Laissez-faire

The Four Styles of Leadership

I. *Authoritarian leadership.* In Authoritarian or Type I leadership, the organizational leader assumes the responsibility for the posing and solving of problems. A leader must have a deep knowledge of the company, a strong vision for the company, and the skills to implement that vision to successfully utilize this style. The late Steve Jobs and his unconventional management of Apple and Pixar is an example of an effective authoritarian leader. His goals for the company rarely embodied a consensus-building approach. Jobs's vision sustained a top-down model in which he retained control of most aspects of the company.

There are three potential advantages of the authoritarian leadership style. First, utilizing a top-down approach means that things can get done rather quickly. Second, implementation of the solution will adhere closely to the original vision, as the leader assumes responsibility for defining problems and finding solutions Third, there is little confusion about who is in charge. Jobs's leadership shows the potential for this style of leadership. Apple's organizational structure under Jobs was meticulous in its simplicity, with all roads leading to Jobs.

This model also has three potential disadvantages. First, followers are not likely to feel empowered. This may be especially difficult for those followers who are highly independent or do not share the leader's vision. Second, leaders employing this style must have the skills to ensure follower buy-in for the vision and goals of the organization. Even the greatest vision will fail without the cooperation of followers. Third, without input from followers or deep knowledge of the organization's capabilities, the leader may not recognize some problems or may propose unviable solutions.

There are some cultures that welcome authoritarian leaders. Latin America, for example, has a history of "caudillos," or strong authoritarian leaders. Venezuela's Hugo Chávez managed to acquire a level of admiration from many Venezuelans that would be difficult to achieve in the United States, where his style of leadership would probably not be as admired. And in a US college or university setting, leaders with a Chávez-like streak are often deeply resented by faculty and many other stakeholders.

Successful examples of Type I leadership hinge on the knowledge, vision, and skills of the leader. Under favorable circumstances the leader is well versed in a company's strengths and weaknesses, understands the environment (for instance, the industry of a particular business), and is able to interpret the organization's vision to key stakeholders—employees, board members, and consumers. The leader has the capacity to understand the needs of followers and clients. Unsuccessful Type I leaders doggedly cling to solutions that are not viable. The success of the organization is tied to the leader's vision for future outcomes and reliant on the capability of that leader to manage change.

II. *Leader-based authoritative leadership.* In Type II leadership, which I refer to as leader-based authoritative, the leader takes primary responsibility for formulating, posing, or otherwise defining problems, but delegates much of the responsibility for solving the problems to followers, who ideally work in collaboration with the leader. This style does not signify that the leader poses problems without listening to followers. On the contrary, it is impossible to gain a sense of the important problems facing an institution without active, careful, and mindful listening. Rather, it confers on the leader primary responsibility for deciding what problems to tackle, when to tackle them, and how extensive the resources should be that are allocated to them.

The potential advantages of this style are threefold. First, it assigns to leadership the primary (but not sole) responsibility for setting the basic agenda. Second, it empowers followers, through shared governance, to solve problems that directly and indirectly affect them. Third, it is more likely to result in followers' acceptance of the process than Type I leadership and hence the ultimate outcomes of a follower-driven committee or task force.

The style also has three potential disadvantages. First, the outcome of the follower-driven committee or task force is likely to be different, in some degree, from what the leader hoped for. In essence, the leader has to hope that the difference is small or that it is positive—producing a better outcome than he or she imagined. Second, the rate of implementation of change is slower than for Type I. Third, the task force may drift and produce a report that addresses a problem other than the one the leader hoped it would solve.

Speaking as a former university administrator, I believe this model to be the preferred one, in many circumstances, among the four styles. In my experience, this model usually works, empowering both faculty and administration to work together for a common good. I have used this model extensively, especially as a provost, and have found that it empowers faculty members to take responsibility for their own destinies. The outcomes of various task forces I have been involved with have ranged from good to outstanding. Many outcomes have been much better than I could have even imagined. But I have also found the model to be slow and even at times frustrating when task forces are reluctant to make the hard decisions that transformational change requires. Patience is essential, on the part of both administration and faculty. So it is important to stay in touch with the task forces and sometimes gently nudge them toward more ambitious agendas of change. There is no guarantee, however, of the outcome one desires.

An example of a Type II leader is Pierre Omidyar, the founder of eBay, who built a platform to address the issue of how to provide for large-scale Internet retailing. Although eBay's platform provides structure for online auctions, the users function as independent contractors who assume responsibility for customer service, purchase fulfillment, and other retail functions.

The success of Type II leadership relies on the leader's ability to correctly define problems and the ability of followers to match solutions to the intended outcomes. It is critical to the process that the leader and followers have a good working relationship based on mutual trust and respect. If the leader formulates problems that are not relevant to followers, their investment in providing appropriate solutions will not be warranted.

III. *Follower-based authoritative leadership.* Type III leadership, which I refer to as follower-based authoritative, essentially reverses the roles in Type II leadership. The leader draws heavily on followers, perhaps through an executive team, to set the agenda for change, and then takes it on himself or herself to figure out how the change should take place. Leaders who follow this model want major follower participation in agenda setting but feel that unless they, as administrators, take charge of implementation, little will actually get done with any deliberate speed.

This style of leadership has three potential advantages. First, it empowers followers to set the agenda on issues that affect them. Second, it is unlikely to lead followers to feel that the agenda is unrelated to or even hostile to their interests. Third, it gets things done at a rate comfortable to the leader, since the leader sets the pace of implementation.

The style has three potential disadvantages, however. First, in a university setting, the administration cedes primary responsibility for setting the agenda of the institution to the faculty. Faculty members typically do not have a bird's-eye, holistic view of the wide range of problems affecting an institution; their view may be more limited in perspective than an administrator's view simply because they do not have contact with as many kinds of stakeholders whose interests may be involved in the setting of priorities for the institution. The set of problems confronted, therefore, may be ones that are of high priority to faculty but of lesser priority to other stakeholders (e.g., trustees or regents, alumni, major donors, corporate or nonprofit partners, and, sometimes, students). Second, some stakeholders, especially trustees or regents, may see agenda setting as an administrative prerogative. Third, problems that an administrator really would like to solve may never even be addressed.

Sam Walton, the founder of Walmart, is an example of the follower-based authoritative leader. Walton was known for soliciting input from employees at all levels of the company, as well as vendors and customers. In this way, he was able to gain insight into potential problems and to work toward solutions using that input. Walton was able to empower employees as stakeholders in the running of Walmart through soliciting input and providing profit-sharing incentives.

As in Type II leadership, in Type III leadership the relationship between followers and leaders is important. The Type III leader must allow followers autonomy in the problem-formulation process, and followers must trust that the leader will propose solutions that adequately address the issues that have been raised. The process depends on the willingness of the parties to balance their interests with the benefits of the organization. Successful examples of Type II and Type III leadership will produce beneficial results for all stakeholders. Conversely, failure to define relevant problems or generate realistic solutions will result in the frustration of one or both parties.

IV. *Laissez-faire leadership.* Type IV leadership, which I refer to as laissez-faire, involves assigning primary responsibility for both problem formulation and problem solution to followers. The main responsibilities of the leader are to allocate resources, serve as a manager, and guide the faculty in its leadership over academic matters.

The potential advantages of this style of leadership are threefold. First, it maximally empowers followers to guide the institution and its future. Second, it may generate a great deal of goodwill on the part of followers, in that they are, to the extent possible, given control of their own destiny. Third, it may make for a very popular leader among the faculty, as it puts leaders where many followers would like them to be—in the deep background.

This style also has three potential disadvantages. First, the leader might be seen by some as abrogating his or her role as an academic leader, leaving it to others to do what he or she was hired to do. Second, it may put followers in a position of greater power than they are prepared to assume, given that their perspective on the organization is often somewhat limited by their role. Third, supervisors above the administrator may begin to question whether they have hired someone with the leadership skills to do the job.

Type IV leadership may also be viewed as a shared or collaborative leadership style. This may be beneficial when the responsibilities of leadership are too great for one leader or in a cooperative agreement among equal stakeholders. In this view a leader may take on a more managerial or administrative role, ensuring that resources are allocated correctly and that the organization is running smoothly. In a successful example of Type IV leadership, leaders and followers share responsibility for problem formation and solutions. In unsuccessful examples, followers would perceive a lack of structure and assume primary management of operations.

An example of a Type IV leader is an administrator who oversees a faculty overhaul of tenure procedures. In such a case, the faculty might decide that their tenure policies are too vague or just not specified, and then decide to find a solution that clarifies these procedures. Administration would be involved in the process only to a minimal extent. A risk would be that the faculty members would make the procedures more clear but not necessarily more rigorous for fear of offending those members who are either coming up for tenure or have been less than productive since obtaining tenure.

Understanding One's Styles and Achieving Flexibility

Leaders do not exist in a vacuum but function within layered contexts that require adjustment depending on resources, followers, and personal abilities and skills. In order to achieve flexibility in the use of styles, one first must come to understand what one's preferred style or styles might be.

The problem, I have found, is that style is as much in the eye of the beholder as it is in any "objective reality" one might envision. Earlier in my career, I did research on romantic relationships, and found that even in a relationship in which two people know each other very well and spend a great deal of time with each other, there is only a weak to moderate degree of correlation between how one believes one is perceived by one's romantic partner and how the romantic partner states he or she perceives one. If even in intimate relationships the correlation between self-perception and other-perception is relatively low, imagine how low it must be for relationships in which the individuals involved know each other quite a bit less.

As a result, a leader who wishes to achieve greater effectiveness through flexibility in styles of leadership must inquire of others as to how they perceive the leader's style. Moreover, these others should be at different levels in a chain or network of command, because it is not unusual for people at one level to perceive you in one way and people at another level to perceive you in an entirely different way.

I would suggest concentrating on your job behavior rather than on what you believe your "traits" to be. Consider, perhaps, the last three major accomplishments in which you take some pride. How did you get those things done? Ask yourself but also ask others, encouraging them to be frank with you and assuring them that they can feel safe in talking to you about how they feel. Such inquiries of others are the only way you will find out how you are perceived. Any change from one way of being to another requires you to understand how you are in the first place. An authoritarian leader may see himself or herself as reaching out to constituencies in a way that the constituencies just do not see; or a laissez-faire leader may view himself or herself as actively in charge while constituents see a leader adrift and possibly disengaged.

There is no one style of leadership that will always produce (a) an optimal educational outcome with (b) the greatest possible speed and (c) to the satisfaction of all relevant stakeholders. In my experience, faculty tend to care a lot about process, so Type I (authoritarian) leadership may cause faculty members to be unwilling to accept the outcomes, even if they are positive, because of what the faculty view as an inadequacy of process. Type IV (laissez-faire) leadership may bring about maximum acceptance on the part of faculty but may produce results that are skewed in favor of faculty interests because of the lack of bird's-eye perspective that administrators and others can contribute to the process. I believe Type III (follower-based authoritative) leadership can work, but the agenda may be limited in scope by faculty's tending to pose problems that are primarily relevant to their own interests. In my experience, Type II (leader-based authoritative) leadership works best, on average, although it certainly is not without risks or shortcomings.

In the end, it may be that different styles work better for different leaders. More importantly, I believe that an administrator may find that alternating among styles works best, depending on the situation and the set of problems at hand. For example, at one extreme, if a problem is particularly urgent and simply does not allow for a long deliberative process, Type I may be the only alternative. At the other extreme, if a problem is not urgent or is clearly relevant most directly to faculty—such as revising faculty-governance procedures—Type IV may be appropriate. Type III may be appropriate for a faculty-driven issue in which there are irreconcilable differences among factions of faculty and it is useful for an authority, such as a dean or provost, to settle the matter.

Although Type I might seem as if it would be most damaging, on average, to faculty morale, I have found that Type IV can be equally damaging. In the case of Type I, faculty may feel disenfranchised and left without a meaningful voice in matters that vitally concern them. But in the case of Type IV, many faculty members may come to feel adrift, as if they are floating in a boat with no clear destination or even direction.

Type II may work best overall, with complementation as needed by Types I, III, and IV. Administrators must decide what style or styles of leadership will bring about optimal outcomes, given the circumstances encountered in their daily work.

Although any style of leadership can fail, Types I and IV leadership are perhaps the most risky and most susceptible to degenerating into balls of clay. Consider a failure of Type I leadership. Recently, a small college announced that it would be shutting down. The surprise was not so much that it was shutting down as that the various stakeholders—faculty, staff, alumni, and friends—had no idea what was coming. How could it possibly happen that a college would reach the point of collapse without the knowledge of any of its stakeholders? This was a case of Type I leadership at the extreme. The president and board succeeded in holding their cards very close to the vest. The outcome was a closure that likely could have been avoided had all of the college's many supporters been aware of its dire financial circumstances. In this case, the extreme of Type I leadership, in my view, resulted in the financial failure of a college that very possibly could have been saved with better leadership.

Now consider an example of Type IV leadership. In one university, a board of trustees was largely out of touch with the educational challenges facing the university. Most of the board members knew little or next to nothing about higher education because they had been selected largely for political reasons, as tends to be the case more and more these days. At one point, the president of the university, in fact although not in principle, was essentially chosen by the faculty. The president then ran the institution largely for the benefit of the faculty. The university diverged further and further from its mission of service to other populations as the faculty, like any other group given the chance, saw opportunities to promote its own interests. The outcome was a mediocre university that managed to become even more mediocre by the year because it failed to adequately optimize outcomes for a broad range of its constituencies. The faculty, for the most part, was happy, but few other constituencies were. We consider below the underlying problem: a culture of mediocracy that is the polar opposite of the values of ACCEL.

When Things Go Very Wrong

Mediocracy, or When Mediocrity Triumphs over Merit

Academics want to talk about mediocrity in academic institutions about as much as the residents of Harry Potter World want to talk about Voldemort. Many of us like to view universities as truly meritocratic environments in which the best prevail and the weak are weeded out or at least properly sanctioned. At the same time, academics have often seen exceptions to this generalization, ranging from mild to flagrant, in which mediocrity is rewarded and excellence is punished. The core academic value of excellence is hijacked.

Joseph Hermanowicz (2013) has shown how, in some environments, mediocrity triumphs. Hermanowicz points out that when mediocre performers capture an academic department (or school or university), two things happen: marginalization of the adept and protection of the mediocre from the adept. The academic unit comes to be run for the benefit of its worst performers. In effect, the normal academic tables are turned to ensure that excellent performers are ostracized and mediocre performers are valued and rewarded. Virtually anyone with experience in university administration has seen departments be hijacked by mediocre performers intent on preserving an environment that makes them look good. The same can happen to schools, colleges, or whole universities.

I use the term *mediocracy* to characterize an environment in which, contrary to academic values, governance is by and for mediocre performers (http://dictionary.reference.com/browse/mediocracy). In a mediocracy, mediocrity is rewarded and excellence is punished. The constituents do not view themselves as mediocre but rather as excelling in ways that outsiders fail to recognize and appreciate. Units that are poorly rated by almost any valid external system of evaluation may nevertheless think of themselves as excellent in their own, externally underappreciated way.

The question that remains is how it is possible that institutions publicly committed to excellence can essentially be hijacked so that their publicly stated goal of academic excellence is subverted and mediocracy is allowed to flourish. My goal here is to describe a set of mechanisms, based on the work of the Yale psychologist Irving Janis (1972) on groupthink.

Groupthink occurs when concurrence among a group becomes so important that realistic appraisals come to be suppressed. Janis uses as examples political fiascoes such as the Bay of Pigs, but he might as easily have used examples of academic institutions or units within those institutions that, contrary to academic norms, value mediocrity. Such a situation can become self-perpetuating. For self-protection, departments hire people like themselves and disparage those with stronger credentials. They might view them as "not fitting in," or as "belonging at, and more likely to accept offers from, more prestigious institutions," or as "not understanding what we are about." In this way, institutions or institutional units that function at a low level continue to function that way.

When groupthink prevails, the in-group overestimates the rightfulness of the group, is closed-minded, and exerts pressure toward uniformity. Janis has referred to eight specific symptoms: (1) illusions of invulnerability, (2) unquestioned belief in the morality or rightfulness of the group, (3) rationalizations of warnings that might question the group's assumptions, (4) stereotyping of those who oppose the group as weak or stupid or biased or just plain evil, (5) self-censorship of ideas that deviate from the group consensus, (6) illusions of unanimity among the group, (7) pressure to conform, with nonconformity viewed as disloyalty, and (8) mindguards, or self-appointed enforcers of group norms who shield the group from those who dissent and who organize others to punish dissenters.

How does this mindset translate into the production and maintenance of mediocrity in academic units or whole institutions? Each of the mechanisms of groupthink is present in the creation and perpetuation a mediocracy.

With regard to self-perceived "rightfulness," denizens of mediocre departments or institutions come to think of themselves not as mediocre but rather as excellent according to their own standards, which they may come to view as superior to the standards of outsiders. The constituents of a mediocracy believe they know something outsiders don't know and that they are guardians of a culture that, in its own way, is superior to the norms set by uninformed, indeed ignorant, outsiders.

Moreover, the participants in a culture of mediocrity are closed-minded. And when knowledgeable insiders or outsiders see things in a different way, their perceptions are discounted or dismissed. Boosters who accept the group norm are praised and rewarded. Participants in mediocre institutions are largely closed to better ways of doing things. In a mediocre culture, insiders who do not conform to the group norms face the choice of either being shunned and rejected or being literally sent away. There is no room for discussion of what should be better, but there is plenty of room for discussion of what is wrong with people who do not accept the group norms.

With regard to the symptoms described above, those who run mediocre departments and institutions often see themselves as invulnerable because they have created the relationships that keep themselves in place. Recent scandals in college athletics show how a culture of invulnerability can persist over many years as athletic directors, coaches, and even higher-level administrators turn a blind eye to the corruption and profit-driven management that has characterized some (but certainly not all) university athletic departments.

Participants in mediocracies typically do not question their own behavior, at least publicly. They question the behavior of insiders or outsiders who dare to cast doubt on the way things are being run. Often one is not even allowed to talk about the problems inherent in governance without risking one's own neck. When there are warnings, from the inside or outside, that things are not as they should be, the typical reaction is to rationalize those warnings—to look for ulterior motives, conspiracies, incompatible value systems, or anything that will call into suspicion the perceptions of the skeptics. Mindguards enforce unanimity of viewpoint. In such environments, it is dangerous to question the accepted norms, and those who do so risk not only disapproval and shunning but also their jobs. Academics who work in such environments are simply not allowed to question them publicly, and certainly not in writing.

Typical arguments for the "superiority" of the mediocracy in an institution may be that (a) the values of the mediocracy better represent the culture of the institution—or the community or the state—than do the values of outsiders, including those of accreditors; (b) there is no need or desire to indulge in the kind of pointy-headed high-brow intellectual endeavors that receive higher external evaluations; (c) the institution could never be at or near the top on some outside scale anyway, and anyone who says it could be is a liar; or (d) the institution is not appreciated and the problem is not with the story but rather with how it is being told to the outside. Sometimes the underlying argument is that any one set of ratings will be worth little because no one set could possibly capture all the unique qualities of the institution. That is true, but when the argument leads to an escape from established academic values, it becomes treacherous. There are certain standards that apply to any institution, such as first-year retention rates; four-, five-, and six-year graduation rates; percentage of students who are employed in jobs that make use of the skills they learned in college; development of critical, creative, and practical thinking skills; and willingness of alumni to support the institution.

The costs of mediocracy are high. First, academic values are undermined. Second, excellent faculty and students will enter a mediocracy only as an absolute last resort, usually at their peril. Third, the excellent people already in an institution will be trying to leave, often with encouragement. Fourth, it will be hard to change the environment because those who try to change it for the better will be viewed as not fitting in and even as a threat. Finally, it will be difficult to attract high levels of external resources because many donors, granting agencies, and potential nonprofit partners will be reluctant to invest in institutions where there is little chance of positive payback.

Converting a culture of mediocrity to a culture of excellence looks as if it should be easy—after all, don't all institutions want to be great? The truth is more complicated. First, performers who are weak do not want to be confronted with colleagues who will make them look bad. If weak performers take over a department, college, or university, they will resist change. Second, weak performers have time on their hands. Because they are not busy doing their jobs constructively, they have the time to marshal resources to fight change, making things difficult for performers who are busy with their work. Third, administrators, even well-intentioned ones, know that their jobs often depend on good or at least acceptable faculty relations, so they may be reluctant to rock the boat. Finally, the governing board may not recognize the problem or may not care about it. The picture they are being shown by the administration is likely to be a rosy one, and the board may not have the knowledge or the will to make the changes that would be needed to transform the institution. Bottom line: in any institution, transformational change is hard work.

In a strong institution, there are remedies against the entrenchment of mediocrity, such as the ceding of control of a department to a chairperson from another department or to a representative of the dean's office. But in a weak institution, the mediocrity may extend from bottom to top. Whereas in some businesses, a poor product means that the business fails, colleges and universities may have protection in loyal fan bases (e.g., certain alumni, donors, and athletic supporters) that businesses do not have. In this case, one would hope that accreditors would come to the rescue, but accreditors deal with minimum standards, not standards for excellence.

Challenges from the outside and even the inside are likely to be met with strong resistance. Positive-change agents may just give up, having better things to do. Challenges from the inside may be few because those who do not accept the mediocrity have either learned to keep quiet or already left.

There is a saying that in the kingdom of the blind, the one-eyed man is king. H. G. Wells (2008), in his 1904 short story "The Country of the Blind," recognized that this is not the case. Rather, in the country of the blind, people with any vision at all are viewed as abnormal and as threats to the social order. In the Wells story, Nuñez, the protagonist, stumbles into the country of the blind. He meets the woman of his dreams. But the elders of the village of the blind think that with all his talk of sight, he is rather crazy. They try to persuade Nuñez to have his eyes cut out; otherwise, he will not be allowed to marry the woman he loves. He escapes, realizing that any vision at all is viewed as a threat to orderly society in the country of the blind. In a mediocracy, any realized talent is similarly viewed as a threat.

There is a solution to the problem of mediocracy, but it may be accepted in environments of mediocracy only if it is imposed. Institutions need to invite teams of evaluators from external institutions that are *aspirational* peers—that is, that by almost any objective standard rank above them—to provide evaluation at all levels, from the lowest rungs of employment to the top administrators and board of trustees. The job of the evaluators is to make suggestions not for reaching minimal standards but rather for reaching standards of excellence, given the target institution's mission. The evaluators must be given free rein to do their evaluations and present them candidly. Then the target institution must take the results seriously. As in the oft-told joke about how many psychologists it takes to change a light bulb—it takes just one, but the light bulb has to want to change—colleges and universities can also change if they want to and have the courage to do so. In order to change, they have to move beyond benefiting only limited constituencies, as often happens when they become prey to academic tribalism.

Academic Tribalism

A second challenge to strong university leadership and progress, and sometimes a cause of mediocre performance, is academic tribalism (Sternberg 2014a). When I was a younger scholar, a very famous cognitive psychologist came to my office to visit me during his colloquium trip to my university. I mentioned with pride that I had just written a new textbook in cognitive psychology. His quick response was, "Bob, you're not a cognitive psychologist anymore."

I was deeply hurt. I had been trained in cognitive psychology by some of the top scholars in the field and had always thought of myself as their protégé. True, I had strayed and done some research on love. What I did not realize was that this straying from the tried-and-true path would lead to expulsion from my academic tribe. Like many academics, I had always been a tribal outcast in the public schools because of my interest in intellectual pursuits. Here I had finally found a tribe that would have me, and they seemed not to want me anymore!

The term "tribe" has been defined in different ways, but here I use it to refer to a group of people who are united by a community of customs and traditions and by adherence to a largely common worldview. Others have also viewed academics as tribal. Hazard Adams (1987) wrote a light-hearted book about tribalism among academics, and Tony Becher and Paul Trowler (2001) wrote a serious academic work about it. The problem with tribalism is that it interferes with the academic mission, in several ways.

1. *Limiting of self-actualization.* Tribalism limits the realization of one's own potential. For example, as long as I viewed myself as a "cognitive psychologist," I was limited in what I could study. Once I freed myself of my tribal affiliation, I could study whatever I wanted to.

2. *Uniformity of point of view.* Tribes tend to have a uniform point of view, at least with regard to the big things. Sometimes this uniformity leads to inability or unwillingness to see other points of view and to a rejection of difference. South Sudan no sooner declared independence from the rest of Sudan than tribes within the new country, such as the Nuer, Murle, and Dinka, starting fighting among each other. In academia, tribes form within and across disciplines and can't understand why anyone would see things another way. In my own field of psychology, scientists and practitioners often have trouble speaking with each other because of their adherence to their own point of view, emphasizing either scientific inquiry or helping clients. In some English departments, one similarly encounters tension between traditional literary scholars and creative writers. In each case, approaches come to be seen, falsely, as mutually exclusive.

3. *Distrust of outsiders.* Tribes tend to be distrustful of outsiders. When I visited an American Indian reservation where two mutually hostile tribes had been placed by the US government, I was struck by the tribes' distrust of each other, even though they had lived on the same reservation for many years. We see this kind of tribalism in academics' tendencies to sometimes disparage or at least feel uncomfortable with those who think differently—scientists' suspicions about humanists and vice versa; academic

departments' suspicion about the athletic department and vice versa; even different tribes within a department, such as zoologists and botanists in some biology departments. Instead of feeling that the approaches are complementary or that each group can learn from the other, there often is a not-so-hidden disdain and rejection.

4. *Hiring and promotion wars.* When multiple tribes coexist within a department, they often battle for resources. In my administrative experience, for example, I have seen hiring and promotion wars between tribes that make it difficult for either side to get its way—between French and Spanish factions of modern-language departments, between theoretical and experimental physicists, and between quantitative and qualitative methodologists in sociology. Even graduate-student slots may be bitterly contested. The result can be that a department is held back because each tribe is so intent on making sure that it, not its competitor tribe, gets additional resources.

5. *Rejection of interdisciplinarity.* Perhaps even worse than being a member of another tribe is a scholar's attempt to be a member of multiple tribes. I saw junior faculty members try, without success, to stay out of a war in a philosophy department between Continental rationalists and British empiricists—they were almost forced to choose sides. I have also seen economists and others who engage in interdisciplinary work be rejected by both groups, because the academics are seen as good for only half the slot they are occupying, thereby "wasting" the other valuable half-slot. Academics may end up praising interdisciplinarity as long as it does not take away valuable positions from their tribe.

6. *Transmission of a tribal value system to students.* Professors may transmit tribal values. I took a course on abnormal psychology from a behaviorist. The engaging professor had little good to say about psychodynamicists (Freudians). I had trouble, as I suspect did other students, separating the professor's tribal viewpoint from "the truth." Similarly, in one of my analytical philosophy courses, the professor would hardly give the time of day to rationalist philosophers. When tribalism passes from one generation of students to the next, it continues to reinforce strongly categorical ways of thinking that prevent students from seeing how different approaches to problems can be useful in tandem or even when melded.

Tribalism does little good for academia other than giving academics a sense of belonging and affiliation. We all like to belong, but academics need to move beyond tribalism to embrace intellectual inclusion rather than exclusion.

How Academic Leaders Can Seem Mediocre Because They Keep Doing What They Did Before

Sometimes academic leaders turn in a mediocre performance not because they are necessarily bad but rather because they keep doing what they did as faculty members. In these cases, there is hope if they can let go of ways that worked before but that no longer work (Sternberg 2011a). Consider ten habits of highly unsuccessful academic leaders that exhibit the negative transfer of training carried over from a leader's pre-administration days. Such administrators cannot adequately lead ACCEL universities because they are still thinking in terms of their needs as faculty members, not in terms of the needs of the broader constituencies for whom they now are responsible.

1. *Visibility.* "Here I am! Here I am!" Academics strive to be visible, and much of the time their advancement through the ranks depends on their visibility to their colleagues at their own institution and to other academics in their field. In contrast, administrators tend to be most effective when they are working behind the scenes and are only modestly visible. The most successful institutions are those that function smoothly—like well-oiled machines—and where administrators don't stick out like squeaky wheels. When administrators become highly visible, it is often because things are not working out.

2. *The role of collaborators.* "I did it! Me! Me!" Effective academics often collaborate, but the greater the number of collaborators one has, the more doubt there is in promotion and tenure decisions over who did what. In publications with many authors, it can become difficult or even impossible to tell who did what, whereas in a single-authored book or article, there is (in theory) no doubt. In contrast, administrators typically can do almost nothing by themselves. They must work collaboratively and as a team in almost everything they do.

3. *Individual glory.* "Am I great or what?" Successful academics bask in glory—of publications, of prizes, of research quoted by the media, of outstanding teaching ratings. Successful administrators, in contrast, often go out of their way to deflect credit and to ensure that others get the glory.

A commonly used technique is to engineer change so that faculty members get credit for ideas, whether the ideas were originally theirs or not. After all, they are the ones who are going to have to live with them.

4. *Strong positions.* "Give 'em an inch and they'll take a mile!" Academics are often rewarded for taking strong positions in professional discourse and debates. Their work may receive less attention if it is viewed as sitting on a fence or as lacking in boldness. Extreme positions get attention, and even if the attention is negative it can sometimes help advance a career. In contrast, administrators making decisions must take into account the interests of diverse stakeholders with very different points of view. Such balancing of interests often results in positions that are middle-ground attempts to achieve some kind of common good. On matters of ethics or principle, there can be no middle ground, but in most of the issues one deals with in administration, any of a number of potential courses of action are ethical and principled, though with very different possible outcomes.

5. *Privacy.* "My personal life is my own business!" The personal lives of academics are typically out of bounds unless they flagrantly misbehave, especially toward their students or colleagues. In contrast, the personal lives of administrators, for better or worse, are usually considered fair game. If an extramarital affair or other personal indiscretion is discovered, for example, it may be viewed as justifiable grounds for terminating an administrator because he or she is bringing unwelcome attention to the university and the moral ground on which it stands. Obviously, such indiscretions become especially problematical when committed with subordinates. In administration, "my personal life is my own business" applies only until one's superiors decide it doesn't, often as a result of unwanted publicity.

6. *Schedule.* "I love the freedom this job gives me to live a balanced life." Many of those who go into academe do so in part because of the flexibility in schedule that it allows—at least for those who do not have mind-numbingly large numbers of courses to teach. Administrative schedules typically are, at best, 9 to 5, allowing much less flexibility, and further usually require one to show up for events on nights and weekends.

7. *Reporting structure.* "No one tells me what to do!" Professors often do not view themselves as working for anyone in particular, other than, perhaps, themselves. They may view themselves as entrepreneurs who create new intellectual enterprises. Although they are usually under a

department chair or head, dean, and so forth, they generally do not view such people as "bosses" but rather as people who should stay out of their way (except when they require additional resources). In contrast, academic administrators have clearly defined supervisors, and if they fail to please their supervisors, they may quickly be in trouble or out of a job.

8. *Degree of latitude in behavior and dress.* "I never got over the hippie look!" Professors are typically allowed a large number of "idiosyncrasy credits" in terms of how they can act and dress. As long as they do not show up nude or too outlandishly dressed, for example, they are generally permitted to carry on with their activities. Administrators, however, are usually expected to wear business attire and to act in ways that are not excessively idiosyncratic. Professors can be annoying in various ways, such as being habitually late for appointments. Such habits would put administrators in jeopardy of their positions.

9. *Focus on one's own teaching and research.* "Enough of my talking about my work; it's your turn: what do you think of my work?" Academics typically focus their greatest attention on their own teaching and research. In contrast, administrators are expected to focus on supporting the teaching and research of their charges. Their main goal is to help the professoriate, staff, and students, not themselves. If they focus too much on their own professional interests, they are viewed as not having successfully made the transition from professor to administrator.

10. *Suffering fools.* "Stuff it, pal!" As an academic, you are expected not to pull punches. If you view someone as foolish, you say so, although perhaps not in so many words. As a reviewer of an article or a commentator on a symposium presentation, you are expected to be quite direct, although not rude. As an administrator, you often have to suffer fools gladly, especially if they happen to be powerful professors, supervisors, or well-heeled donors.

On the whole, the habits described above are learned and are largely a result of different reward systems for professors and administrators. Professors are typically rewarded for behavior that is sufficiently individualistic that their own personal contributions shine through. If they are too communal, they may be appreciated but will have difficulty getting through the reappointment-tenure-promotion process. Administrators are usually rewarded for behavior that is sufficiently communal that it helps a wide swath of students, faculty, and staff. If they are too individualistic, they may be viewed as promoting themselves rather than the common good of the university.

The greatest problem all universities face is a simple one: inertia. Their stakeholders—administrators, professors, staff, alumni, even students—are used to things being done in a certain way. Over time, stakeholders learn to optimize, or at least satisfice, in whatever environment they have. They are then loath to change that environment because they have made it work for them, to the extent possible. They don't want to start over and take the risk that things will actually get worse. So things stay the same because it is just so much easier for stakeholders if they stay the way they have been, almost without regard to how functional that way is.

A background as a professor does not always prepare one for life as an academic administrator. As an administrator, one often has to unlearn many of the habits acquired as a professor. One also has to learn to think in new ways. As a professor, one tries to market one's research and teaching. As an administrator, one has to market the mission, perhaps the ACCEL mission, of a whole university. We consider marketing next.

13

Marketing Higher Education

Nonprofit higher education is under threat like never before. Costs for higher education are rising at a rate that simply may not be sustainable over the long term. For-profit universities have provided platforms that enable individuals, especially those in the workforce, to obtain degrees with an ease and convenience formerly not possible. Silicon Valley entrepreneurs are looking for ways to provide quality online education at a fraction of the current cost. Some of them even question the value of a college education: as mentioned earlier, Peter Thiel is actually paying students not to go to college and to start businesses instead.

As costs to colleges and universities rise, state legislatures have been cutting allocations in the public sector in a way never seen before, at the same time constraining the rate at which tuition may rise; low interest rates reduce returns on endowments; newly limited funding of grant proposals reduces income through indirect costs; and philanthropy is constrained in many cases by flat or even falling personal incomes. What's to be done?

This chapter is based on Sternberg 2012b.

We in the higher-education sector can learn a lot from the Swiss watch-making industry (Sternberg 2012b). In the 1980s, the Swiss watch industry was in serious trouble. Swiss watchmakers—who had dominated the industry for decades and, in some cases, for centuries—were being routed by Japanese watchmakers, who were producing watches that could do much more than the Swiss ones, and at a fraction of the cost. Why pay hundreds or even thousands of dollars for a Swiss watch that told the time and possibly the date when you could get the time, day, and date from a Japanese product, not to mention additional features such as a stop-watch, alarm, multiple time zones, and sometimes more? Even worse for the Swiss industry, the Japanese quartz (battery-operated) watches were often more accurate in telling the time than the Swiss hand-wound or self-winding models.

Swiss watchmakers might have gone bust—in much the way some of us fear for the newspaper and magazine industries today—except for their creative redefinition of what it means to own a Swiss watch. Recognizing that the Japanese were out to capture their market, the Swiss watchmakers set out to redefine what it meant to own a Swiss watch. The Swiss watch was to become what a classical stringed instrument had become—the symbol of quality. It is difficult if not impossible to distinguish the sound of a Stradivarius from that of a well-made modern instrument, but musicians are willing to pay a huge premium for the perception of quality in the classical instrument. Swiss watchmakers similarly capitalized on their brand equity, knowing that they had only a limited amount of time to do so before becoming irrelevant. They needed users of their products to personally identify with them—to see their Swiss watches as extensions of themselves. Similarly, an ACCEL university has to be seen as an extension of the people in the university—as their embodiment through the concept of a university.

Different watchmakers emphasized different images. For example, Rolex Oyster watches present a bold image of luxury and privilege. Patek Philippe watches, generally even more expensive than Rolexes, tend to present an image of the highest quality accompanied by understated elegance and the durability of a single watch over generations. A Blancpain watch is even more understated, and known for being handmade by a single maker. Tag Heuer has become a symbol of the young achiever on the way up.

Longines offers quality at a more modest price, while Swatch watches are funky and relatively inexpensive. An ACCEL university is as much a brand as any particular kind of watch.

What are the lessons in brand equity to be learned for higher education?

1. *Waiting to see what happens does not work.* The Swiss watchmakers could not tarry or their market would have been gone for good. Neither can higher education today wait around and hope for the best. Some newspaper and magazine publishers waited; you can see how well it worked out for them! There are too many threats to nonprofit higher education to adopt a stance of wait-and-see. You can't wait to change while your market share steadily evaporates.

2. *Quality institutions will survive only if they effectively market their brand.* The Swiss watch brands had (and still have) a worldwide reputation for superiority. The watchmakers, however, needed to persuade their customers that quality matters. This was no easy task. Many products today, such as personal computers, have become largely mass-marketed products of generic quality. Some manufacturers, such as IBM, left the business, recognizing that relatively few PC customers would pay a premium for quality. Cheap watches can be bought by the hundreds before you reach the cost of a good Swiss watch. Moreover, all the watches tell time. The Swiss watchmakers, therefore, needed to persuade customers that their product was a statement about the wearer—much like a piece of jewelry. (Indeed, some non-Swiss brands, such as Cartier and Bulgari, are known primarily for their association with jewelry.)

You may be thinking that you would never seek to purchase a premium watch. But how about some other product that is more luxurious than you really need—a premium car, bicycle, house, home appliance, television, cell phone, clothing, or even branded rather than generic food or drugs? Most of us seek a premium version of something because, for whatever that thing is, we want better quality, or at least our perception of it. With higher education, students often feel their choices are limited, relative to their resources, when it comes to price.

When students pay the high and, in some institutions, astronomical costs of a college education today, they understandably feel that they are paying a premium price, whether they want to or not, and they expect to get their money's worth. You might think that the premium branding strategy applies only to elite institutions. But today, because students perceive almost all of higher education as commanding premium prices, they want a product that delivers. Having a strong value proposition applies to all institutions, not just elite ones. Thus, institutions of higher education need to market their brand to bring pride of ownership and belonging to their students. They need to develop personal identification with the brand. Generic institutions without a clear and differentiated value proposition are the ones most likely to be hurt.

3. *Quality is, in part, in the eye of the beholder.* How does one actually know that, say, a Rolex or a Patek Philippe is a superior watch? For the large majority of buyers, that knowledge is gotten through the superior functioning and durability of the watch and through the watchmaker's reputation. It is not enough to be good: the customer must be persuaded, as Detroit automakers are learning today after many lean years in which they saw their brand equity decimated. Not only do you need to excel; you must be recognized for your excellence. Good marketing and good public relations are necessary but generally not sufficient to persuade stakeholders of quality. Thus, colleges and universities need transparent systems of accountability that will persuade stakeholders of the quality the institutions claim.

4. *Institutions will succeed to the extent that they identify, pursue, and market their unique niche.* Institutions at the top of the reputational heap—the Yales and the Stanfords, say—have marked out their niche, trying to be the best possible in a wide variety of disciplines. Most institutions of higher learning, however, have neither the financial resources nor even the will to become the best across the board. Instead, they need to do what the Swiss watchmakers did—find a niche in which they excel and then sell themselves as powerfully as they can to those who identify with what they have to offer.

As one example, colleges could start planning an "ethical leadership track," to be administered jointly by academic and student affairs and to be readily and freely available to all students—undergraduate and graduate. It would combine the study of ethical leadership in the academic sphere with activities developed by student affairs that immediately apply what one learns in the classroom to one's activities on campus.

In this way, educators might hope to better integrate the academic and student-affairs sides of a university, a task that is not always easily accomplished. In particular, certain courses would be identified as participating in the track and would include principles and case studies in ethical leadership as applied to the particular discipline being studied. Thus, students would not have to take additional courses but rather would elect courses and course sections relevant to the track. They would see directly how ethical leadership cross-cuts academic disciplines. And through their student-affairs activities, such as community service, student government, athletics, journalism, or whatever, they would apply what they learned. They would then be accountable in the academic work for showing how they applied what they learned on the academic side to the student-affairs side.

5. *Consistency is needed in quality and in messaging.* For the best watchmakers, every watch is of superb quality. There are few or no duds, and if there is a dud, it is quickly replaced, no questions asked. Moreover, the watchmakers deliver on quality: there is an active market for quality Swiss watches dating back to the early 1900s. If the old watches are serviced, they still work and keep accurate time. And they bring high prices, even a century later. Similarly, colleges and universities need to produce graduates who show to employers and other stakeholders in the higher-education system that they have the skills and work ethic to cope effectively with the work demands of the present and the future.

Similarly, messaging has to be strong and consistent. In earlier times, it was relatively simple to make different pitches to different audiences—to try to be everything to everybody. But with the advent of the Internet, information spreads around the globe literally at the speed of light. As some political candidates have discovered, whatever you say anywhere to anybody is fair game. You can't afford to be indecisive about what you stand for. Some institutions cannot decide who or what they are: they have too many messages, too many logos, too many moving parts working at cross-purposes to each other. The Swiss watchmakers that have succeeded have been consistent in producing high-quality products as well as a distinctive and unified brand message, sometimes offering diverse options (models) within the context of that overall message.

To some readers, it may seem offensive to think of a college or university in terms of a construct of brand equity. But in an age of rapid advances and intense competition, institutions of higher learning can no longer afford to be quixotic or otherwise naive. Enhancement and effective communication of brand equity is what saved Swiss watch companies. It is what will save quality institutions of higher education.

In my view, the ACCEL university has unique and valuable brand equity. Universities that market themselves in terms of the ACCEL mission compete in a way that can attract resources unavailable to those with more narrow or boring missions.

14

It's Not Only Students
Who Need to Learn

A Model of Institutional Change for Assessing Universities as Learning Organizations

In universities, we are acutely aware of the need for students to learn (Bok 2008). Student learning is measured by grades but also, now, by standardized tests and other kinds of measures such as electronic portfolios (Sternberg et al. 2011). Faculty learning is measured primarily by assessment of CVs. But how about the learning of a university?

Universities also need to learn (Thorp and Goldstein 2013). Whereas educators have become very attuned to rankings of universities on the basis of where universities are perceived to be, they have been less attuned to the question of whether universities are learning organizations—whether they are modifiable and can change (Bok 2013). Change is happening very rapidly in the field of higher education, whether the issue is MOOCs, criteria for accreditation, measurement of learning outcomes, or models for charging tuition or allocating financial aid (Selingo 2013; Zemsky 2013).

All organizations need to learn to keep up with rapid change in society (Senge 2006). I present here a model for assessing the potential of universities to learn and change. I focus on universities, but all the points made apply equally to colleges lacking graduate programs; indeed, the points apply to other kinds of organizations as well. First, I discuss prerequisites for learning institutions. Then I survey attitudinal variables. Finally, I talk about mediating variables that affect whether change can actually occur.

Prerequisites for Learning Institutions

Universities, like many institutions, have difficulty implementing change (Christensen and Eyring 2011). Learning institutions require three prerequisites for change (Sternberg 2000, 2015b).

Ability to Change

In order to learn, an institution has to be able to change. Not all organizations are. There can be several reasons why universities are unable to change, except perhaps cosmetically. One is lack of resources: they just lack the money or other resources they need to be able to change in meaningful ways. A second reason can be an administration, from the board of trustees downward, that enforces a culture of stagnation. Trustees may remember what the institution was like when they attended it and want it to remain the same. Or administrators may feel that their jobs will be threatened if the institution changes in any serious way. Or the professoriate may be extremely conservative and view itself as protecting the culture of the institution, no matter how stagnant it has become. An institution cannot learn if its management or other stakeholders cannot or will not let it.

Self-Efficacy: Belief in the Ability to Change

An organization may be able to change but not believe that it can. And if it does not believe it can change, it almost certainly won't. Just as we meet people who lack essential belief in their own ability to change ("I just can't lose weight"; "I'll never stop smoking"; "It's not worth trying to get a job because no one will ever want to hire me"), so are there institutions that lack the self-efficacy for learning and change. If stakeholders in a university lack self-efficacy for change, little else matters, even if the institution in fact could change if people believed it could.

Courage to Change

An institution may want to change but not have the courage to do so. Why does institutional learning and its resulting change require courage? Because when you change, inevitably you give up some of the old to make way for the new. And there inevitably are many individuals and groups that have a strong vested interest in what already exists. What professor, for example, wants to see her department abolished? What administrator wants to see his job eliminated? Sometimes people are game for change, as long as it does not affect them, with the result that nothing really changes because people do not have the courage to move from where they are to where they need to go.

A "Mineralogical" Framework for Institutional Learning and Change

Consider a cultural framework for institutional learning and change (Sternberg 2000) as it applies to universities. (Measurement within the framework is described in Sternberg 2000.) The framework assesses three factors:

1. How much desire is there for actual change in this institutional culture as a whole?
2. How much desire is there for the appearance of change in the culture of the institution?
3. What is the perceived quality or potential quality of the institution?

If, to simplify things, we respond to each of these questions with a value that is either "low" or "high," then we end up with 2^3, or eight different kinds of institutional cultures with respect to learning and resulting change. The argument here is that the eight kinds of institutional cultures differ rather dramatically in how much learning and change they permit. Of course, a university need not be a pure case; it may be a mixture of kinds of institutional cultures (with respect to learning and change). Although these are certainly not the only possible cultures with respect to learning and change, they encompass some of the major institutional types with respect to learning and change. It is possible that the same framework could apply to individuals as well, if one viewed an individual as a complex system.

Institutional cultures may sometimes be at least partially "domain-specific." In other words, one department or unit of the organization will fall into one category, another department (or other unit) into another category. The institution may be modifiable with respect to some areas but not others.

The Rusted-Iron Institution

The rusted-iron institution is low in desire for actual change, desire for appearance of change, and perceived quality. The rusted-iron institution is the antithesis of a learning organization. Its constituents simply abhor change or, for whatever reason, think it is impossible for their institution. The mood of the institution is variable, depending on circumstances. In my experience, rusted-iron institutions fall into two broad groups.

One possible mood is despondence. Such universities may feel lost, hopeless, or somehow wrecked. Sometimes their constituents feel that they are beaten down by bureaucracy, low morale, or institutional calcification. People in the institution who are despondent may simply have given up on it. Not infrequently, rusted-iron institutions are ones that have seen brighter days, but for which those days are long gone.

A second possible mood, oddly, is self-satisfaction. As we saw in chapter 12, people who are self-satisfied may take pride in being mediocre, or believe that tradition trumps quality or that others don't see what value they see. In this case, the organization essentially takes pride in its mediocrity. Taking pride in mediocrity is not as far-fetched as it sounds. The insular internal view of an institution may be that it is fine, whereas the external view is that it is anything but fine. In 1970, the late senator Roman Hruska of Nebraska said of G. Harrold Carswell, a nominee for the Supreme Court: "Even if he were mediocre, there are a lot of mediocre judges and people and lawyers. They are entitled to a little representation, aren't they, and a little chance?" This attitude prevails in some rusted-iron institutions. There is always plenty of room for mediocrity. In this case, one simply dismisses external views as misguided or irrelevant.

One would think that such an institution would have trouble attracting students, but it may well attract those who are satisfied with a culture of mediocrity, especially if the price reflects the quality of instruction. Or it may attract those who cannot afford anything better or who simply don't know any better.

In his work on groupthink, mentioned earlier, Irving Janis (1972) described the concept of mindguards, people whose job it is to ensure conformity within a group. In the case of a rusted-iron organization, there are likely to be a lot of mindguards, individuals who view themselves as guardians of tradition. They believe they represent the almost sacred culture of the institution, and guard it religiously. What they may not say is that they are threatened by any changes that will make them look bad. For example, unproductive faculty members often do not want productive colleagues because those colleagues may put the unproductive ones to shame.

For-profit businesses that are rusted-iron organizations are unlikely to have a long life. They are overtaken by the competition. Rather, rusted-iron organizations that survive for any length of time are more likely to be nonprofits, likely ones that have some kind of lock on their business, such as state universities or those that have a long tradition and loyal alumni. One often marvels that they stay bad so long, but unless and until they encounter serious competition that threatens their business model, they may have few incentives to change and many incentives to stay as they are.

Various signs indicate a rusted-iron university. Among these signs are an entrenched bureaucracy, apathy, a decayed physical plant, employee burnout, lack of desire on the part of stakeholders for change or belief in the futility of trying to change, lack of follow-through on agreements, indifference to those who are served, and lack of resources. The prognosis for change in an educational institution showing these signs is poor.

In the case of Rusted Iron University, a state university, the organization is not well regarded nationally but has built a series of myths around itself as providing services that other universities cannot provide. Because the services are provided inexpensively to consumers, it maintains itself. It also receives state support, so that if it cannot meet its expenses through student tuition and fees, it can get a bailout from the state. It has various clientele: students who utilize its services because they are easily available; students who use it because members of their family have in the past; people who want cheap services but may tell themselves that they are getting quality; and students who simply do not realize that the services are inferior because they have no comparison.

Employees of the university fear change because it would highlight their own mediocre performance. Because many people in the state do not know any better or because they have a long family tradition of sending their children to the institution, they continue to send their children to the university regardless, in part because of its bargain-basement price and despite its bargain-basement quality.

The Granite Institution

The granite university is low in desire for actual change, low in desire for appearance of change, but high in perceived quality. Its mood is one of smugness. Its self-belief is that the institution is sure and solid and that change would only chip away at it just as erosion chips away at rocks and beaches. The institution may feel that it is great but misunderstood or that it is a university that works and does not need to be snobbish like some great universities.

Some signs of a granite institution are an emphasis on entrenched traditions, a focus on keeping employees and possibly unions in line, pride in always having done things the way they're now being done, old facilities, and grimness in the attitudes of personnel. The prognosis for this university, like the prognosis for the rusted-iron institution, is poor.

The greatest challenge with a granite university is the pride people take in the entrenchment of mediocrity. One might look to trustees to change things, but in my experience, they often are embodiments of the culture. Real go-getters don't want to be trustees of such institutions, so the people who will get on board and the people who will even be asked are likely to be those who support and perhaps grew up intellectually in the culture.

The prognosis for a granite institution is in some ways worse than that for a rusted-iron one. In a rusted-iron institution, new leadership may bring hope of change. In a granite institution, new leaders who talk about change are not likely to last long because they threaten the mediocrity that is at the core of the institution's culture.

Granite University is also public. Many stakeholders believe it to be one of the finest state-supported universities in the region. Few people outside the state share this view. At one time, the university was well regarded, but that was before state budget cuts forced it to dismantle programs and terminate employees. In some institutions where these events occur, stakeholders become painfully aware of the loss of quality. At Granite University, however, living in the past is a way of life. Some people even say that going there is like going back in time a hundred years. The large majority of constituents are proud of what the university once represented, believing that it still is what it was in the past. Those individuals who recognize that the university has changed for the worse are, for the most part, afraid to speak up. Their fear stems from the "tall poppy" phenomenon: poppies that grow higher than the others are cut down to size. The same can apply to people.

The Amber Institution (with Internal Insects)

The amber institution is low in desire for actual change, high in desire for the appearance of change, and low in perceived quality. Its mood is one of frustration. Its self-belief is that that it is internally flawed and that change might therefore destroy it. As in amber jewelry with insects inside, you can't get rid of the insects without destroying the amber. So you either learn to like the insects or you get yourself new jewelry. Thus, the amber institution believes that it has internal flaws: if they were to be removed, it would result in the destruction of the organization. Amber institutions, unlike granite ones, know they have problems but feel they cannot solve them. That said, they would like the institution to appear to change, or at least for people to love the amber without noticing the internal insects.

Some signs of an amber institution are an inured and sometimes overly long-serving academic leadership, obvious structural flaws in organization, hyperstability in the face of dissension, and inaccessibility of the power structure of the organization. The prognosis for change is medium-low.

Amber University, a large private institution, is suffering from falling enrollments because it draws its students primarily from a region in which the population of university students has been declining but in which there are a number of universities rather similar to itself. The university is in the lower middle of the prestige rankings. Its academic leadership has been stable for many years although the top position has changed recently. Because it has a very small endowment, it is largely tuition-dependent. Partly as a result of its having hired consultants, it is very conscious of branding. It has had several different marketing campaigns, each trying less than successfully to differentiate it from its competition. The marketing campaigns make it look almost like a different university each time, but it remains essentially the same. The faculty and staff have expressed concern that the university puts too much money into marketing itself and not enough into actually improving its educational product.

The Opal Institution

The opal institution is low in desire for actual change but high in desire for the appearance of change and high in self-perceived quality. Its mood is one of self-righteousness. It often believes it is at the top and that any changes can only make it worse. Opal institutions are often rated highly, with the result that they fear that change will hurt their ratings.

This institution is like an opal in that if regarded from different perspectives, it takes on different appearances and looks as if it is changing, when in fact, it's always the same opal. Only the appearances are different. The power structure of the organization believes that changing the organization, like changing an opal, is likely to only make it worse. It fares best when left alone but viewed from many different angles so that it appears to be in flux when it is not.

Signs of an opal institution may be large amounts of capital, a shiny physical plant, many (sometimes under- or ill-used) resources, slickness of management, clear emphasis on appearances, high salaries at the top of the organizational structure, and a surprising lack of mission. Prospects for change are moderate to low.

Opal University is a highly rated private institution in any set of rankings one may look at. It has a large endowment and can afford to hire top professors and constantly update its physical plant. Its endowment was hurt in the crash of 2008 but has since recovered, to a large extent. Although most of its faculty and students are liberal politically, it is quite conservative institutionally. New programs must go through what seems like an endless set of committees before being approved, and sometimes the rationale for turning down new ideas amounts to little more than "that's not what we do here." Its reputation will always bring it excellent students because a degree from the institution has substantial "market value" when students go looking for jobs. But the institution, a very old one, risks falling seriously behind the times because it does not want to learn from the times—or from its mistakes.

The Cubic Zirconium Institution

The cubic zirconium institution is high in desire for actual change but low both in desire for the appearance of change and in perceived quality. The mood of the organization is fraudulence: as is the case with a cubic zirconium, no one wants others to know that it's fake, so viewers are, where possible, kept at a distance. Its self-belief is, "We're kind of a fraud; we can't let outsiders get too close, lest they find out." It may try to hide that its faculty is weak, including by not even disclosing publicly who the faculty members are. It may graduate only a tiny fraction of the students who matriculate but not publicly disclose its first-year retention or six-year graduation rates. It may accept anyone who enrolls but have an admissions office that pretends admission is only for the chosen few.

Signs of a cubic zirconium organization are resistance to scrutiny, a history of resistance to change, descriptions that emphasize show rather than substance, and employees who are reluctant to talk to outsiders—and who may not even be publicly identified.

Cubic Zirconium University is a publicly traded, for-profit institution. Although it has a considerable number of students and is nationally known, it is identified at least as much for its aggressiveness in recruiting and for its utilization of federal scholarship dollars as it is for the programs it offers. It has been subject to some scrutiny from accreditors beyond that normally given to many other universities. Its full set of faculty members is not publicly disclosed, and some, probably many, are thought to be faculty members at other institutions who are moonlighting, not necessarily with the approval or even the knowledge of their primary employers. The institution appears to graduate a relatively small proportion of its students but does not make public the information that would allow outsiders to easily evaluate its success in getting its students through. The prognosis for change is rather low.

The Slightly Imperfect Diamond Institution

The slightly imperfect diamond institution is high in desire for actual change, low in desire for the appearance of change, and high in perceived quality. Its mood is one of denial. Its self-belief is that it has some particular imperfection or set of imperfections and if only it could dispense with the imperfection(s), it would be a fine institution. The nature of the imperfection differs among institutions, but it is the scapegoat for the university's woes. The organization is like a slightly imperfect diamond in that it has, from its own point of view, one not entirely apparent flaw, which it would just as soon deny, if it could. The typical view of this kind of institution is that the slight imperfection spoils the institution but it tries to do as well as it can, given the circumstances. Prospects for change are moderate.

What are possible imperfections? They include an autocratic president, a board of trustees that is out of sync with the institution, a weak student body, poor athletic facilities (or athletic facilities that are so good that they draw all the attention away from other parts of the institution), or a lack of adequate finances in an institution that has a history of excellence.

Signs of the slightly imperfect diamond organization are praise of the system coupled with veiled digs at the imperfection, deflection of probing questions about the imperfection, attempts to deny the problem of the imperfection, and generally favorable indications but subtle hints that something is wrong. Sometimes, if the problem is dealt with, the institution really can become better. Other times the imperfection is merely a symptom of more serious underlying problems. Prospects for change are moderate to good if the imperfection can be dealt with.

SI Diamond University is a state institution of renown, with many stakeholders who believe that the university would thrive were it not for one problem: the governor and the state legislature are starving it of funds. At one time, the university was extremely well funded—indeed, it was among the best-funded of universities in the country—but today that funding has been greatly reduced. The governor and legislature argue that the issue is not that they have a beef with the university but rather that certain costs, such as of prisons, health programs, and pensions, are fixed, so that it is variable-cost items like universities that suffer when times are lean. Everyone acknowledges that the substantial cuts in funding have hurt the university, but no one is clear as to what to do about it. Meanwhile, the university is closing students out of courses, sometimes resulting in their taking an extra year to finish their requirements; laying off faculty; failing to replace essential staff members; increasing deferred maintenance; and decreasing financial aid. The university is changing but not as a result of learning; rather, it is changing for the worse as it is starved of funds.

The Lead Institution

The lead institution is high in desire for actual change, high in desire for appearance of change, but low in perceived quality. Its mood is one of superstition, essentially the hope that a rabbit can be pulled out of a hat. Its self-belief is that it needs to find a way, metaphorically, to change lead into gold. The university has an almost alchemical or magical view that some quick fix will turn it into the kind of organization it wants to be. Often it wants change quickly, of a kind that would take many years and perhaps decades to achieve. Prospects for change are modest.

Signs of a lead institution are impatience, magical beliefs with respect to possibilities for change, lack of interest in understanding interventions, lack of understanding of programs for change, and an emphasis on doing, not planning.

Lead University has a new president who was brought in to make it great. This private institution is generally at the lower levels of many rankings charts and does not have a history of striving for excellence. But the new president convinced the search committee that he had the vision and the leadership skills to take the university from near the bottom of the charts to the upper end, or at least the top third. The problem is that his excellent salesmanship is not matched by the quality of faculty, students, or even board to realize the goals he has set for the institution. The president seems to seriously believe that he can transform the institution, but he is finding that although people want the institution to become great, they just do not know how to get there and cannot help him as much as he had hoped.

The Diamond-in-the-Rough Organization

The diamond-in-the-rough institution is high in desire for actual change, desire for appearance of change, and perceived quality. Its mood is one of hopefulness. Its self-belief is that it is really good and can be even better.

Signs of a diamond-in-the-rough institution are willingness to devote resources such as time and money to change, recognition of the importance of planning, accurate understanding of its strengths and weaknesses, and receptiveness. The diamond-in-the-rough institution views itself in just this way, as a diamond that has a great deal of value but needs to be shaped and formed.

Diamond-in-the Rough University is a large university that historically was in the higher ranks but not the top ranks in university ratings. It has undergone a remarkable transformation in the last decade, moving itself up to become one of the most highly ranked private universities in the country. Several ingredients combined to enable it to do this: a large endowment and some key donors who were willing to give huge chunks of money to enable the university to achieve its goals; an extremely dynamic and internationally visible president who set high goals and had the support of his board, faculty, and alumni; an excellent urban location that naturally attracts students and faculty members who would like to live where the university is situated; a substantial expansion of faculty with compensation packages that enabled the university to attract some of the very best scholars in the world; and excellent graduate and professional schools that have done highly visible research that has helped enhance the university's reputation.

Our society needs diamond-in-the rough institutions that are flexible and modifiable. The reason is simple: society will change whether or not our institutions do. Although we can talk about planning for five, ten, or even twenty years out, none of us can know for sure what the world will look like in the future, nor what universities will need to look like in the future. The best an institution can do is to be flexible and respond to society's needs as they emerge, retaining at all times the fundamental values that underlie ACCEL.

Mediating Variables

Change in a university can come from a board of trustees, a president, a faculty senate, or any number of sources of leadership. How difficult will change be? Change is very hard to achieve in universities, even if the prerequisites described above are met and the institution is a diamond in the rough. Among the reasons for this difficulty are five mediating variables that affect the extent to which change is likely to happen.

1. *Legitimacy of the change agent.* Change will be difficult if the agent of change is not perceived as legitimate, for example, a president appointed outside what stakeholders of the university consider to be due process, or a faculty senate that is unrepresentative of the faculty as a whole.

2. *Credibility of the change agent.* Change can be hampered if a change agent is perceived as lacking credibility, for example, a president who appears to be solely a political appointment, or a provost who is in charge of academics at an institution but lacks serious academic credentials.

3. *Ownership of change.* Change will be impeded if stakeholders in a university do not feel ownership of the change, for example, if change is forced on them by a board or president without serious consultation.

4. *Rate of change.* Change may be stymied if the rate of change is too fast or too slow. The problem with change that is too fast is that people cannot adequately absorb it and are likely to feel that the train has left the station without them. But change that is too slow leaves stakeholders with the feeling that nothing much is happening other than talk—that there really is no train leaving the station but rather one that is just stuck in place.

5. *Cultural compatibility of change.* Perhaps most important is the compatibility of change with the culture of the institution. What is particularly vexing about this issue is that sometimes it is the culture itself that needs change, but cultures are remarkably resistant to change and typically endure beyond any one set of people who are embedded in them. That is, you can hire new leaders or even new faculty members with diverse viewpoints, but the culture often lives on despite, or sometimes because of, the new hires.

Meaningful organizational change is difficult and complex (Kotter 2012). It requires certain prerequisites—actual ability to change, belief in the institution's ability to change, and courage to change. It helps if the institution wants to change, wants to appear to change, and has some confidence in its quality or potential quality. And meaningful change is more likely when the change agent has legitimacy and credibility, and when the change has broad ownership, occurs at a suitable rate, and is culturally compatible.

Change agents should at the very least be aware of these issues before they attempt to change an institution. Institutions can learn and change, but typically they do so reluctantly and in fits and starts rather than through a smooth, continuous process. The framework provided here may provide some guidance as to how meaningful institutional learning and change can take place. Any institution of higher learning can become an ACCEL institution. The question is whether its constituents want it to, and if so, whether they have the courage and the will to change.

In my career, I have kept seeking out the ball of gold mentioned in the Stephen Crane poem in the preface. But as one gets closer and closer to the center of university leadership, it becomes harder and harder to see a true ball of gold. One may see clay, or if one is lucky, bronze or silver. I believe there is a ball of gold there. It is in the ACCEL university. But what I have learned, in the end, is that we don't find that ball of gold. Like the alchemists, we seek to create it. And although what we create may never be a ball of pure gold, if we work at it and adhere to the guidelines in this book, we can come pretty close. In the next chapter, I speak specifically about what one can do to get to the ball of gold.

PART V
PUTTING THEORY INTO PRACTICE

15

Transforming a University into an ACCEL University

What One Can Do Right Now

How do you translate the ideas in this book into a plan of action to transform a university into an ACCEL university? Incrementally. But the greatest obstacle is just translating thought into action. Most universities are rather far away from being ACCEL universities. But through a series of incremental steps, they can become ACCEL universities. Here I suggest steps one can take, with each step based on a chapter of the book. Each step starts with a question to ask oneself and others. The details of the answers are in the chapters.

Ask how the university teaches students to translate thought into action (Introduction). The university needs to get away from the phony dichotomy between teaching for the life of the mind (e.g., philosophy, English literature) and teaching for real-world practice (e.g., engineering, applied mathematics). It's this simple: if students can't see how to use what they learn, they won't learn it. So if instructors are teaching material that they don't see how students can use, the students certainly won't see how either. Instructors need to teach general education—whether it's Plato in philosophy or Adele in modern culture—but their focus always has to be on how students can use what they learn to negotiate the challenges of their lives as active concerned citizens and ethical leaders. But if students are not learning how to think adaptively as well as how to negotiate a particular job, they will be out of date when the demands of the marketplace change over time. They will be good for only their first job.

Ask about access (chapter 1). Thomas Jefferson pioneered the concept of access in higher education, realizing that with an excellent education students could realize their potential. Ask whether your university provides access and how it ensures that those who are qualified are encouraged to gain access to the resources of the university.

Ask about the mission statement (chapter 2). The mission statement for a university describes where the university is trying to go. If you like the idea of an ACCEL university, ask whether the mission statement is compatible with such a university, and if it is not, consider forming an exploratory task force to canvass stakeholders of the university to see whether they would be interested in modifying the mission statement to increase its compatibility with the goals of ACCEL. Many universities further have strategic plans that are created or re-created every decade or so. If you can place goals from ACCEL in the strategic plan, you will have greater justification for setting out to accomplish those goals. Again, such goals can be set only with broad input from the various stakeholders of the university.

Examine how university students are learning not just to memorize material but also how to think creatively, analytically, practically, and wisely about it (chapter 3). Negotiating the challenges of everyday life means creatively generating novel ideas to deal with challenging tasks, analyzing whether the ideas are any good, practically implementing the ideas and convincing others of their worth, and ensuring that the resulting actions benefit a common good, not just one's own interests or those of one's inner circle. A university needs to ensure, concretely, that students are learning inside and outside the classroom how to think in all of these ways.

Ask what the university is doing to achieve deep, not merely shallow, diversity (chapter 4). Deep diversity is about differing life backgrounds, differing worldviews, differing cultural origins. Shallow diversity is merely about racial, ethnic, religious, or other quotas, without consideration of what such differences mean. Shallow quotas give only the appearance of meaningful diversity, although regrettably our society has, for the most part, bought into such shallow notions. You don't learn to think in new ways from someone else merely because his or her ethnicity, socially defined race, or religion is different. Such diversity can be a start but not a finish. You learn to think in new ways because someone else brings different cultural backgrounds, assumptions, ideologies, and worldviews to your life.

Ask what kind of student would contribute most to, and learn the most from, an education in the university (chapter 5). As a society, we have foolishly and mindlessly become locked into standardized tests whose main function is to predict academic success, especially in the first year. Obviously, you don't want to admit students who cannot do the academic work. But no researcher, ever, has found that college grades are particularly good predictors of who will become an active concerned citizen or ethical leader. Do you vote for political candidates based on their GPAs? If you want to admit students who will make a difference to the world, you have to stop using standardized tests as a crutch to compensate for the fact that you never asked whom you really want to receive an education in your university.

Ask whether financial-aid policies, in view of college costs, are allowing those who would contribute and learn most from the university environment to actually matriculate and graduate (chapter 6). Our society's notions about financial aid tend to be as shallow as our notions about diversity. Universities will give "merit" aid because of standardized test scores that have no relation to the mission of the university, or simply because someone comes from a certain part of the country. If the university gives merit aid, make sure that the merit truly reflects the mission of the ACCEL university. If the university gives financial assistance based on need, ensure to the extent possible that the aid is distributed fairly. More and more, selective universities are becoming bastions of the rich and the poor, with the middle class shut out. Some of the wealthiest universities are working on this problem, but all universities need to work on it, within their means.

Ask how instruction develops students' skills in thinking creatively, analytically, practically, and wisely, and how it helps students develop passion for something that interests them (chapter 7). Such teaching generally doesn't just happen. Instructors usually need to learn how to teach to students with diverse learning needs, and then the instructors need to be rewarded for their successful efforts.

Ask whether assessments of learning, whether for specific courses or for purposes of accreditation, match instruction that is geared toward developing creative, analytical, practical, and wise thinking (chapter 8). It is challenging to teach for diverse skills and even more challenging to develop assessments. Yet it can be done, especially through portfolios and projects. If the assessment does not match the instruction, students will quickly learn that the rewards come not from studying for the way instruction is done but rather from studying for the way assessment is done.

Ask what steps are being taken to optimize retention and graduation (chapter 9). What concrete steps is the university taking to increase retention and graduation rates? I refer to "optimization" rather than "maximization" because there probably are some students who should drop out. The particular university environment just does not suit them. But we should be past the days when we leave students to sink or swim. If we accept students into our university, we have a responsibility to do what we can to help them succeed through their own efforts.

Ask whether university athletics, to the extent they exist, are helping to fulfill the overall mission of the university or are running in a direction different from that mission (chapter 10). Athletics can help fulfill the mission of a university or can sabotage that mission. If the university is seeking to be an ACCEL university, it has to act with the same integrity in athletics as in academics.

Ask whether assessments of faculty take into account their development of active concerned citizenship and ethical leadership in their students, and whether the faculty role-model these skills (chapter 11). Students model what they see, not what they are told. Assessments of faculty should reflect the extent to which faculty help fulfill the mission of the university, whether in research, teaching, or service. Great research sets a model for high standards of academic excellence in moving forward the frontiers of knowledge. Great teaching sets a model for developing ACCEL skills in students. And great service sets a model for the same kind of citizenship we would hope to see in our students.

Ask whether university governance role-models the same kinds of skills it hopes to instill in students (chapter 12). When students, faculty, staff, alumni, or any other group loses confidence in the integrity of university governance, it becomes very difficult to instill ACCEL skills in students, because the university itself seems not to be demonstrating the behavior it seeks to inculcate in others. In particular, autocratic or laissez-faire leadership over a long period of time makes adherence to the ACCEL model very challenging.

Ask whether the marketing of the university reflects its mission (chapter 13). Because universities compete for students (and faculty), it sometimes becomes tempting to market a university simply in terms of whatever seems to attract the most new students or the best faculty. But if the marketing of the university does not reflect the university's mission, eventually the university starts to lose the mission because people fail to see it in the way the university presents itself.

Ask whether the university is governing itself in a way that allows sufficient flexibility to achieve its goals or to get back on track if it is straying from its goals (chapter 14). Universities tend to stray from their mission either when they become so rigid that they cannot move forward as needed to adapt to societal changes or when they become so loose that they can move almost anywhere without a way to get back on the preferred path. Universities can reach a ball of gold—an ACCEL ball of gold—if they have the will and flexibility to do so.

Do it (chapter 15).

References

Adams, H. 1987. *The Academic Tribes*. 2nd ed. Champaign-Urbana: University of Illinois Press.

Amabile, T. M. 1996. *Creativity in Context: Update to the Social Psychology of Creativity*. Boulder, CO: Westview Press.

Apuzzo, M. 2015. A U.S. Tax Investigation Snowballed to Stun the Soccer World. *New York Times*. http://www.nytimes.com/2015/05/30/sports/soccer/more-indictments-expected-in-fifa-case-irs-official-says.html?_r=0.

Archibald, R. B., and D. H. Feldman. 2014. *Why Does College Cost so Much?* New York: Oxford University Press.

Arum, R., and J. Roksa. 2011. *Academically Adrift*. Chicago: University of Chicago Press.

——. 2014. *Aspiring Adults Adrift*. Chicago: University of Chicago Press.

Association of American Colleges and Universities. 2013. Employers More Interested in Critical Thinking and Problem Solving Than College Major. Washington, DC: Association of American Colleges and Universities. http://www.aacu.org/press/press-releases/employers-more-interested-critical-thinking-and-problem-solving-college-major.

Astin, A. 2011. In "Academically Adrift," Data Don't Back up Sweeping Claim. *Chronicle of Higher Education*. http://chronicle.com/article/Academically-Adrift-a/126371/.

Bandura, A. 1997. *Self-Efficacy: The Exercise of Self-Control*. New York: Worth.

——. 2016. *Moral Disengagement*. New York: Worth.

Baum, S. 2014. Higher Education Pays Off, So Why the Misunderstanding? http://www.urban.org/urban-wire/higher-education-pays-so-why-misunderstanding.

Becher, T., and P. R. Trowler. 2001. *Academic Tribes and Territories*. 2nd ed. Maidenhead, UK: Open Universities Press.

Beckett, S. 1982. *Waiting for Godot*. New York: Grove Press.

Binet, A., and T. Simon. 1916. *The Development of Intelligence in Children*. Trans. E. S. Kite. Baltimore, MD: Williams and Wilkins.

Bok, D. 2008. *Our Underachieving Colleges: A Candid Look at How Much Students Learn and Why They Should Be Learning More*. Princeton, NJ: Princeton University Press.

——. 2013. *Higher Education in America*. Princeton, NJ: Princeton University Press.

Bowen, W. G. 2013. *Higher Education in the Digital Age*. Princeton, NJ: Princeton University Press.

Branch, T. 2011. The Shame of College Sports. *The Atlantic*. http://www.theatlantic.com/magazine/archive/2011/10/the-shame-of-college-sports/308643/.

Brands, H. W. 2006. *Andrew Jackson: His Life and Times*. New York: Anchor.

Cacioppo, J. T., and R. E. Petty. 1982. The Need for Cognition. *Journal of Personality and Social Psychology* 42, 116–131.

Chickering, A. W., and G. D. Kuh. 2005. *Promoting Student Success: Creating Conditions So Every Student Can Learn*. Occasional Paper No. 3. Bloomington: Indiana University Center for Postsecondary Research.

Christensen, C. M., and H. J. Eyring. 2011. *The Innovative University: Changing the DNA of the University from the Inside Out*. San Francisco: Jossey-Bass.

Csikszentmihalyi, M. 2013. *Creativity*. New York: Harper Perennial.

Darley, J. M., and C. D. Batson. 1973. From Jerusalem to Jericho: A Study of Situational and Dispositional Variables in Helping Behavior. *Journal of Personality and Social Psychology* 27, 100–108.

Darley, J. M., and B. Latané. 1970. *The Unresponsive Bystander: Why Doesn't He Help?* New York: Appleton Century Crofts.

Deci, E. L., and R. M. Ryan. 2012. Self-Determination Theory. In *Handbook of Theories of Social Psychology: Vol. 1*, edited by P. A. M. Van Lange, A. W. Kruglanski, and E. T. Higgins, pp. 416–437. Thousand Oaks, CA: Sage.

Delbanco, A. 2013. *College: What It Was, Is, and Should Be*. Princeton, NJ: Princeton University Press.

Dweck, C. 2007. *Mindset: The New Psychology of Success*. New York: Ballantine Books.

Federici, M. P. 2012. *The Political Philosophy of Alexander Hamilton*. Baltimore, MD: Johns Hopkins University Press.

Fischer, K. 2014. A College Degree Sorts Job Applicants, but Employers Wish It Meant More. *Chronicle of Higher Education*. http://chronicle.com/article/The-Employment-Mismatch/137625/#id=overview.

Fraser, S. 1995. *The Bell Curve Wars*. New York: New Republic Books.

Galton, F. 1883. *Inquiry into Human Faculty and Its Development*. London: Macmillan.

Gardner, H. 2011. *Frames of Mind: The Theory of Multiple Intelligences*. 3rd ed. New York: Basic.

Golden, D. 2006. *The Price of Admission*. New York: Crown.

Grigorenko, E. L., P. W. Geissler, R. Prince, F. Okatcha, C. Nokes, D. A. Kenny, D. A. Bundy, and R. J. Sternberg. 2001. The Organization of Luo Conceptions of Intelligence: A Study of Implicit Theories in a Kenyan Village. *International Journal of Behavioral Development* 25(4), 367–378.

Grigorenko, E. L., E. Meier, J. Lipka, G. Mohatt, E. Yanez, and R. J. Sternberg. 2004. Academic and Practical Intelligence: A Case Study of the Yup'ik in Alaska. *Learning and Individual Differences* 14, 183–207.

Hermanowicz, J. 2013. The Culture of Mediocrity. *Minerva* 51, 363–387.

Herrnstein, R. J., and C. Murray. 1994. *The Bell Curve*. New York: Free Press.

Hoover, E. 2004. SAT Scores "Launder" Students' Backgrounds, Study Finds. *Chronicle of Higher Education*. http://www.calstate.edu/pa/clips2004/june/3june/sat.shtml.

Humphreys, D., and P. Kelly. 2014. *How Liberal Arts and Science Majors Fare in Employment: A Report on Earnings and Long-Term Career Paths*. Washington, DC: Association of American Colleges and Universities.

Janis, I. L. 1972. *Victims of Groupthink*. Boston: Houghton-Mifflin.

Kahneman, D. 2013. *Thinking: Fast and Slow*. New York: Farrar, Straus and Giroux.

Kahneman, D., and A. Tversky. 1971. Subjective Probability: A Judgment of Representativeness. *Cognitive Psychology* 3, 430–454.

Karabel, J. 2006. *The Chosen: The Hidden History of Admission and Exclusion at Harvard, Yale, and Princeton*. New York: Mariner.

Kaufman, J. C., and R. J. Sternberg, eds. 2010. *Cambridge Handbook of Creativity*. New York: Cambridge University Press.

Klein, S., O. L. Liu, J. Sconing, R. Bolus, B. Bridgeman, H. Kugelmass, A. Nemeth, S. Robbins, and J. Steedle. 2009. Test Validity Study Report. Retrieved from Fund for the Improvement of Postsecondary Education, http://www.voluntarysystem.org/docs/reports/TVSReport_Final.pdf.

Kotter, J. P. 2012. *Leading Change*. Boston: Harvard Business School Press.

Kozhevnikov, M., C. Evans, and S. M. Kosslyn. 2014. Cognitive Style as Environmentally Sensitive Individual Differences in Cognition: A Modern Synthesis and Applications in Education, Business, and Management. *Psychological Science in the Public Interest* 15(1), 3–33.

Kuh, G. D., J. Kinzie, J. H. Schuh, E. J. Whitt, and Associates. 2010. *Student Success in College: Creating Conditions That Matter*. San Francisco: Jossey-Bass.

Lemann, N. 1999. *The Big Test: The Secret History of the American Meritocracy*. New York: Farrar, Straus and Giroux.

Lorin, J. 2014. Student Debt: The Rising U.S. Burden. http://www.bloombergview.com/quicktake/student-debt.

Maki, P. L. 2010. *Assessing for Learning*. Sterling, VA: Stylus.

McKenna, L. 2015. The College President-to-Adjunct Pay Ratio. *The Atlantic,* September 24. http://www.theatlantic.com/education/archive/2015/09/income-inequality-in-higher-education-the-college-president-to-adjunct-pay-ratio/407029/.

McLoughlin, Michelle. 2005. Yale Psychologist Designs Test, a Challenger to the SAT. *USA Today*. http://usatoday30.usatoday.com/news/education/2005-03-05-sat-rainbow_x.htm.

Meacham, J. 2013. *Thomas Jefferson: The Art of Power*. New York: Random House.

Milgram, S. 2009. *Obedience to Authority.* New York: Harper Perennial.

Mischel, W. 2014. *The Marshmallow Test: Mastering Self-Control.* New York: Little, Brown.

Nisbett, R. E. 1993. *Rules for Reasoning.* New York: Psychology Press.

Okagaki, L., and R. J. Sternberg. 1993. Parental Beliefs and Children's School Performance. *Child Development* 64(1), 36–56.

Pashler, H., M. McDaniel, D. Rohrer, and R. Bjork. 2008. Learning Styles: Concepts and Evidence. *Psychological Science in the Public Interest* 9(3), 106–119.

Pintrich, P. R. 2000. An Achievement Goal Theory Perspective on Issues in Motivation Terminology, Theory, and Research. *Contemporary Educational Psychology* 25(1), 92–104.

Reicher, S. D., S. A. Haslam, and J. R. Smith. 2012. Working toward the Experimenter: Reconceptualizing Obedience within the Milgram Paradigm as Identification-Based Followership. *Perspectives on Psychological Science* 7, 315–324.

Reisman, D. 1963. *The Lonely Crowd.* New Haven, CT: Yale University Press.

Rosenthal, R., and L. Jacobson. 1992. *Pygmalion in the Classroom.* Expanded ed. New York: Irvington.

Rothstein, J. 2004. College Performance Predictions and the SAT. *Journal of Econometrics* 121, 297–317.

Schmitt, N., F. L. Oswald, B. H. Kim, A. Imus, S. Merritt, A. Friede, and S. Shivpuri. 2007. The Use of Background and Ability Profiles to Predict College Student Outcomes. *Journal of Applied Psychology* 92, 165–179.

Selingo, J. J. 2013. *College (Un)Bound.* New York: New Harvest.

Senge, P. 2006. *The Fifth Discipline: The Art and Practice of the Learning Organization.* New York: Doubleday.

Simonton, D. K. 2004. *Creativity in Science.* New York: Cambridge University Press.

Smith, E. E., and D. L. Medin. 1981. *Concepts and Categories.* Cambridge, MA: Harvard University Press.

Spearman, C. 1927. *The Abilities of Man.* New York: Macmillan.

SportsYeah. 2015. The 13 Most Shocking NFL Scandals. http://www.ranker.com/list/13-most-shocking-nfl-scandals/sportsyeah.

Stanovich, K. E. 2010. *What Intelligence Tests Miss: The Psychology of Rational Thought.* New Haven, CT: Yale University Press.

Steele, C. M., and J. Aronson. 1995. Stereotype Threat and the Intellectual Test Performance of African Americans. *Journal of Personality and Social Psychology* 69(5), 797–811.

Stemler, S. E., E. L. Grigorenko, L. Jarvin, and R. J. Sternberg. 2006. Using the Theory of Successful Intelligence as a Basis for Augmenting AP Exams in Psychology and Statistics. *Contemporary Educational Psychology* 31(2), 344–376.

Sternberg, R. J. 1973. Cost-Benefit Analysis of the Yale Admissions Office Interview. *College and University* 48, 154–164.

——. 1977. *Intelligence, Information Processing, and Human Abilities: The Componential Analysis of Human Intelligence.* Mahwah, NJ: Erlbaum.

——. 1988. *The Triarchic Mind: A New Theory of Human Intelligence.* New York: Viking.

——. 1990. *Metaphors of Mind.* New York: Cambridge University Press.

——. 1997a. *Successful Intelligence.* New York: Plume.

——. 1997b. *Thinking Styles*. New York: Cambridge University Press.

——. 2000. *Making School Reform Work: A "Mineralogical" Theory of School Modifiability*. Bloomington, IN: Phi Delta Kappa Educational Foundation.

——, ed. 2002. *Why Smart People Can Be So Stupid*. New Haven, CT: Yale University Press.

——. 2003a. WICS: A Model for Leadership in Organizations. *Academy of Management Learning and Education* 2, 386–401.

——. 2003b. *Wisdom, Intelligence, and Creativity Synthesized*. New York: Cambridge University Press.

——. 2004a. Good Intentions, Bad Results: A Dozen Reasons Why the No Child Left Behind (NCLB) Act Is Failing Our Nation's Schools. *Education Week* 24(9), 42, 56.

——. 2004b. *Psychology 101½: The Unspoken Rules for Success in Academia*. Washington, DC: American Psychological Association.

——. 2007. A Systems Model of Leadership: WICS. *American Psychologist* 62(1), 34–42.

——. 2008a. Interdisciplinary Problem-Based Learning: An Alternative to Traditional Majors and Minors. *Liberal Education* 94(1), 12–17.

——. 2008b. The WICS Approach to Leadership: Stories of Leadership and the Structures and Processes That Support Them. *Leadership Quarterly* 19(3), 360–371.

——. 2010a. *College Admissions for the 21st Century*. Cambridge, MA: Harvard University Press.

——. 2010b. Teaching for Ethical Reasoning in Liberal Education. *Liberal Education* 96(3), 32–37.

——. 2011a. 10 Bad Habits. *Inside Higher Ed*. http://www.insidehighered.com/advice/2011/12/21/essay-professorial-traits-administrators-need-drop.

——. 2011b. The Flaw of Overall Rankings. *Inside Higher Ed*. http://www.insidehighered.com/views/2011/01/24/sternberg.

——. 2011c. Who Is Really Adrift? *Inside Higher Ed*. https://www.insidehighered.com/views/2011/02/08/a_critique_of_academically_adrift_and_the_test_behind_many_of_the_findings.

——. 2012a. Ethical Drift. *Liberal Education* 98(3), 60.

——. 2012b. Lessons from Swiss Watch-Makers. *Inside Higher Ed*. http://www.insidehighered.com/views/2012/10/10/essay-how-colleges-could-learn-swiss-watch-makers.

——. 2013a. The End Is Not Nigh for Colleges. *Chronicle of Higher Education* 59(22), A56.

——. 2013b. Leadership for Academic Administration: What Works When? *Change* 45(5), 24–27.

——. 2013c. Research to Improve Retention. *Inside Higher Ed*. http://www.insidehighered.com/views/2013/02/07/essay-use-research-improve-student-retention.

——. 2013d. Self-Sabotage in the Academic Career: 15 Ways in Which Faculty Members Harm Their Own Futures, Often without Knowing It. *Chronicle of Higher Education* 59(34), A36–A37.

——. 2013e. When a Better Ranking Is a Bad Thing. *Inside Higher Ed*. http://www.insidehighered.com/views/2013/11/07/essay-when-good-rankings-lead-colleges-wrong-direction.

——. 2014a. Academic Tribalism. *Chronicle of Higher Education.* http://chronicle.com/blogs/conversation/2014/02/26/academic-tribalism/.

——, ed. 2014b. *The Modern Land-Grant University.* West Lafayette, IN: Purdue University Press.

——. 2014c. Murky Environments in Academe. *Chronicle of Higher Education.* http://chronicle.com/article/Murky-Environments-in-Academe/147057/?cid=atandutm_source=atandutm_medium=en.

——. 2014d. Three Traditions of Democracy in Relation to American Higher Education. *Liberal Education* 100(2), 42–49.

——. 2015a. Epilogue: Why Is Ethical Behavior Challenging? A Model of Ethical Reasoning. In *Ethical Challenges in the Behavioral and Brain Sciences: Case Studies and Commentaries,* edited by R. J. Sternberg and S. T. Fiske, pp. 218–226. New York: Cambridge University Press.

——. 2015b. A Model of Creative Institutional Change for Assessing Universities as Learning Organizations. *Creativity Research Journal* 27, 254–261.

——. 2015c. Still Searching for the Zipperumpazoo: A Reflection after 40 Years. *Child Development Perspectives* 9(2), 106–110.

——. 2015d. Teaching for Creativity: The Sounds of Silence. *Psychology of Aesthetics, Creativity, and the Arts* 9(2), 115–117.

Sternberg, R. J., and M. Barnes. 1985. Real and Ideal Others in Romantic Relationships: Is Four a Crowd? *Journal of Personality and Social Psychology* 49, 1586–1608.

Sternberg, R. J., B. E. Conway, J. L. Ketron, and M. Bernstein. 1981. People's Conceptions of Intelligence. *Journal of Personality and Social Psychology* 41, 37–55.

Sternberg, R. J., and D. K. Detterman, eds. 1986. *What Is Intelligence?* Norwood, NJ: Ablex Publishing.

Sternberg, R. J., and S. T. Fiske. 2015. *Ethical Challenges in the Behavioral and Brain Sciences.* New York: Cambridge University Press.

Sternberg, R. J., G. B. Forsythe, J. Hedlund, J. Horvath, S. Snook, W. M. Williams, R. K. Wagner, and E. L. Grigorenko. 2000. *Practical Intelligence in Everyday Life.* New York: Cambridge University Press.

Sternberg, R. J., and E. L. Grigorenko. 2007. *Teaching for Successful Intelligence.* 2nd ed. Thousand Oaks, CA: Corwin Press.

Sternberg, R. J., E. L. Grigorenko, and L.-F. Zhang. 2008. Styles of Learning and Thinking Matter in Instruction and Assessment. *Perspectives on Psychological Science* 3(6), 486–506.

Sternberg, R. J., and T. I. Lubart. 1995. *Defying the Crowd: Cultivating Creativity in a Culture of Conformity.* New York: Free Press.

Sternberg, R. J., K. Nokes, P. W. Geissler, R. Prince, F. Okatcha, D. A. Bundy, and E. L. Grigorenko. 2001. The Relationship between Academic and Practical Intelligence: A Case Study in Kenya. *Intelligence* 29, 401–418.

Sternberg, R. J., J. Penn, and C. Hawkins, with case studies by Sally Reed. 2011. *Assessing College Student Learning.* Washington, DC: Association of American Colleges and Universities.

Sternberg, R. J., C. Powell, P. A. McGrane, and S. McGregor. 1997. Effects of a Parasitic Infection on Cognitive Functioning. *Journal of Experimental Psychology: Applied* 3, 67–76.

Sternberg, R. J., and the Rainbow Project Collaborators. 2006. The Rainbow Project: Enhancing the SAT through Assessments of Analytical, Practical and Creative Skills. *Intelligence* 34(4), 321–350.

Sternberg, R. J., B. Torff, and E. L. Grigorenko. 1998. Teaching Triarchically Improves School Achievement. *Journal of Educational Psychology* 90, 374–384.

Sternberg, R. J., and W. M. Williams. 2001. Teaching for Creativity: Two Dozen Tips. In *Plain Talk about Education*, edited by R. D. Small and A. P. Thomas, pp. 153–165. Covington, LA: Center for Development and Learning.

Stolberg, S. G., and S. Labaton. 2009. Obama Calls Wall Street Bonuses "Shameful." *New York Times*. http://www.nytimes.com/2009/01/30/business/30obama.html?_r=0.

Subotnik, R. F., D. E. Karp, and E. R. Morgan. 1989. High IQ Children at Midlife. *Roeper Review* 3, 139–144.

Supiano, B. 2013. Employers Want Broadly Educated New Hires, Survey Finds. *Chronicle of Higher Education*. http://chronicle.com/article/Employers-Want-Broadly/138453/.

Terman, L. M., and M. H. Oden. 1959. *The Gifted Group at Mid-Life: 35 Years' Follow-Up of the Superior Child*. Stanford, CA: Stanford University Press.

Thorp, H., and B. Goldstein. 2013. *Engines of Innovation: The Entrepreneurial University in the Twenty-First Century*. Chapel Hill: University of North Carolina Press.

Tylicki, D. 2011. MLB History: 20 Most Shocking Scandals in Baseball History. http://bleacherreport.com/articles/941589-20-most-shocking-scandals-in-baseball-history.

Wadsworth, G. H. 2012. Sky Rocketing College Costs. http://inflationdata.com/Inflation/Inflation_Articles/Education_Inflation.asp.

Weinstein, R. S. 2002. *Reaching Higher: The Power of Expectations in Schooling*. Cambridge, MA: Harvard University Press.

Wells, H. G. 2008. The Country of the Blind. In *The Complete Short-Story Collection*. Seattle, WA: CreateSpace.

Wieder, B. 2011. Thiel Fellowship Pays 24 Talented Students $100,000 Not to Attend College. *Chronicle of Higher Education*. http://chronicle.com/article/Thiel-Fellowship-Pays-24/127622/.

Wikipedia. 2015. Jacksonian Democracy. http://en.wikipedia.org/wiki/Jacksonian_democracy.

Yang, S., and R. J. Sternberg. 1997. Taiwanese Chinese People's Conceptions of Intelligence. *Intelligence* 25, 21–36.

Zemsky, R. 2013. *Checklist for Change: Making American Higher Education a Sustainable Enterprise*. New Brunswick, NJ: Rutgers University Press.

Zhang, L.-F., and R. J. Sternberg. 2006. *The Nature of Intellectual Styles*. Mahwah, NJ: Erlbaum.

Zhang, L.-F., R. J. Sternberg, and S. Rayner, eds. 2012. *Handbook of Intellectual Styles*. New York: Springer.

Zimbardo, P. 2008. *The Lucifer Effect: Understanding How Good People Turn Evil*. New York: Random House.

Index